The Total Business Manual

MODERN ACCOUNTING
PERSPECTIVES AND PRACTICE

Gary John Previts, Series Editor

55.00

The Total Business Manual
A Step-by-Step Guide to Planning, Operating, and Evaluating Your Business

E. JAMES BURTON, PhD, CPA
Professor of Accounting
Middle Tennessee State University
Murfreesboro, Tennessee

W. BLAN McBRIDE
President
Professional Growth Associates, Inc.
Tallahassee, Florida

John Wiley & Sons, Inc.

New York • Chichester • Brisbane • Toronto • Singapore

In recognition of the importance of preserving what has been
written, it is a policy of John Wiley & Sons, Inc. to have
books of enduring value published in the United
States printed on acid-free paper, and we exert
our best efforts to that end.

This publication is designed to provide accurate and
authoritative information in regard to the subject
matter covered. It is sold with the understanding that
the publisher is not engaged in rendering legal, accounting,
or other professional service. If legal advice or other
expert assistance is required, the services of a competent
professional person should be sought. *From a Declaration
of Principles jointly adopted by a Committee of the
American Bar Association and a Committee of Publishers.*

Library of Congress Cataloging in Publication Data:

Burton, E. James.
  The total business manual: A step-by-step guide to planning,
operating, and evaluating your business / E. James Burton, W. Blan
McBride.
     p.   cm.—(Modern accounting perspectives and practice)
  Includes bibliographical references.
  ISBN 0-471-87927-4 (cloth)
  1. Industrial management—Handbooks, manuals, etc. 2. Business
enterprises—Finance—Handbooks, manuals, etc.   I. McBride, W.
Blan.   II. Title.   III. Series: Modern accounting perspectives and
practice series.
HD31.B852   1991
658—dc20   91-4760
                                                          CIP

Printed in the United States of America

10 9 8 7 6 5 4 3 2 1

PREFACE

This book is a product of more than 50 years of combined business, seminar, and teaching experience. It has been written in simple, practical language so that the average small-business owner can apply its principles to his/her business. While it has been written for practical application, it is firmly rooted in sound business theory.

Who will benefit from this book? Business owners with little if any academic training in the area of business may use it to understand concepts that are presented in business periodicals, newspapers, and seminars. He/she will find it a reference source that explains many things that have been heard but not understood for some time. Those with academic training in business will find theory applied to real contexts. Though the basic truths encountered here will not be new, an understanding of their applications will be greatly enhanced.

The authors have successfully implemented the concepts presented in this book in a variety of business situations. Mr. McBride has been an engineer, a plant manager for a large manufacturing firm, the owner and operator of a small-job shop operation, the owner and operator of a customs products operation, an inventor, a college teacher, and a seminar presenter. Dr. Burton is a Certified Public Accountant who has also owned and operated, or participated as a member of the board of directors of, an accounts receivable management firm, a real estate development partnership, a consulting firm, an equipment manufacturing firm, and a drapery manufacturing firm.

Perhaps the most effective way to use this book is as a reference source. We would suggest that you first read the book through once, implementing the concepts section by section; it is not casual reading but rather a manual, intended for a reading-doing-reading-doing approach. Then, when you have trouble or concerns in a particular area, consult the specific chapter addressing that problem to find solutions.

We express our appreciation to Mr. Bill Bilenky for his very able assistance with the preliminary compilation of these materials. Bill's legal perspective and expertise were quite valuable as we assembled the thoughts that resulted in this book. Also, both Bob Gilliland and Carol Corbett made major contributions to the process.

However, we reserve our deepest gratitude for the many clients who helped us to apply and to refine our thoughts and techniques in practical application. It is because we have seen these things work for these clients that we know they can work for you, our reader.

E. JAMES BURTON, PH.D.
W. BLAN MCBRIDE

CONTENTS

Contents

INTRODUCTION

This book was conceived from hundreds of hours of seminars and consulting sessions with thousands of participants and clients. It was promoted by an intimate knowledge of what business schools teach, how they teach it, and what they fail to teach.

The book is *not* for everyone. It is written for a specific and targeted audience. Those who will benefit most from it will be:

Owners, operators, managers of manufacturing, multilocation wholesale/ retail, or multilocation or multiservice service businesses. There will probably be three or fewer key decision makers in the business, who will want to apply more professional management techniques to their growing business.

The book has been arranged in three sections for your specific use. Don't let these section titles fool you: the book will be productive for businesses that are just being started as well as those with operational history already in place.

Section I, Preparing to Operate the Business, focuses on the proper preparation for beginning a new period of operations (tax year, budget year, new product introduction, etc.) as well as for introducing a new business to the world. The tools and techniques discussed are those which help establish standards and expectations for the operations.

Section II, Operating the Business, pays attention to key operational decisions that must be carried out on an ongoing basis. Each of the chapters deals with pertinent decisions critical to any type of business.

Section III, Evaluating the Operations of the Business, deals with measuring operations against the expectations generated in Section I. Not only will these tools help evaluate how well the business has been performing, but they will also serve as significant inputs for the next period's expectation-setting process.

Though not everything covered in a business school MBA curriculum is, or was intended to be, addressed here, the most relevant topics are; therefore the book serves as an update for those who have business school training and an introduction for those who haven't.

You certainly don't need to be a math wizard or a computer guru to understand the "quantitative" material presented here. We explain these approaches and use them as means, not as ends.

Best wishes for improving, implementing, and benefiting from your decisions—and for making lots of money.

The Total Business Manual

I

PREPARING TO OPERATE THE BUSINESS

Section I, like each of the remaining two sections, contains five chapters. The chapters in this section—

Planning

Forecasting

Breaking Even and Profit Planning

Investing in Long-Term Assets and Capital Budgeting

Budgeting for Operations

—are arranged in a progression from the general to the specific.

All of the information generated from the tools in Chapters 2 through 5 is part of the planning process. Planning is discussed first; subsequent chapters pick up on some of the more useful, if not always well-understood, tools available.

If this planning approach is new to you, read Section I in its entirety before attempting to implement any of the tools. If you are using this book as a refresher or reference manual, choose the area in which you are having a problem and begin there. In any case read at least the whole chapter before starting to implement so you will have all of the ideas in proper context.

1

Planning

Everyone plans! Every business person looks forward in time and has in mind those things that need to be accomplished for the betterment of the business. These thoughts are specific and personal to the planner; they focus on the areas of major interest to you, rather than cover the whole business (marketing people focus on marketing, finance people on finance, etc.). Such plans are often based on "guesstimates" rather than on factual data. Unless communicated, your thoughts as the planner will not be of much use to other people in the business, or serve as motivating tools for others.

Planning, which has as its prescribed end a business plan, should be practical rather than conceptual. When a business plan is written, it is available to all potential users both inside and outside the business. The process of recording thoughts causes the planner carefully to develop schedules to support any estimates or projections being made. The plan becomes a goal-setting device for the rest of the business as well.

The process of writing also spurs you to consider all areas of the organization and integrate them into the plan. The plan is available not only for internal users but also for external users, who may be considering funding the business, or for other external needs such as regulation.

Note: A major part of the material contained in this chapter is abbreviated from *Total Business Planning: A Step-By-Step Guide With Forms* (Revised) by E. James Burton and W. Blan McBride (John Wiley & Sons, 1991). You may wish to consult this book for a fuller discussion of various points.

THE PLANNING COMMUNICATIONS PROCESS

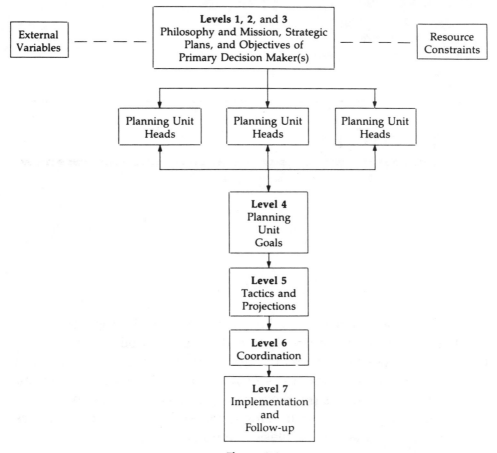

Figure 1.1

There are at least six good reasons why you need a business plan.

1. A business plan is an effective management tool for making major decisions. It sets out in detail what you intend to do and how you intend to do it, and serves as the framework for making decisions on how to accomplish the established objectives.

2. A business plan is an effective means for measuring actual performance. By comparing periodic measurements of accomplishment with expectations, you can determine how effectively the business is performing.

3. A business plan is a basis for rewarding performance. If individuals have been assigned responsibilities, and the accomplishment of those responsibilities can be measured, then appropriate and effective rewards can be determined.

4. A business plan helps motivate managers who have contributed to its development. Once a manager has "signed up" to the business plan, it is in that manager's best interest to see to it that the plan is accomplished.

5. A business plan is an educational tool. The process of developing a business plan helps the members of the team better understand the components involved and how they work together.

6. A business plan is a means of communicating expectations and demonstrating results. It informs personnel as to what is expected of them and how they will be measured. It shows them the results of their work according to the plan.

PROCESS VS. DOCUMENT

Much of the value of a business plan derives from the process you go through to develop it. A business planning process is a combination of brainstorming, daydreaming, research, analysis, communications, and position-paper writing. If implemented properly, a business planning process provides an opportunity for every level of management to be involved in determining how that business will be conducted over a period of time. A business plan has been described as a written document that spells out in detail where the company's business is and where it is intended to go. It should allow the management team to identify opportunities and threats, recognize strengths and weaknesses, reconcile conflicting views, and arrive at a set of agreed upon objectives, goals, and tactics in a systematic, realistic manner. As one dissects the components involved in that definition, it becomes obvious that a great deal of effort and time are necessary to construct a good business plan.

A business planning process is like a pyramid. At the top of the pyramid is a senior management team that must decide on key issues to guide the business through a long planning future. Below the senior management team is a larger tier of management. This tier expands upon the concepts put forth by the senior management team, building an increasingly more detailed plan of how these concepts should be accomplished. At each additional management level, the number of people involved increases and the planning becomes more detailed.

Even in a smaller business, which may have only a few involved decision makers, the business planning process can be very revealing. As the key decision makers in the business begin to communicate their beliefs as to "What business we are in" and the philosophy under which

MANAGEMENT LEVEL   DETAIL LEVEL

Senior Management   Philosophy, Mission,
                                        Objectives

Fewer
People &
Less Detail

Middle Management   Status, Goals

First Level   Tactics,
Management   Projections

More People & Greater Detail

PLANNING PYRAMID
Figure 1.2

the business ought to be run, there are often significant disagreements or misunderstandings that need to be resolved. The business planning process usually brings these misunderstandings or disagreements to the surface so that they can be worked on and a consensus can be reached.

DEFINITIONS

A common set of definitions will facilitate the understanding of the process in the plan being discussed here. The following list of terms and definitions may be helpful to you:

Philosophy. The set of basic beliefs that establish the parameters (boundaries of behavior) for the business and its personnel. It is a statement of what the business does and does not do. A statement of philosophy often begins with "We believe . . ." and follows with "therefore . . ."

Mission Statement. The mission statement is the primary focus of the business and answers the question, "What business are we in?"

Objective. Objectives are the aim or end of an action, the results to be accomplished. For the business as a whole, the objectives answer the question, "Where do we want to go?"

Status. The status is an assessment of the present position of the business and answers the question, "Where are we?"

Goals. Goals are the ends toward which a particular unit of the business strives; they are a step toward accomplishing an objective. For a particular unit of the business, goals answer the question, "Where do we, as a part of the business, want to go in keeping with the overall objectives of the business?"

Tactics. Tactics are methods of using resources to reach goals. They help to answer the question, "How do we get there?"

Projections. Projections are quantitative assessments and estimates of the results expected from the use of various tactics. These answer the question, "How will we know when we are there?"

PLANNING PROCESS: LEVELS ONE TO SEVEN

Of course, you will need to modify your planning process according to the type and the size of the business involved; still, it is possible to lay out a generalized framework within which the planning process can be developed. The planning process can be thought of as a seven-level process.

Group		Level
Senior Management	PHILOSOPHY/MISSION	1
Senior Management	STRATEGIC PLANNING	2
Senior Management	CORPORATE OBJECTIVES	3
Planning Unit Management	STATUS/GOALS	4
Planning Unit Supervisors	TACTICS/PROJECTIONS	5
Plan Coordinator	COORDINATION	6
Everyone	IMPLEMENTATION AND FOLLOW-UP	7

Figure 1.3

Level One

The first level in a planning process is the development of the philosophy and mission of the business. Often, management of the business will have unpublished philosophy and mission statements. For the long-range growth and development of the business, it is important that each of these items be specifically developed and written down so that they can be used by other people within the business for guidance.

The development of the philosophy and the mission statement are the responsibility of the senior management team. The senior management team (even if it consists of only one person—you) should take the time to consider the development of the philosophy and the mission statement in written form. There are forms and questions in the appendices to this chapter that will be helpful in the development of a philosophy statement and a mission statement.

Level Two

Strategic planning consists of an analysis of the competitive environment to determine what market factors are most important to customers, which factors are controlled by which competitors, what market moves others are making, and, therefore, what you should do to position yourself in the market. This requires a lot of information and considerable analysis. Forms such as that shown in Figure 1.5 may be helpful.

Level Three

Objectives are the key accomplishments that you have set out for the business as a whole during the planning period. It is probably best that no more than four key objectives are stated. If you are able to find the resources to commit to the accomplishment of four significant objectives, and if those objectives are attained in any given period, the business will have had a very good year. By limiting the number of objectives, you will be able to focus on the most important aspects of your undertaking and avoid dissipating your resources.

Level Four

At the fourth level of the business planning process, additional tiers of management are brought in. With a clear explanation from senior

PRODUCT MATRIX ANALYSIS

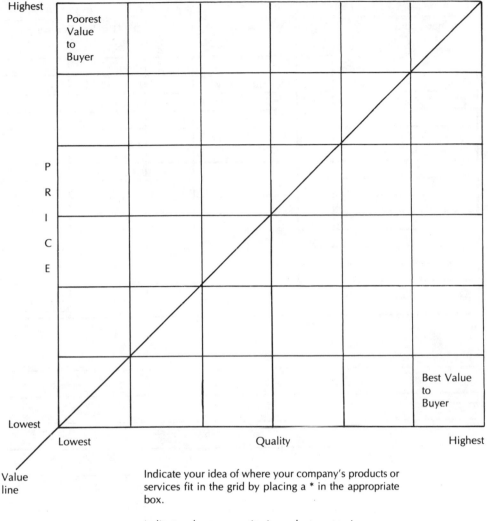

Indicate your idea of where your company's products or services fit in the grid by placing a * in the appropriate box.

Indicate where competitor's products or services are on the grid.

Figure 1.4

management of the philosophy/mission, strategic plans, and objectives of the business, the other managers will be able to assess their present condition (status) and determine the goals for their particular parts of the business. Their goals should support the corporate objectives. Clear statements of these goals are very important to help additional people in the units determine how to meet the objectives.

STRATEGIC FACTORS ANALYSIS

Customer/Client _____   Product/Service _____

Companies	Rank					
	Price	Quality	Delivery			

Summary

_____

_____

_____

_____

_____

From *Total Business Planning* by E.J. Burton and W.B. McBride © 1991 John Wiley & Sons, Inc.

Figure 1.5

SUGGESTIONS FOR USE

Strategic Factors Analysis

1. Identify specific customer/client or a specific customer/client group. Insert in upper left corner.

2. Identify specific product/service to be offered. Insert in upper right corner.

3. Identify the strategic factors considered important to the identified group in suggestion 1. Enter these as column headings along with *Price*, *Quality*, and *Delivery*.

4. Rank these strategic factors in order of importance, and enter your numerical results into the column headings labeled *Rank*.

5. Compare answers with others and attempt a consensus.

6. List yourself as the first entry under *Companies*; then, in descending order of market share, continue with a list of your competitors.

7. Compare answers with others and attempt a consensus.

8. Insert numbers into the matrix indicating each competitor's ranking with respect to each strategic factor.

9. Compare answers with others and attempt a consensus.

10. Identify rankings which are likely to be subject to attempts at change or which may be likely to change due to economic environment factors. Identify direction of such changes with arrows.

11. Compare answers with others and attempt a consensus.

12. In the space provided, write a short summary of the above described situation.

From *Total Business Planning* by E.J. Burton and W.B. McBride © 1991 John Wiley & Sons, Inc.

Figure 1.6

STRATEGIC PLAN OF ACTION

With specific reference to your competitors, what do you most want to accomplish? (State the accomplishments as specific results.)

1. _____

2. _____

3. _____

What course of action will you follow to cause these to happen?

1. a. _____

    b. _____

    c. _____

2. a. _____

    b. _____

    c. _____

3. a. _____

    b. _____

    c. _____

From *Total Business Planning* by E.J. Burton and W.B. McBride © 1991 John Wiley & Sons, Inc.

Figure 1.7

Level Five

At this point in the planning process the largest number of people in the business is brought into the process. The people who have to make things happen within the departments should be involved in establishing the "How do we make them happen?" and "What does it look like when they have happened?" parts of the plan. This should be an opportunity for the personnel in the business to put their creativity to use, to look at a number of different tactics, and to examine what the results of using those various tactics will be.

Level Six

Ultimately, it is time to take all of the information you have gathered and to put it into a final document. This is the process of coordination.

Planning Unit

To be completed by: _____

PRODUCT PLANNING RECORD

Product _____ For Year of 19 ____

		Year		
		Present		
1) Units Sold —Actual				
2) —Projected				
3) Unit Sales Price —Actual				
4) —Projected				
5) Unit Variable Cost —Actual				
6) —Projected				
7) Unit Gross Margin —Actual				
8) —Projected				
9) Total Revenue —Actual				
10) —Projected				
11) Promotion Expense —Actual				
12) —Projected				
13)				
14)				
15)				
16)				

Problems may be indicated by:

- Declining number of units sold
- Declining total revenue
- Declining margins

- Increasing price reductions to maintain sales
- Increasing costs as a percent of sales

- Increasing promotion expense as a percent of sales
- Significant variances between actuals and projections

From *Total Business Planning* by E.J. Burton and W.B. McBride © 1991 John Wiley & Sons, Inc.

Figure 1.8

Planning Unit

To be completed by: _____

SALESPERSON'S SALES FORECAST FOR 19____

Customer   Salesman

Product(s)	Units Projected				
	Quarter 1	Quarter 2	Quarter 3	Quarter 4	Annual
———					
———					
———					
———					
———					
———					
———					
———					
———					
———					
———					
Totals					

- Summarize by division
- Summarize by product

From *Total Business Planning* by E.J. Burton and W.B. McBride © 1991 John Wiley & Sons, Inc.

Figure 1.9

Planning Unit
_____

To be completed by: _____

SALES FORECAST SUMMARY FOR 19____

Units Projected

Product(s)	Quarter 1	Quarter 2	Quarter 3	Quarter 4	Annual
_____					
_____					
_____					
_____					
_____					
_____					
_____					
_____					
_____					
_____					
_____					
_____					
_____					
Totals					

From _Total Business Planning_ by E.J. Burton and W.B. McBride © 1991 John Wiley & Sons, Inc.

Figure 1.10

KEY SEGMENT PERSONNEL PROJECTIONS

Planning Unit

Position Title	Number of Employees		Increase
	Current Yr. 19 __	Planning Yr. 19 __	(Decrease)

From *Total Business Planning* by E.J. Burton and W.B. McBride © 1991 John Wiley & Sons, Inc.

Figure 1.11

In the development of the objectives and goals of the business, all participants should keep in mind the eight characteristics of well-stated objectives and goals.

1. *Consistent*. Objectives and goals should be consistent with all of the planning levels described above as well as any other stated objectives and goals.
2. *Clear*. Objectives and goals should be stated in such a way that the reader understands the writer's intentions.
3. *Concise*. Objectives and goals should focus on one and only one issue so as to avoid confusion and conflict.
4. *Actionable*. Objectives and goals should be stated in such a way that permits specific actions to be taken toward their accomplishment.
5. *Measurable*. Objectives and goals must be subjected to performance standards and, if possible, those standards should be stated in quantitative terms.
6. *Monitorable*. Objectives and goals should be broken into specific segments so that they can be evaluated periodically for accomplishment.
7. *Positive*. Objectives and goals should be stated in active, not passive, terms.
8. *Motivating*. Objectives and goals should have an element of vision and commitment so that they motivate personnel toward higher accomplishment levels.

Level Seven

Implementation and follow-up are critical. Without diligent and prudent implementation, the best plans are to no avail. Therefore, a major part of the planning effort must be devoted to how to make it happen, how to know if it is happening, what to do if it isn't happening, and what rewards are appropriate for those who do make it happen. These should not be afterthoughts but rather part of the plan.

While much of the foundational planning occurs at the top of the organization, the majority of the implementation occurs at the "bottom," on an individual basis. Each person must know exactly what is expected of him or her by what date, and how it will be measured. Figures 1.12 and 1.13 are a part of a system devised by the authors for this purpose.

Figures 1.14 and 1.15 are also a part of that system. These are designed to quantify, to the maximum extent possible, the planning outcome ex-

INDIVIDUAL PERFORMANCE EXPECTATIONS

SUMMARY OF TACTICS/ACTION STEPS ASSIGNED

Name: _____   Page ___ of ___

Department: _____   Acknowledged by: _____

Date: _____

GOAL ID #	TACTIC/ACTION STEP ASSIGNED	COMPLETION DATE	EVIDENCE OF COMPLETION

© 1987 Professional Growth Associates, Inc., Tallahassee, FL.

From *Total Business Planning* by E.J. Burton and W.B. McBride © 1991 John Wiley & Sons, Inc.

Figure 1.12

INDIVIDUAL PERFORMANCE EXPECTATIONS

INSTRUCTIONS

_____   _____
Due Date   Planning Coordinator

Each Responsible Manager should complete an Individual Performance Expectations (IPE) sheet for each Employee to whom one or more Action Steps has been assigned for one or more Goals.

Primarily, the IPE sheet is a consolidation of information from the Goal Action Plan Sheets. It is intended to help the Employee and Manager understand and track the Tactics/Action Steps for which an individual is responsible.

As the Responsible Manager you should:

1. Complete the Name and Department information.

2. List the Goal ID #, the Tactic/Action Step Assigned, the Completion Date by which this step should be done, and the Evidence of Completion for _each_ item assigned to this person. This information can be taken from the Goal Action Plan Sheets.

3. Complete the "Page ___of ___ " indicators for each page for each person.

4. Give a copy of each Employee's IPE to that Employee and discuss the expectations.

5. Have each Employee sign and date (Acknowledged by and Date) the original IPE and return it to you. The Employee should retain a copy.

6. Keep a copy and give the original to the Planning Coordinator by the Due Date.

7. At least quarterly, review the IPE sheets with each of your employees as a part of the plan progress review.

© 1987 Professional Growth Associates, Inc., Tallahassee, FL.

From _Total Business Planning_ by E.J. Burton and W.B. McBride © 1991 John Wiley & Sons, Inc.

Figure 1.13

pectations. Having a quantitative measurement system allows everyone to grasp quickly how well they are doing against plan and to note where adjustments are needed.

Results can be noted at the individual level, the unit level, and the organization level. Figure 1.16 shows a sample outcome from the quantitative measurement at the organization level.

Putting the measurement in graphic form, much like the standard United Way barometer that is so often used to note progress toward a contribution goal, is very effective. Figure 1.17 illustrates how this is done using the numbers from Figure 1.16.

Following Figure 1.17 is the outline of a business plan. For your specific purpose you may reorganize, add to, or delete sections of this outline. However, this will serve as a guide for the plan you want to put together.

GOAL WEIGHTING AND PROGRESS CHART

FYE: _____

Due Date _____ Planning Coordinator _____

Please complete the indicated columns and return to the Planning Coordinator on or before the Due Date.

Columns to be Completed

Responsible Person: _____

| 1 | 2 | 3 | 4 | 5 | 6 | 7 | 8 | 9 | 10 | 11 | 12 |

Corp. Obj. No.	Weight to Objective	Goal No.	Weight to Goal	Cumulative Completion Percentage*							
				Exp. 1st Qtr.	Act. 1st Qtr.	Exp. 2nd Qtr.	Act. 2nd Qtr.	Exp. 3rd Qtr.	Act. 3rd Qtr.	Exp. 4th Qtr.	Act. 4th Qtr.
										100%	
										100%	
										100%	
										100%	
										100%	
										100%	
										100%	
										100%	
										100%	
										100%	
										100%	
										100%	
										100%	
										100%	
XX	XX	XX	100%	XX	XX	XX	XX	XX	XX	XX	XX
Col 1	Col 2	Col 3	Col 4	Col 5	Col 6	Col 7	Col 8	Col 9	Col 10	Col 11	Col 12

* Exp = Expected at beginning of plan year   * Act = Actual at end of quarter

Expected columns to be completed fully. Actual columns to be completed at the end of the quarter.

© 1987 Professional Growth Associates, Inc., Tallahassee, FL.

From *Total Business Planning* by E.J. Burton and W.B. McBride © 1991 John Wiley & Sons, Inc.

Figure 1.14

GOAL WEIGHTING AND PROGRESS CHART

FYE: _____

INSTRUCTIONS

_____   _____
Due Date   Planning Coordinator

You have received a summary of all the Goals for your responsibility area with a Goal Identification number assigned and a Goal Weighting and Progress Chart listing all your Goals by Identification Number. If this is not so, please contact the Planning Coordinator immediately.

The Goal Listing Sheet is a summary of the Goals you have established for yourself and your responsibility area. It is for your information.

Goal Weighting and Progress Chart Instructions:

1. Columns 1, 2, and 3 have been completed for you.

2. Looking at your Goal Listing Sheet and considering the weight assigned to the related Corporate Objectives, (Col. 2), assign a weight (portion of 100%) to each listed Goal. Place the assigned weight in Col. 4 beside each Goal number (Col. 3).

3. Note that the sum of all Goal Weights for your Department must be 100%.

4. For each listed Goal, complete Cols. 5, 7, and 9 with the **cumulative** percentage of that Goal which you plan to attain by the end of the indicated quarter. Note that Col. 11 already indicates the planned cumulative percentage completion at the end of the 4th quarter to be 100%.

5. The same sheet will be used at the end of each quarter for you to record the Actual Completion of each Goal. However, at this time, Cols. 6, 8, 10, and 12 should be left blank.

6. When you have completed the above, make a copy of this sheet for your records and return the original to the Planning Coordinator by the Due Date above.

© 1987 Professional Growth Associates, Inc., Tallahassee, FL.

From *Total Business Planning* by E.J. Burton and W.B. McBride © 1991 John Wiley & Sons, Inc.

Figure 1.15

OBJECTIVE	WEIGHT	RELATIVE COMPLETION	YEAR-END WEIGHTED COMPLETION	VARIANCE
OBJECTIVE 1	20.00%	82.67%	16.53%	−3.47%
OBJECTIVE 2	30.00%	100.00%	30.00%	0.00%
OBJECTIVE 3	40.00%	60.00%	24.00%	−16.00%
OBJECTIVE 4	10.00%	100.00%	10.00%	0.00%
TOTAL	100.00%		80.53%	−19.47%

Figure 1.16

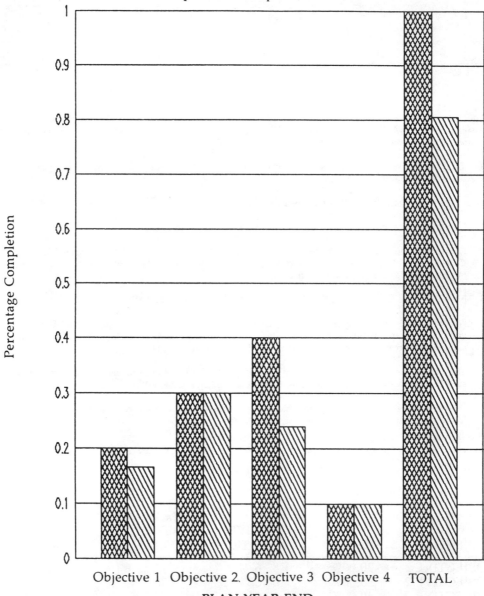

SAMPLE

Comparison of Expected to Actual

Figure 1.17

BUSINESS PLAN OUTLINE

1. *Cover sheet.* (with appropriate descriptions):
   Business name
   Business address
   Business phone
   Principals
   Date
2. *Sign-up page.* Every manager who helps make the plan should sign it, thereby encouraging commitment to the plan.
3. *Executive summary.* This is what sells someone on reading the remainder of the plan. It should be about two double-spaced, typed pages and contain the essence of the plan. Remember: consider for whom it is written, what is being requested from them, and why they should be interested in doing it.
4. *Table of contents.* Make it specific and complete. Some readers may judge the completeness of the plan from the detail provided in the table of contents.
5. *Major assumptions.* Any assumptions vital to the plan should be stated here. Also include brief contingencies for actions to be taken if the assumptions are violated.
6. *Background section.* If this is a start-up venture, a brief explanation should be made of how the idea (project, product, new territory company, etc.) originated. If this is an operating plan, this section may supplement the major highlights with additional detail in an appendix.
7. *Definition of the business.* It is important that you be able to state succinctly what the business is. This is distinct from what the business does (a listing of functions, products, or services), and should be geared to answer the question: *What need are we meeting?* The philosophy and mission are placed here.
8. *Definition of the market.* Having stated *what* need you are fulfilling, you can now define *who* has that need. Your definition will indicate the target of your marketing effort and will give demographic characteristics. Your market penetration projections should be included along with an analysis of the competition. Your strategic planning assessments will be placed here.
9. *Description of products or services.* Identify needed products or services. The description(s) of the product or services should fully explain to the reader why, given the previously stated information, your products or services will be demanded. You may append catalog sheets, pictures,

etc. Basically, this is psychographic information—why people will buy your products or services.

10. *Management structure.* Having described the business, the market, and the product, it is time to indicate who will make things happen. A start-up or financing plan will require more detail than will an operating plan. Resumes and other details of personal backgrounds should be left to an appendix. This section should sell two things: *that you have the right people* and *that they are properly organized.*

11. *Objectives, goals, and tactics.* State what you intend to accomplish and how. Include varying amounts of detail based upon the purpose of the plan, but focus this section on the "crunch factors." Much of the detail can be placed in the appendices. Areas of objectives or goals to be covered in this section include (but are not limited to):

   a. Sales forecasts.

   b. Marketing plans.

   c. Manufacturing or servicing plans.

   d. Quality assurance plans.

   e. Financial plans.

12. *Financial data.* The plan is future oriented. Therefore, this section should focus on projections and pro formas. Historical financial information necessary to understanding the plan should be referenced in an appendix. The items to be included are:

   a. Cost-volume-profit analysis.

   b. Income projections—pro forma:

   • monthly for planning year.

   • quarterly for second year.

   • annual for third year.

   c. Cash flow analysis—pro forma:

   • monthly for planning year.

   • quarterly for second year.

   • annual for third year.

Appendices. Appendices give supporting detail to the content section as well as adding material of interest not otherwise included. If there is proprietary information (patent, research and development, formulas, market research, etc.) the distribution of which you may wish to control, it would be wise to place that information in detachable appendices to include:

1. Narrative history of the company.

2. Management structure. Additional resumes, organization charts, etc.

3. Detail of objectives, goals, and strategies:
   - products and services.
   - research and development.
   - marketing.
   - manufacturing.
   - administration.
   - finance.
4. Historical financial information (three to five years if possible).
5. Tax returns (three to five years if possible).
6. Letters of recommendation or endorsement.
7. Report forms and schedules.

SUMMARY

Planning is a function carried out in varying degrees by people as individuals as well as people banded together to form organizations or businesses. Most plans are conceptualizations of what a person intends to do in the short- or long-term future. A business plan operates in the same manner. But, unless written, the plan may be of little use externally or even internally. The physical process of writing a plan encourages consideration of most of the elements of a good plan.

Creating a business plan is an ongoing, continuous process, the implementation of which will determine how the business will be run over time. The plan should be originated from the top down, with upper management providing direction and objectives and lower levels of management fleshing out detail and definition.

The step-by-step generation is done in seven levels. Level one is the development of philosophy/mission. Level two is the strategic assessment of the competitive environment. Level three is the creation or statement of the major objectives of the firm or business. Level four is the setting of goals for the particular parts of the business. Level five is the assimilation of the people who have to execute the plan to establish how will it be made to happen. Level six is the generation of a tangible document, formalizing the plan as envisioned. The objectives of the business should be consistent, clear, consise, actionable, measurable, monitorable, positive, and motivating. Level seven is implementation and follow-up on what has been planned.

While there is no set format for a business plan, many text writers offer a variety of suggestions. What they all seem to have in common is a structured format for the presentation of how the business got here, what assumptions were being made, where it intends to go, and how it expects to get there.

Remembering that the business plan may also serve the purpose of trying to "sell" the business to bankers, investors and potential trade creditors, it is best to write for the specific audience expected to read the document. You may wish to tailor a version of the plan to the specific audience. This can be done by changing the emphasis and detail in certain parts of the plan. If, for example, the business is seeking a short-term loan from a bank, the firm's liquidity and cash flow prospects should be emphasized (especially if they are favorable).

APPENDIX A: HISTORY QUESTIONNAIRE

To be completed by: _____

Completing these questions will help to show how we became what we are and why we are positioned to do what we have planned to do.

1. Date of company's founding. _____

    _____

2. Original founder(s) of business, name of business, location of business, and purpose of business. _____

    _____

3. Changes in name, location, and/or purpose, along with corresponding dates. _____

    _____

    _____

4. Major economic or environmental events which have affected company. _____

    _____

    _____

5. Dates and explanations of major additions to or divestitures of business. _____

    _____

    _____

6. Major obstacles and problems the business has faced. _____

    _____

    _____

7. Turning points, and causes of greatest periods of growth and profitability. _____

    _____

    _____

From *Total Business Planning* by E.J. Burton and W.B. McBride © 1991 John Wiley & Sons, Inc.

APPENDIX B: STATUS QUO QUESTIONNAIRE

To be completed by: _____

1. If the company operates in the coming year in the same manner as this year, identify those areas under your budgeting control (budget lines) which:

    a. Must be increased

    _____

    b. Could stay the same

    _____

    c. Are targets for cost reductions

    _____

2. Again assuming the present methods of operations:

    a. Identify two conditions over which you have little control that keep your area from making a greater profit contribution.

    _____

    _____

    b. State two changes which you have (or can get) authority to change that should make your area more profitable.

    _____

    _____

    c. By what date(s) could the above changes reasonably be made?

    _____

    _____

From *Total Business Planning* by E.J. Burton and W.B. McBride © 1991 John Wiley & Sons, Inc.

APPENDIX C: THIRTY QUESTIONS TO ASSIST WITH STRATEGIC PLANNING

1. Who are our five major customers (or classes of customers)?

    a. _____

    b. _____

    c. _____

    d. _____

    e. _____

2. What are the common characteristics of these five?

    a. _____

    b. _____

    c. _____

3. Why do they buy our product?

    a. _____

    b. _____

    c. _____

4. Who are three potential customers (or classes of customers) who do not currently do business with us?

    a. _____

    b. _____

    c. _____

5. Why don't these three do business with us?

    a. _____

    b. _____

    c. _____

6. Are there any obvious ethnic, age, religious, gender, or other biases in our customer base?

    _____

    _____

From *Total Business Planning* by E.J. Burton and W.B. McBride © 1991 John Wiley & Sons, Inc.

7. What is our most effective sales channel?

    _____

    _____

    _____

8. What products are our greatest revenue producers?

    a. _____

    b. _____

    c. _____

9. What products are our greatest profit producers?

    a. _____

    b. _____

    c. _____

10. If customers could not buy what we sell (even from a competitor)
    what would they do?

    _____

    _____

    _____

    _____

Demographics—Who buys?

11. Are our products purchased primarily by any particular age group?

    _____

12. Are our products purchased primarily by any specific ethnic group?

    _____

13. Are our products purchased primarily by one gender?

    _____

14. Are our products purchased primarily within any geographic area(s)?

    _____

15. Are our products purchased primarily by any income level group?

_____

16. Are sales of our product(s) tied to sales or use of any other products?

_____

17. Are sales of our product tied largely to any occupational category?

_____

18. What is the education level of our primary purchasers?

_____

19. Who (according to the above categories) are the heaviest users of our product?

_____

Psychographics—Why do they buy?

20. What are the benefits each class of customer (see above) derives from using our product?

_____

_____

21. Which _advertising_ has been most effective?

_____

_____

22. Whose _endorsement_ might cause a person to buy our product(s)?

_____

_____

23. What types of _packaging_ have produced the most sales?

_____

_____

24. What is the buyer's _hot button_?

_____

_____

Channels—Where do they buy?

25. Which distribution channel produces the most sales revenue?

    _____

    _____

26. Which distribution channel produces the most gross profit?

    _____

    _____

27. What has been the greatest change competitors have made in dis-
    tribution channels?

    _____

    _____

28. What has been the most effective change we have made in distribution
    channels?

    _____

    _____

29. Why was the change (in question 28) so effective?

    _____

    _____

30. Is there a level in the distribution link which can be eliminated?

    _____

    _____

From *Total Business Planning* by E.J. Burton and W.B. McBride © 1991 John Wiley & Sons, Inc.

APPENDIX D: INTERNAL DATA MONITORING

Item Monitored	Last Period	Current Period	Desired Pro Forma
Financial			
1. Profit Margin (Earnings/Sales)			
2. Asset Turnover (Sales/Assets)			
3. Capital Structure (Assets/Equity)			
4. Return on Equity [(1) × (2) × (3)]			
5. Accounts Receivable Turnover (Sales/Accounts Receivable)			
6. Accounts Payable Turnover (Purchases/Accounts Payable)			
7. Current Ratio (Current Assets/Current Liabilities)			
Operational*			
8.			
9.			

*Examples of operational data to be monitored might include:

- Backlog
- Down-time
- Rejects
- Calls received

From *Total Business Planning* by E.J. Burton and W.B. McBride © 1991 John Wiley & Sons, Inc.

__2__

Forecasting

$\mathbf{A}$s stated in the previous chapter, any businessman who seriously intends to improve the likelihood of success engages in some form of planning. Since you do not know with certainty what the future will bring, the on-going process of making decisions will involve estimates and projections based upon past experiences, others' advice, and some old "seat-of-the-pants" guessing. Like personal plans for the weekend, plans for the future are based upon forecasts. The forecast provides the skeleton that you flesh out with operating, financial, and sales expectations.

Forecasting, with all its potential mathematical complexities, statistical manipulations, and scientific underpinnings, still has a little magic and intuition to it. The weather forecast for the weekend may be conducted on a grand, "scientific," scale with weather satellites, color weather radar, and sophisticated modeling, but whether it will rain at the cottage on Saturday is still just an educated guess. Likewise, a forecast of the economy and the market will be both scientific and intuitive.

In business, forecasting is often associated with quantitative projections of specific numbers such as sales, gross profits, operating expenses, etc. Certainly these projections are a necessary element. However, there is a qualitative component as well, which does not lend itself to numeric outcomes but is equally essential.

Forecasting is a learned skill; it is the assimilation of data into a usable estimation of what the future will *probably* be. Better data does not guarantee better forecasts but it does improve the probability. Good forecasts are the result of two elements: good data and meaningful analysis. These two elements are the foundation of the four basic steps of good forecasting:

- Compilation of accurate fundamental data (sometimes called the bench mark).
- Preparation of the data for analysis purposes.
- Application of one or more forecasting methods to analyze the data.
- Application of sound judgment and intuition to develop the forecast.

Because there are many good books written on the mathematical/statistical aspects of forecasting, which is a complex and time-consuming subject on its own, we will discuss these matters briefly and refer you to other sources to deal with those complexities. This chapter focuses on *using* forecasts.

Some representative references you may want to consult for help with the "math" part of forecasting are (from simple to complicated):

1. *Budgeting Fundamentals for Nonfinancial Executives and Managers*, Allen Sweeny and John Wisener, Jr., McGraw-Hill Paperbacks.
2. *Budgeting for Profit*, John C. Camillus, Chilton Better Business Services.
3. *Business Cycles and Forecasting*, Carl A. Danten and Lloyd M. Valentine, Southwestern Publishing Company.
4. The instruction manual from your computer spread-sheet package.
5. *Information for Decision Making: Quantitative and Behavioral Decisions* (Second Edition), Alfred Rappaport, editor, Prentice-Hall.

Initially, you have to decide what you are trying to forecast:

- a short-term projection—less than a year,
- an intermediate plan—two to five years, or
- a long-term commitment of over five years.

At first, it seems unlikely that you will try to forecast the future for more than five years. But some large, capital-intensive businesses must forecast beyond that period. An electric utility, for example, which may invest billions of dollars in just one power plant, faces construction cycles of five to seven years. At the time of completion, the company hopes to have adequate demand to pay both a return *of* its investments and a return *on* its investment.

Closer to home, you may have to look five to seven years out if you are starting from scratch to research and develop a significant new product.

Once the planning or forecasting horizon is established, you have to make the second essential decision: "What is it we want to forecast?" For the power plant, as with many products, the question may have many answers:

- The peak and average demand for power by year, until project retirement.
- The regulatory environment established by the government and how much it will allow to be recovered through rates during construction.
- The projected costs from completion of construction through the operating life of the plant.
- The environmental concerns faced in the generation of electricity from other energy sources.

These questions may not seem to be comparable to your forecasting problems. However, upon closer examination, the concerns are not dissimilar. For the smaller business the forecasting demands might be:

- Peak and average demand for the product.
- What government regulation might be imposed (quotas, import restriction, tariffs, etc.)?
- What will the investment market be like—what will money cost?
- What design changes or product innovations may result?
- What air or water pollution problems may the business processes encounter (e.g., waste disposals)?
- What can we expect from competitors?

This series of concerns points up the need to forecast the external environment. The external environment consists of all those factors outside the business that may affect the ability of the business to produce, market, and sell a product or service.

While the external environment has an impact on the business, it is not the only environment that the business must survey. The business is also affected by many internal forces:

- *Labor costs.* Some of the considerations to be included in the forecasts are:
  1. Employee/benefits related costs.

   2. Government requirements.
   3. Safety costs.
   4. Hours of work required.
   5. Automation impacts.
   6. Unions impacts.
   7. Productivity changes.
   8. Turnover/retirement.

- *Material Costs.* In this case, other elements must be evaluated to make an estimate of future costs:
   1. Availability—whether resources are scarce or plentiful.
   2. Transportation.
   3. Substitute commodities.
   4. Disposal of wastes.
   5. Product redesign/engineering changes.
   6. Cost reductions.
   7. Scrap and rework.

- *Overhead Costs.* Some of the concerns involved include:
   1. Taxes.
   2. Utilities.
   3. Maintenance/building repair.
   4. Cleaning.
   5. Materials handling.
   6. Warehousing and shipping.

COMPILING ACCURATE DATA

With good information, some insight, and intuition most people can generate a meaningful forecast. You may have the necessary insight or intuition but still wonder where the information needed for forecasting comes from. It is obtained from the same two environments that affect the future operations of the business: inside sources and outside sources.

Information from internal sources:

- *Company records.* These records are the basic internal data sources for the firm. Internal company records can be readily and consistently generated by automated or manual manipulations of production, financial, personnel, advertising, inventory, purchasing, and other data.

- *Product sales records.* These can be sorted and arranged by customer, product, sales region, county, city, product class, salesman, individual brand, and other.

- *Sales personnel*. Salesmen and regional sales managers can develop important information at a grass-roots level from customers, jobbers, distributors, and other local people such as bankers.

Information from external sources:

- *Government publications of statistical data*. Often government publications are the original source data used and summarized by other sources. Caution should be used to ensure that the data are the most current available. The government is continuously updating and refining its reports.
- *Secondary sources*. Many business publications, such as *Fortune, The Wall Street Journal, Business Week, Newsweek,* and *U.S. News and World Report,* are first-rate sources of statistical data; however, the information printed in these sources is often derived (and interpreted) from primary government publications. Going to the primary source is preferable.
- *Information and data from trade associations*. This data is compiled and generated from members of the trade association, paid for by members, and generally distributed to members.
- *Trade publications*. Information, data, and analysis are published in trade journals, trade papers, or magazines and consumer publications. It may be provided at no charge or for a subscription fee.
- *Syndicated services*. Again, data, information, and analysis are accumulated by syndicated services, which sell this material to subscribers. Usually this information is restricted to subscribers.

The phrase "to subscribers only," used by a number of the best publications, makes it sound as if there are few free data sources. However, in a great number of cases, the public library is either a subscriber or may be associated with another library that is a subscriber. Because most libraries are funded through public money, they offer easy and free access to the publications that are limited to "subscribers only." In fact, librarians will always assist in locating relevant, timely data and information. Public libraries, particularly college and university libraries, are great sources of current information.

PREPARING THE DATA FOR ANALYSIS

A forecast is the end result of a continuous process aimed at predicting the future. Since you cannot consistently predict the future with any certainty, the process has a feedback step built into the procedure to permit you to reconsider the projections based upon changed data. Forecasting should be continuous and ongoing and not static. Because the value of any forecast is based upon the degree to which it can provide useful information for the decision-making process, the best information about the market and the demands it places upon you should be input into the process.

There is no one hard and fast forecasting process. But the following eight steps are generally applicable to most forecasting efforts. These can be expanded or contracted to fit your needs.

1. List the basic facts about past trends and forecasts.
2. Establish the causes of changes in past actual demand.
3. Analyze the causes of deviations between previous forecasts and past actuals.
4. Determine factors that are likely to affect future demand.
5. Based only upon information available to you *before* that period, generate a forecast for a *past* period. Then measure your accuracy and reliability against the known results. Make any necessary changes to your process until it is an acceptable predictor of the *actual* results of the past period. This allows you, via a trial run approach, to construct a proven effective process on known data.
6. Create a forecast for the future using your revised methodology from step 5.
7. Monitor the performance of the forecast against actual outcomes and determine the causes of variation from the forecast.
8. Revise the forecast when new data or obvious methodology errors appear.

Stating an eight-step process for the generation and use of a forecast makes it appear as if there is a beginning and an end. In reality, it is a continuous process throughout the life of any product and continues through a transition period into new products.

Some of the major external factors to be considered in the forecasting process are:

Competitor/Market Analysis:

• The primary data requirement is the size of the market or potential market—locally, regionally, or nationally.

- The number of direct competitors and those producing similar products that may target different parts of the market because of product differentiation.

- The relative position in the market and an analysis of the objectives stated in your business plan.

- Results of any test marketing programs and the information generated concerning national or regional market acceptance.

- Estimation of competitive reaction to product introduction.

In undertaking a test market analysis, you try to estimate what will happen in your target by experimenting in reasonably representative smaller markets. You experiment with different advertising and promotional campaigns and observe the effectiveness of the programs. Getting some actual reactions to plans for the product's introduction market-wide should lessen the risk of product failure. Usually by this stage in the process of product introduction the product is well defined and capable of being produced in quantity.

Often, however, you are interested in opening a retail outlet or providing a service and don't have the luxury (and the considerable expense) associated with test marketing. In such cases, in order to improve the chances of success, you may still wish to conduct a small market survey.

For example, a businessman in a city of 96,000 is considering opening a Scandinavian furniture and accessories store. At present there is no store of its kind in the city. He has visited most of the specialty stores in the community and has reasonably assured himself that except for a few isolated products in a few stores he could expect no immediate competition. While this is interesting, it does not assure success—it means there is no *current* competition, but it could also mean that someone had tried and failed to provide the product.

What do you do next? Information normally available in the public library may be very helpful to you. A survey of the U.S. Census will give the cities in the U.S. with populations comparable to that of the city in which you seek to start the business. Next, a review of the telephone directory yellow pages for those cities (also often available in the library) quickly identifies cities with Scandinavian furniture stores. In this manner, a data base of comparable businesses in similar cities can be compiled, with names, addresses, and phone numbers.

The owners of some of these businesses may be willing to share their experiences, if they feel secure that they are not providing a potential competitor with information. If the businesses or cities are not at too great a distance, you can visit them to obtain valuable pricing and marketing information.

In summary, the concerns of the retail store are not unlike the manufacturer:

- You determine if you have competitors, and who they are.
- You segment the furniture and accessories market and settle upon the business of Scandinavian furniture and accessories.
- You evaluate the possibility or probability of new entrants into the market segment.

One final consideration is determining how and in what areas the business can compete. If you're entering a market with established competition, you should prepare an evaluation of how and on what variables the competitors compete. This is called Strategic Competitor Assessment and is part of the Strategic Factors Analysis (see Chapter 1, Figures 1.5 and 1.6).

A pertinent question for a Strategic Competitor Assessment is: Do the firms compete on the basis of

- costs (cost-plus construction)
- price (roofing shingles)
- technology (personal computers, watches, and calculators)
- service (accounting firms, lawyers, and consultants)
- distribution (fast food)?

By discovering the variable of most importance, you will have valuable information on which to base your business plan. And, you will know the area of data collection of primary importance to your forecasting needs.

In some areas, technological breakthroughs have occurred with such speed that new products are developed and marketed in a matter of months. The digital wristwatch is such a product. With the rate of innovation and concentration on product features (at low prices) it is difficult to predict future market conditions. The wristwatch market at one time was distinguished by two features: cost and accuracy. With the introduction of sophisticated electronic technologies, the issue of accuracy of movements has been significantly reduced as a differentiable issue. With the tremendous reduction in the costs of technology and the high market competition, prices have been driven down to the level that the product is often considered disposable. It may be cheaper to buy a new watch than to purchase replacement batteries.

Though historical information may show a frequency of product innovation and introduction this may not be useful in periods of great change. The difficulty may be compounded if the product is subject to seasonal demand. Technological innovations reduced to new product introduction are timed to coincide with high product demand periods.

Another technological innovation consideration is the entry of existing technology into new products and markets. The microprocessor is a technology that has been introduced into many new product configurations. Such introductions have changed the competitive factors and differentiated products, thus influencing markets significantly.

- Microprocessors control the fuel consumption of automobiles, directly resulting in a new competitive element of "better gas mileage."
- Microprocessors in microwave ovens allow the user to pop in a frozen mass at 8:00 A.M. and arrive home at 5:00 P.M. to a prepared meal.
- A microprocessor plays games with the kids, teaches French to a teenager, and balances the checkbook. It will even let Mom or Dad do the family tax return for the year.
- The microprocessor tucked neatly away in the thermostat in the hall can control the heat and air conditioning in the house, taking advantage of time-of-day utility rates, outside climate, and day and night differentials.
- A microprocessor in the home or office security system can detect fire, intrusions, and threats to security while informing the appropriate agency of the condition.

Microprocessors have almost limitless applications to existing products. These applications of existing technologies present a lower risk than the introduction of a new technology because both the existing technology and the existing product have established market acceptance.

It is also important to forecast for technological innovation and application. This factor can bring about product obsolescence and decreased marketability faster than almost any other influence.

A final major consideration concerning technology changes may be reflected in psychographic marketing factors.

- What benefits do your customers derive from using your product? What projected benefits do you anticipate adding and when?

- What adjectives do your customers use in describing your product and what adjectives do you want them to apply?
- Whose endorsements will help promote sales of the product as configured in the future?
- Where are the products currently purchased and how will that change with a change in technology?

The answers to these questions may indicate a product configuration for an electronic wristwatch that also has an alarm, night light, stop watch, waterproof case, calendar, and day/date functions. Advertising and marketing can be planned for many different approaches and markets based upon the psychographic ("hot button") factors indicated.

The business should take two points into consideration with regard to governments.

- What new governmental regulations may affect the way you currently do business?
- What continuing and future regulations can be anticipated to have an impact on your business?

No business is immune from governmental regulation. Typical interventions include:

- Product safety.
- Licensure (certification).
- Taxation.
- Employee considerations:
  —OSHA.
  —Social security.
  —Unemployment compensation.
  —Insurance.
  —Pensions and other benefits.
- Regulation of output.
- Price controls.
- Import/export quotas and regulations.
- Operating authority (permits).
- Duties (import) and inspection.

Each of these (and other) categories has an associated cost, and in some cases established future requirements. For example, in the case of employee social security benefits, rate increases and ceilings have been established for future periods. These, of course, affect costs and therefore future product pricing. Each must be forecast for the planning horizon.

Whereas some governmental impacts may be predicted with reasonable accuracy, others, such as the currency exchange rate, may create serious problems. The results of governmental activity are not easily projected and even experts have difficulty in predicting governmental behavior, not to mention the impacts of that behavior. However, a reasonable attempt is better than no attempt.

APPLICATION OF FORECASTING METHODS

Beginning in the 1920s, government and, later, private companies began compiling data and conducting quantitative analysis of the national economy. The intent of the studies was to devise a system that would signal changes in the business environment, warn of downturns, and predict the end of recessions. From the data collected, monthly, quarterly, and annual series on prices, employment, and production were generated as indicators of business health.

A number of data series, such as employment, indexes of consumer and wholesale prices, and manufacturers' orders are published in the nation's newspapers. These indicators are followed closely by many professionals, especially during periods of change in business activities.

Economic indicators have been grouped into three types: leading, coincidental, and lagging.

- *Leading*. These indicators provide advance warning of possible changes in business activities.
- *Coincidental*. These reflect the current performance of the economy.
- *Lagging*. These confirm a change previously signaled in the economic business activity.

Coincidental indicators are perhaps the most common and familiar. They include (For some products or services these may also be leading or lagging indicators):

- Gross National Product.
- Industrial production.
- Personal income.
- Retail sales.
- Employment.

Whereas coincidental indicators are used to determine whether the economy is currently experiencing contraction, expansion, or stability, leading indicators are necessary for forecasting. Leading indicators help forecasters assess short-term trends in the coincidental indicators. In addition, leading indicators help planners and policy makers anticipate changes in the economy: they may indicate up-turns or down-turns in business. Anticipating down-turns helps the business take corrective action and plan for the tightening of economic conditions. In the event that an up-turn is suggested, the business could prepare to take advantage of the improvement in business conditions.

Housing starts is a key leading indicator for economic activity in some industries. Others include:

- New orders for durable goods.
- Construction contracts.
- Formation of new business enterprises.
- Hiring rates.
- Average length of workweek.

Using indicators for forecasting has been refined and developed by professional forecasting businesses that use sophisticated mathematical and statistical models to generate projections. For many smaller businesses, a manual algorithm, or a step-by-step approach, can produce effective projections. It is set out in the following steps:

1. Plot a time series of the industry's historical experience (sales per year, units per month, etc.).

2. Remove any seasonality by using some averaging or smoothing method. (Irregularities due to some obviously unusual problem such as a war may also require adjustment.)

3. Fit a trend using linear regression (least squares) or the eyeball method.

4. Repeat these steps for national, regional, local, or industrial or trade association data of a causal nature. For example, sales of replacement auto parts is related to sales of new autos in previous periods. The intent here is to find a comparative series.

5. If there is a historical relationship in the cycle pattern between that which you want to predict (sales of replacement parts) and the other data (sales of new cars),
   a. obtain forecasts of the other variable(s), and

   b. forecast the cycle for your variable based upon the cycle for the economic variable.

6. Project the trend line determined in step 3 and add the cycle generated in step 5.

7. Remember the seasonal variations you may earlier have attempted to remove for simplicity.

8. Test the projection for reasonableness.

One of your concerns may be which indicators will be most relevant for comparative purposes. As mentioned throughout this book, trade association data and information is often most relevant and comparable. It is usually most appropriate for market share and market size determinations.

Comparative indicators can come from evaluation of demographic information about your product. By answering the following questions, you may be able to generate forecasts based upon the growth patterns of these factors.

- What particular age group purchases your products?
- Are your products purchased by a specific ethnic group?
- Is your product purchased more frequently by either gender?
- Is the product geographically restricted?
- Are the products purchased by people of a particular income level?
- Are sales of the product tied to the sales of other products?
- Are the sales related to any one occupational category?
- What is the educational level of purchasers of the product?
- Who (according to the above categories) are the heaviest users of your product?

Applying Judgment and Intuition

One method for testing the reasonableness of your forecasts is the use of scenarios. The use of scenarios offers you a technique designed to help you face the possible unpleasant situations that may occur.

A scenario is a story about the future that uses current facts and trends. The conclusion to the story is presented in a form that is easy to understand. It is important to remember that in scenario preparation, evaluation of the possible outcome initially has to be suspended so that discussion of the problem can occur objectively. Prejudging a scenario has a chilling effect upon brainstorming. It is through creative brainstorming—always to be encouraged—that scenarios are created.

SUMMARY

Forecasting is a combination of science and intuition, or, if you will, art. Its objective should be the generation of multiple forecasts based upon different scenarios. Getting involved in scenario generation helps managers steer clear of thinking there is only one way to run the business. It allows for creative, alternative planning.

The necessary analysis of the market, competitors, the economy, and the firm itself enlightens management as to the position of the firm in the market and price structure; how demand works; how the economic cycle affects the business plans; and how the firm can integrate these elements to forecast for better planning.

APPENDIX: LINEAR REGRESSION

The term "linear regression" often scares people off. The more familiar expression, "least squares estimate," a form of linear regression, is less frightening and most people have been exposed to it. Many inexpensive calculators will make linear regression determinations after entry of the data.

Linear regression determines the placement of a line that minimizes the sum of the squares of the deviations of the actual data points from the straight line of best fit. The linear equation of the form—

$$Y = MX + B$$

—is determined for the line. M is the slope of the line and B is the Y intercept. If the relationship is set up so that the cost of production is the Y axis and the units of production are the X axis, the Y intercept (the point of zero production), should approximate the fixed costs. In this model, the slope, M, is the change associated with an incremental change in production. This would indicate the variable cost. As the mathematics are somewhat complicated, we have developed the following worksheet (Figure 2.1) to ease the operation.

LEAST SQUARES LINE OF REGRESSION

PERIOD	COLUMN 1 Units	COLUMN 2 Total Costs	COLUMN 3 Col. 1 Squared	COLUMN 4 Col. 1 × Col. 2
1				
2				
3				
4				
5				
6				
7				
8				
9				
10				
11				
12				
13				
14				
15				
TOTAL				

Figure 2.1

Some example data to fill in Figure 1 follows:
Assume for a given 12-month period the following data:

Month	Units	Costs
Jan	500	1200
Feb	200	700
Mar	300	1100
Apr	600	1500
May	100	600
June	400	1100
July	500	1500
Aug	200	500
Sept	400	1000
Oct	450	1200
Nov	300	800
Dec	550	1700
Total	4500	12900

With this data, we can now use the form "Least Squares Line of Regression" to calculate the slope/intercept form of the equation of the "best-fit" line. Instructions for use of the form follow.

INSTRUCTIONS:

A) For each period, enter units produced in column 1 and costs in column 2.

B) Square each figure in column 1 and enter the result in column 3.

C) Multiply each figure in column 1 by the corresponding figure in column 2 and enter the product in column 4.

D) Sum columns 1 through 4. Also determine the number of periods used.

E) Now substitute the values obtained into the following two equations:
  1) Sum of column 2 = (number of periods) (a) + (sum of column 1) (b).
  2) Sum of column 4 = (sum of column 1) (a) + (sum of column 3) (b).

F) To get (b), multiply equation 1 by (sum of column 1)/(number of periods) to produce equation 3. Subtract equation 3 from equation 2 and solve for (b).

G) To get (a), substitute (b) above into either equation 1 or 2 and solve for (a).

H) The figures thus obtained are used to construct the graph as follows:
   a = the cost at zero units of production
   b = the additional cost incurred with each unit of production

The example data have been placed into Figure 1 format. Column 1 contains production quantities and column 2 contains costs incurred. Let's assume that the periods are months so that we can ignore inflation and avoid adjusting the cost for it. This takes care of step (A).

Columns 3 and 4 have been filled in from steps (B) and (C). Totals are figured as called for in step (D) and the number of periods is 12. Figure 2.2 represents this information.

LEAST SQUARES LINE OF REGRESSION

PERIOD	COLUMN 1 Units	COLUMN 2 Total Costs	COLUMN 3 Col. 1 Squared	COLUMN 4 Col. 1 × Col. 2
1	500	1,200	250,000	600,000
2	200	700	40,000	140,000
3	300	1,100	90,000	330,000
4	600	1,500	360,000	900,000
5	100	600	10,000	60,000
6	400	1,100	160,000	440,000
7	500	1,500	250,000	750,000
8	200	500	40,000	100,000
9	400	1,000	160,000	400,000
10	450	1,200	202,500	540,000
11	300	800	90,000	240,000
12	550	1,700	302,500	935,000
13				
14				
15				
TOTAL	4,500	12,900	1,955,000	5,435,000

Figure 2.2

The equations in step (D) are:

$$(1) \quad 12{,}900 = 12a + 4500b \text{ and}$$

$$(2) \quad 5{,}435{,}000 = 4500a + 1{,}955{,}000b.$$

In step (F) we multiply equation (1) by 4500/12, or 375, and get equation (3):

$$(3) \quad 4{,}837{,}500 = 4500a + 1{,}687{,}500b$$

Subtracting equation (3) from equation (2) we get:

$$
\begin{array}{r}
5{,}435{,}000 = 4500a + 1{,}955{,}000b \\
\underline{4{,}837{,}000 = 4500a + 1{,}687{,}500b} \\
598{,}000 = \qquad\quad 267{,}500b \text{ and } b = 2.236
\end{array}
$$

In step (G) we substitute this value for (b) into either equation and find (a). Using equation (1):

$$12{,}900 = 12a + 4500 \,(2.236)$$

$$a = 236.5$$

The resulting graph is shown as Figure 2.3.

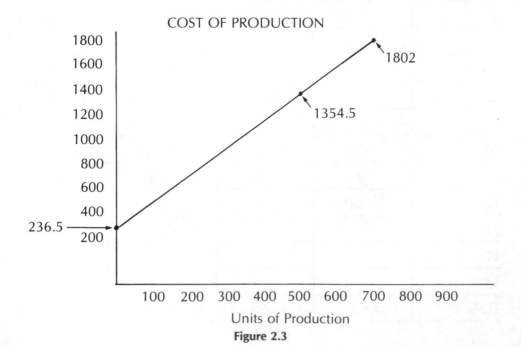

Figure 2.3

The graph is constructed as follows:

A) Find the point at which the line will cross the vertical axis. This is (a) or 236.5. Because it crosses the vertical axis at zero units of production we can use this as an approximation of fixed costs. Mark this point on the graph.

B) Compute another point on the line. Take an arbitrary level of production such as 700 units and multiply this number by (b). This gives an approximation of variable costs. Add fixed costs to this figure. Example: (700) (2.236) + 236.5 = 1802. This figure will be the total costs of production at that level of production. Plot this point on the graph. Connect the two points.

_3

Cost-Volume-Profit Relationships

The most common utilization of the cost-volume-profit relationship (C-V-P) has been to determine a break-even point. Business schools generally teach that the C-V-P relationship is a straight-line function. That is, you break even at the point of intersection of the total cost line and total revenue line. In certain situations that is an accurate reflection of reality. In other circumstances the truth is a bit more complex.

Figure 3.1 shows a typical straight-line version C-V-P relationship—the traditional break-even analysis. But break-even analysis can be a far more functional tool than a simple straight-line determination of a quantity where break-even occurs. The familiar equation for this graph is the sales quantity at which sales revenue equals the sum of fixed costs plus variable costs:

$$\text{BE Sales Revenue } = \text{ Fixed Costs } + \text{ Variable Costs.}$$

Another way to look at the two individual lines is to say that total cost (TC) is equal to the fixed cost (FC) plus the variable cost per unit (VC) times the quantity (Q):

$$TC = FC + (VC \times Q).$$

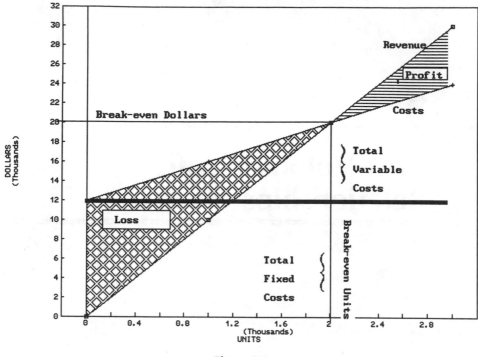

Figure 3.1

The equation for the total revenue (TR) line is simply the price (P) times the quantity sold:

$$TR = P \times Q.$$

The break-even point occurs where total revenue (TR) exactly equals total cost (TC):

$$TR = TC.$$

After the break-even point, total revenue exceeds total cost, and profits accrue.

The graph and the equation are, however, much more versatile tools than just break-even predictors. They can help you answer questions such as:

1. What price is necessary if given quantities are predicted?
2. What sales level is necessary to produce a given profit?
3. What effect will changes in variable costs have on profits?

4. What increase in sales volume is necessary to cover an increase in costs?

5. What effect does a change in fixed costs have on profit and break-even?

Although the answers to these questions are extremely useful, there are severe limiting assumptions associated with the straight-line model:

1. The selling price remains constant regardless of the quantity sold.

2. All costs are classifiable as strictly fixed or variable.

3. The fixed costs remain constant for all levels of production up to capacity.

4. Total variable costs vary directly with the volume produced.

5. The cost of inputs, policies, and technologies remain constant.

6. Production is always equal to sales (i.e., no inventory is carried).

In most cases you cannot meet the conditions of these assumptions; therefore this graph and equation may be of limited help. However, each condition and each assumption can be compared to the actual situation and a judgment made as to how well the graph represents it. The usefulness of any forecasting tool is measured by how reliable and accurate it is as a predictor. If the tool is an accurate predictor, you should evaluate the cost of compiling the necessary data against the benefits derived from making better decisions. If the tool is not accurate, it is not worthwhile no matter how small the cost.

As with any tool, the more it is pushed, the more complex its application becomes and the more costly the compilation of needed data. Fortunately, to a point, as the complexity increases the reliability and accuracy also increase. By making the use of the tool just a little more complex, the following helpful questions may be answered:

1. What selling price yields the greatest profits?

2. What effect would a change in the selling price have on revenues or on profits?

3. Should the firm attempt to raise its sales volume?

4. At what volume should the firm consider raising capacity?

In order to answer these questions, the model must be changed from the classic straight-line model to the curved-line model, which will be addressed later in the chapter.

It is clear that the simple break-even analysis can be useful in determining the point in units or in dollars where break-even occurs. In addition, the model has certain strategic planning and analysis value for solving capital budgeting problems and as an aid in making other management decisions.

SOME BASIC USES FOR COST-VOLUME-PROFIT RELATIONSHIPS

C-V-P can be used as an inexpensive screening device. Other financial models, such as discounted cash flow, require the use of more expensive, harder-to-get data. Before incurring the cost of gathering this data, a simple C-V-P analysis may initially tell whether it is worthwhile to do more intensive and costly analysis.

You can use C-V-P as a simple test for product specifications and designs. Each design has cost implications and costs often affect price and market feasibility. C-V-P analysis based on projected costs and expected selling prices permits comparison of possible designs before specifications are frozen and product or process lines are implemented. For example, C-V-P analysis can be used for a new product with an uncertain projected sales volume; the decision can be made whether to build parts on a temporary hand-tooled basis or to invest in expensive automated production tooling.

The hand-tooled method typically has higher variable costs but lower fixed costs. This will often result in a lower break-even quantity for a project, lower risks, and lower potential profits. Generally, the more automated and technology-intensive your process is, the higher the sales necessary for break-even. The obvious cause is that the initial fixed cost is significantly higher than in hand-tooling but the variable cost per product unit is correspondingly less. C-V-P analysis permits the examination of these trade-offs; alternatives may be compared and evaluated against one another.

You can also use C-V-P analysis as a substitute for estimating an unknown factor in making project decisions. In any decision concerning a project there are many variables that you must consider and estimate in reaching a decision (demand, cost, price, and other factors). Usually, costs can be approximated for a process or product, and only two variables remain: selling price and demand.

Because selling price and demand are related, demand is difficult to estimate. If demand can be estimated, profit is a simple calculation. The break-even point occurs at zero profit; therefore, it is simple to calculate the minimum demand above which a project becomes a reasonable undertaking. Of course, simply having calculated the demand estimate does not assure you the market share required. But break-even does give you a way to look at uncertainty and to fix a reasonable target quantity.

APPLYING C-V-P TO OTHER AREAS

While one use of C-V-P is to determine the sales necessary to generate a given profit level, you can also use the model to determine other useful information, such as the maximum out-of-pocket costs that should be put into the product.

For an understanding of how these different functions work, certain factors need to be defined.

Contribution on a per-unit basis (CM) is defined as the selling price per unit (P) minus the variable cost per unit (VC):

$$CM = P - VC$$

Break-even volume is equal to the total fixed cost (FC) divided by the contribution on a per-unit basis. Thus break-even volume (BV) equals fixed cost divided by contribution margin:

$$BV = \frac{FC}{CM}$$

Contribution margin as a percent of revenue (CM%) is equal to the selling price per unit (P) minus the variable cost per unit (VC) divided by the selling price (P):

$$CM\% = \frac{(P - VC)}{P}$$

Break-even in terms of dollars (B$) is equal to the total fixed cost (FC) divided by the contribution margin percentage (CM%):

$$B\$ = \frac{FC}{CM\%}$$

For example, if the selling price of an item was $10.00, with a variable cost of $7.50, the contribution on a per unit basis is equal to:

$$CM = \$10 - \$7.50 = \$2.50$$

If the fixed costs necessary to manufacture such an item are $250,000, the break-even volume would simply be:

$$BV = \frac{\$250,000}{\$2.50} = 100,000 \text{ units}$$

The CM% would be

$$(CM\%) = \frac{(\$10 - \$7.50)}{\$10} = 25\%$$

The B$ would be:

$$B\$ = \frac{\$250,000}{.25} = \$1,000,000$$

Using the formulae that have been generated, we will now look at the maximum out-of-pocket cost problem.

Problem. Suppose you can forecast sales with a reasonable degree of assurance and estimate you can sell 150,000 items per year. What out-of-pocket expenses can you incur and still break even? First we change the break-even formula to find and use those factors we know. Take the formula:

$$BV = \frac{FC}{CM}$$

Multiply both sides by CM to get:

$$BV \times CM = FC$$

Then solve for CM:

$$CM = \frac{FC}{BV}$$

Now we simply find the contribution margin for the product:

$$CM = \frac{\$250,000}{150,000 \text{ units}} = \$1.67$$

By subtracting the CM of $1.67 from the selling price of $10.00 we get $8.33, the variable cost the firm can incur on each unit and still break even at 150,000 units and a $10.00 selling price.

Determining Potential Selling Price for a Product. Again, assume the variable cost for producing the product is $7.50 per unit, and there are $250,000 in fixed costs. Add to that data the "known" sales volume of 150,000 units, and a desire to make a profit of $100,000 per year. What is the minimum selling price? The CM is equal to the fixed costs, divided by the break-even volume (CM = FC/BV). In our example, CM would be equal to $250,000 of fixed costs plus $100,000 of profit (treated as a fixed cost) divided by 150,000 units. Therefore: CM = $350,000/150,000, or CM is equal to $2.333. The minimum price should equal the variable cost plus the fixed cost: $7.50 + $2.333 = $9.833. (Remember: Up to the BV point all of the CM goes to meet FC. Therefore, the $2.333 per unit on the first 150,000 units is FC per unit.) Therefore, $9.84 is the selling price, which can be compared to the existing market price to determine whether the product has a good chance for selling, or if specifications must be altered to get the price down. This approach works well as an initial basis for bidding on projects.

Advertising Decisions

Advertising decisions may also be evaluated using C-V-P. Advertising is generally a contractually fixed cost. Any additional fixed costs raise the firm's break-even point, and thus require additional revenues or lower variable costs to compensate for the increase in expenditures. As already shown, the money for fixed-cost coverage comes from the contribution margin.

In our example, the contribution margin is 25 percent. Four additional dollars of revenue are required to cover each additional dollar of fixed cost. So, if you make a $25,000 expenditure for additional advertising, you would need to recover four times $25,000, or $100,000, in additional sales just to cover the cost of the additional advertising. You are not trying to guess how much sales will be generated from the additional advertising; you are evaluating the necessary increase in sales to justify an incremental expenditure for advertising.

Analysis of Credit Request

The model may also be used to determine whether to grant a request for credit. All that is required is an understanding of how to evaluate a credit application.

For example, a potential distributor for a product approaches you and requests to be considered for credit purchases. This distributor expects to purchase 400 units per month and requests terms of net 30 days, and conservatively estimates his account will turn over eight times per year. How do you evaluate whether to extend credit to this potential distributor?

Whenever a new account is taken on, the potential loss to you is the variable cost of the balance carried. The fixed costs are considered "sunk" and taking on an additional credit customer does not significantly affect the sunk costs. However, you incur the additional cost of carrying and administering the account. If we assume the carrying costs amount to ten percent of the average balance, and the administrative costs are fixed at $1,000.00 per year for each new account, the average expected balance is found by taking total sales and dividing by turnover. The average expected balance in our case would be equal to 400 units times $10 per unit times 12 months, divided by 8 (expected turnover per year).

$$\text{Average Expected Balance} = \frac{\$48,000}{8} = \$6,000$$

The fixed cost associated with taking on this account is 10 percent of the average balance, plus the administrative costs:

$$FC = (\$6,000 \times 10\%) + \$1,000 = \$1,600$$

To these fixed costs must be added the variable cost of the average balance. Therefore, in this case, 75 percent of the $6,000 would be the associated variable cost. So the variable cost would be equal to:

$$VC = \$6,000 \times 75\% = \$4,500$$

(The 75 percent is derived when the $7.50 per unit variable cost is divided by the selling price of $10.00. As noted earlier, you incur $2.50 per unit fixed cost up to the break-even point, regardless of whether credit is granted or, for that matter, any of the product is sold.) Therefore, the potential total cost, including possible loss of the outstanding balance, is:

$$\$4,500 + \$1,600 = \$6,100$$

Going back to an earlier analysis where we determined the contribution margin percentage of this product to be 25 percent, we concluded that it required four additional dollars of revenue to cover one dollar of additional total cost. The marginal break-even analysis for taking on this new customer would be four times the expected total cost. Therefore, the B$ for the account is equal to four times $6,100, or $24,400.

Thus the firm needs $24,400 in sales to the distributor to assure the account will at least break even if properly paid. Since the expected yearly sales are calculated as: 400 units times $10.00 per unit times 12 months, or $48,000, the firm should reach break-even in approximately six months. It is at this point that managerial judgment should consider whether a six months' break-even is a reasonable period for a distributor and the probability that this distributor will pay properly.

Although this is not a statistically sophisticated approach to granting credit, it does show a measure of the expected exposure to loss that an account will incur. Break-even analysis may be used to evaluate competing credit applications. A simple test could be which application has the shortest break-even time. To ensure a good decision, comparative decisions between competing potential distributors can be made using past experience.

Other Applications

C-V-P analysis can also be used to compare variable cost changes and fixed cost changes for various products. It is applicable to determinations and analysis of such variable costs as material, labor, and overhead. By looking at the contribution margin percentage, you can readily determine the marginal sales required to break even on the costs of additional labor increments, material cost increases, or even the addition of a new supervisor or other managerial position.

Profit Margins

In our original example, we determined that the contribution margin percentage for our product was 25 percent (CM% = 25%). This assumed you were operating at zero profit (the necessary assumption for break-even). Now, if you wish to determine at what quantity level a 10 percent profit margin could be expected, the model can be modified to accommodate that question.

Since the model assumes zero profit at CM = 25 percent, to calculate the break-even quantity for a 10 percent profit we simply assume that the 25 percent contribution margin percentage is reduced by the profit percentage; in other words, we wish to find that quantity which produces a contribution margin percentage of 15 percent. The formula: BE = FC/CM% is used. Since the fixed cost in the original model was $250,000, we divide it by 15 percent to get the break-even dollars of $1,666,670. Since the selling price was $10.00 per unit, the break-even quantity would be 166,667 units.

Of course, you must be careful to determine whether that break-even quantity is within plant capacity and whether it can be sold within your market share. If you do not control enough of a market share to sell 166,667 units, it would do little good to produce them and expect a profit.

PROOF

At 166,667 units		
Total Revenue @ $10/unit		$1,666,670
Total Costs:		
Fixed Costs:	$ 250,000	
Variable Costs @ 7.50/unit:	1,250,003	1,500,003
Net Profit Before Tax		$ 166,667

$$\text{Net Profit \%} = \frac{\$166,667}{\$1,666,670} = 10\%$$

AN ALTERNATIVE APPLICATION OF THE C-V-P ANALYSIS

In periods when competition for market position and sales becomes fierce and when cash flow is restricted, C-V-P analysis can be employed to evaluate cash or near-cash items to test or screen whether to discontinue, divest, or drop a product or location that might be detrimental from a cash flow standpoint. Cash flow C-V-P analysis can be done quickly and easily when trying to make shut down decisions.

Assume that Jones Ice Cream Company has four retail locations. Location 2 is in an area that is being redeveloped and where new roads are being put in. Traffic has been significantly cut and entry and exit from the location is very difficult. All construction should be completed in nine months.

	Cash Costs Per Month Open	Cash Costs Per Month Closed	Relevant Cash Costs
Rent	$1,200	$1,200	-0-
Insurance	300	200	$ 100
Minimum Personnel	1,600	200	1,400
Utilities	800	100	700
	$3,900	$1,700	$2,200

Assuming the gross margin on ice cream sales is 50 percent, the location must create $2,200/.50 = $4,400 sales per month for Jones Ice Cream Company to be as well off keeping Location 2 open as it would be to close it for the construction period. (Costs which do not differ between alternatives are not relevant to the decision.)

THE CURVED-LINE C-V-P ANALYSIS

Assumptions

The curved-line C-V-P analysis does not have some of the restrictive assumptions applicable to the straight-line case. The relevant limiting assumptions for the curved-line model are:

1. Policies, technology, and prices are constant.
2. Product mix is constant.
3. Production is equal to sales (no inventory level changes).

In this case it is no longer necessary to have a constant selling price; costs that are strictly fixed or variable; a constant fixed cost for all volumes; a direct relationship between variable cost and volume; or constant prices for raw materials and other inputs. If the assumptions for the curved-line C-V-P analysis do not fit the model you are trying to evaluate, it is better to try another evaluation method than to force the facts into the analysis.

One of the more interesting nonlinear pricing problems is the cost of quantity discounts. The question seldom asked is: "How do we determine how to set quantity discounts?" One answer to this question may be: "We determine quantity discount policies by estimating the Economic Order Quantity (EOQ) for the buyers of our product." This can be done by determining buyers' periodic demands from our records, and estimating their holding costs. Another method is using the EOQ techniques described later in the inventory chapter and the pricing guides in the pricing and marketing chapters to develop price breaks for use in maximizing profits.

What Does It Look Like?

The curved-line C-V-P analysis is also commonly called the economist's description of the total cost/total revenue relationship. It looks more complex than the linear version and to some degree it is. However, with the advent of the graphing programs on microcomputer spreadsheets, the construction of the curved-line model is no more difficult than the linear model, provided you have the data.

Figure 3.2 shows how a computer generated curved-line break-even graph might look. Note that it has two break-even points: one at a relatively low volume and one at a higher volume, which is likely to be close to capacity. One of the difficulties of constructing this graph from actual data is that most people try to stay in the most profitable range and therefore have little actual data at the lower or higher ends of the scale.

In order to generate this curve some hypothetical data may have to be added to actual data that are available. If so, there are some cautions you should observe. First, unless the market demand is extremely strong for

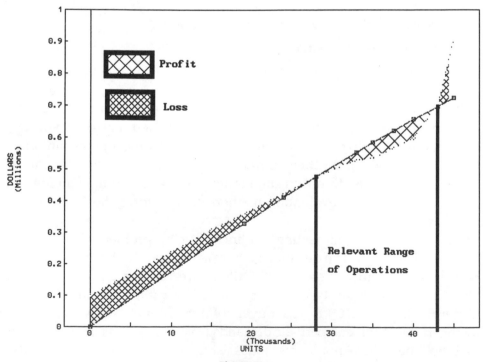

Figure 3.2

your product or service, you probably have to decrease your selling price to increase your unit sales. Failing to factor these price reductions into your data will result in inflated revenue estimates at high volumes. Second, as you approach capacity production, costs have a tendency to increase, sometimes dramatically (overtime, expediting, premiums for materials). Failing to factor in these cost increases will result in deflated cost estimates at high volumes. This combination of high revenue estimates and low cost estimates might indicate decisions that could prove unhealthy. Beware of these tendencies. It is important that you get good data.

Data Generation

The quality of the data you use has a direct relationship to the quality of the information generated by that data. The following method can be employed with little modification to many sales and revenue data collection problems. The methods described in the previous chapter on forecasting obviously apply here as well.

Step 1. Identify the person or persons most likely to be the best predictors of sales for your products.

A good candidate may be your regional sales manager. As an example, the regional sales manager may have had a good career with the company starting as field repairman and working his way up through sales to his current position. If so, he probably knows the products well and may have kept good records on sales of products for the last few years.

Step 2. Identify the range of selling prices around which you intend to gather information. (You may have to go back and change these prices later if there is a market share problem).

Example: Smith Company has decided to market its "Fairy-Tale" cassettes in the $12.50 to $17.50 price range based upon a market survey of competitive products.

Step 3. Pick several equally spaced prices within the price range relevant to the product.

Example: Smith decides to get sales quantity estimates for $1.00 increments between and including $12.50 to $17.50. They assume there are different markets into which they can sell at different price points. Obviously, they plan to sell as many units as possible at the highest price points before dropping the price. Therefore, each price drop will create marginal unit sales that Smith would not get at the higher price points.

Step 4. Have the selected person(s) predict the total quantity the firm could expect to sell at each selected price point.

Example: The estimator(s) gave the following:

Price/Unit	Total Units	Marginal Units
$17.50	15,000	15,000
16.50	28,000	13,000
15.50	35,000	7,000
14.50	40,000	5,000
13.50	43,000	3,000
12.50	45,000	2,000

Step 5. Multiply the price/unit by the marginal units to obtain marginal revenue (additional revenue generated from sales obtained by dropping the price).

Obtain the total revenue by a step-wise addition of the marginal revenue column (the total revenue at $15.50 is the marginal revenue at $17.50 + the marginal revenue at $16.50 + the marginal revenue at $15.50):

Price/ Unit	Total Units	Marginal Units	Marginal Revenue	Total Revenue
$17.50	15,000	15,000	$262,500	$262,500
16.50	28,000	13,000	214,500	477,000
15.50	35,000	7,000	108,500	585,500
14.50	40,000	5,000	72,500	658,000
13.50	43,000	3,000	40,500	698,500
12.50	45,000	2,000	25,000	723,500

The resulting Total Revenue line is shown in Figure 3.3. If you were to assume that all 45,000 units could be sold at $17.50 per unit the revenue estimate would be $787,500. Figure 3.4 shows the resulting inflated revenue estimate from this error.

Sometimes a price-based method will prove to be ineffective. The predictors might say that it is easier to predict the price given the quantities desired.

Example: The products of the Evans Company are educational and foreign language lesson tapes. An alternative method for determining the curve is to proceed with the following method.

After identifying the persons within the organization:

Step 1. Identify the relevant range of sales and stick closely to that in gathering information. (Here the market share question is not a problem.) Assume the per-unit costs are lowest when production is in a range of 25,000 to 30,000 units per year.

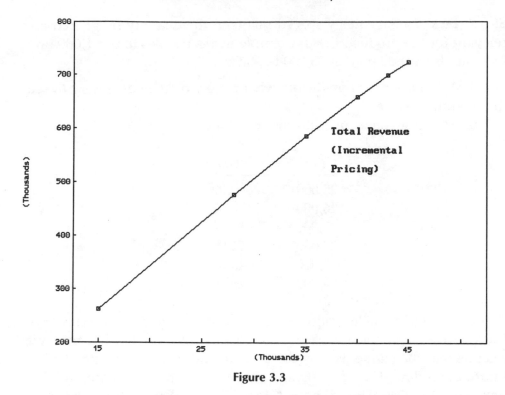

Figure 3.3

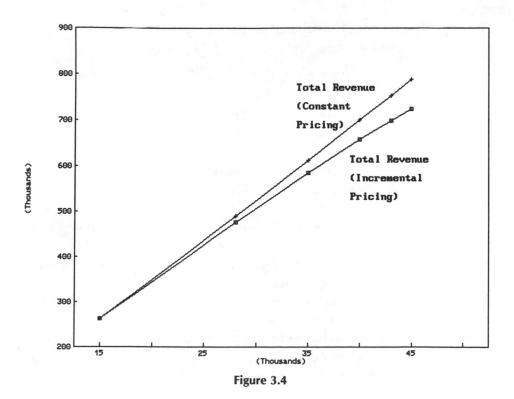

Figure 3.4

Step 2. Pick several equally spaced points in the quantity range that are relevant for the product. In our example Evans decides to use 1,000 unit increments in the range of 25,000 to 30,000.

Step 3. Ask the selected predictors what price would be necessary to sell the quantity selected.

The predictor comes up with the following prices.

Units	Price/Unit
25,000	$60.00
26,000	58.00
27,000	55.00
28,000	51.00
29,000	46.00
30,000	40.00

Step 4. Multiply the selling prices by the corresponding quantity to produce the expected revenue for each selected quantity. In this instance we assume that the market is very competitive and there is virtually perfect information flow. Therefore, Evans can set only one price with which it will have to stick. They cannot "cream the market" as in a previous example.

The expected revenues for the educational tapes would be:

Units	Total Revenue
25,000	$1,500,000
26,000	1,508,000
27,000	1,485,000
28,000	1,428,000
29,000	1,344,000
30,000	1,200,000

Step 5. Plot the points representing the revenues and quantities on a graph as before.

In this case we are using the quantity as the independent variable and determining price as the dependent variable. In the first example we were using price as the independent variable and making quantity the dependent variable. In either case, we expect (and hope) to get a curve. Setting the quantity and estimating the price may be a better planning tool, since we can often generate better cost figures if we work within efficient production levels.

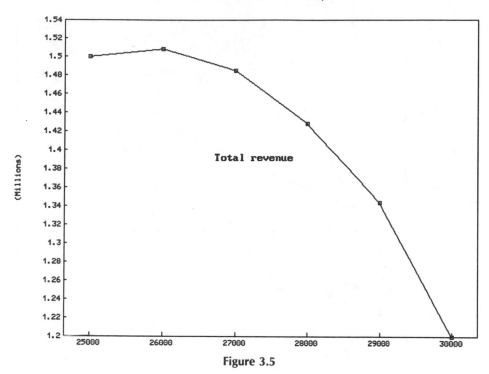

Figure 3.5

It is obvious that this market is very sensitive to price. Evans is better off, from a total revenue point of view, at lower volume/higher price. In fact, if costs are more than $8 per unit, they may be better off at 25,000 units.

Generating the Cost Line

As with the revenue line, there are several methods to generate the cost line.

1. The simplest method is to obtain an estimate of total costs for an expected volume. This is the first information needed. Draw a line from that total cost point (Point A) to the point on the vertical axis associated with the fixed costs, assuming zero production (Point B). This is often called Standby Costs because it indicates expenditures that would continue in the short term even if operations were to be shut down.

In this manner, we arrive at a linear approximation based upon two pieces of data. But why use only two data points when you have more available?

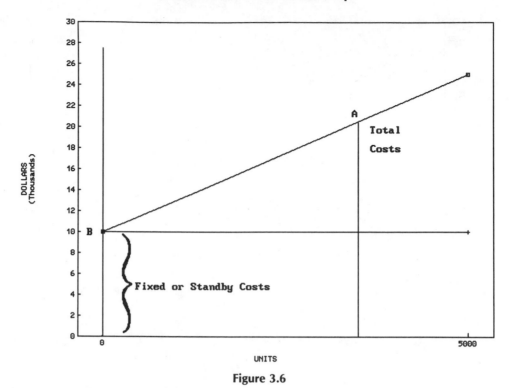

Figure 3.6

2. Obtain total cost figures and quantity figures for several previous
   periods and plot these points on a graph, as has been done in Figure
   3.7. This approach should be used with some caution:
   A. Short periods of time should be used to minimize the effects of
      inflation.
   B. In looking at those periods you should assure yourself that significant
      learning effects have already taken place and that the process has
      stabilized.

Once you have obtained several cost figures and associated quantity
figures and have plotted the points you will want to draw a line that
seems to fit the data best. There are two easy methods for doing this:

- The eyeball approximation, or TLAR (That Looks About Right) method.
  In this method you try to fit a line that to you seems to best approximate
  the relationships.

- Linear regression. There are many canned linear regression programs
  available on some very inexpensive pocket calculators. An example
  using the Hewlett-Packard 12C calculator is included in the Appendix
  to this chapter. We have also provided a form in the Appendix to

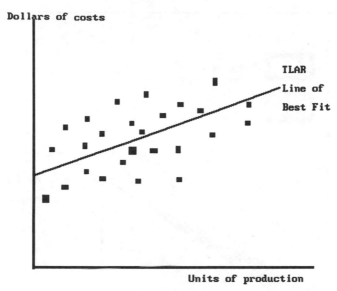

Figure 3.7

Chapter 2 for the calculation of least squares linear regressions. A screen-by-screen example using Lotus 1-2-3™ to produce a regression is also provided in the Appendix to this chapter.

WHAT DOES IT ALL MEAN?

Plotting the total cost and total revenue curves on the same graph generates useful information for planning. Before getting into the strategic planning implications of the cost-volume-profit relationships, it should be noted that there are three points of interest on the curve shown in Figure 3.8. There is the break-even point at the lower end of the curve, BE1, where, for the first time, a quantity production will put the firm in a position where total revenues equal total costs. From this point, as the quantity produced increases, total revenues exceed total costs, and there is a profit. Ultimately, a second break-even point, BE2, is reached. Again, total cost equal the total revenues and above this level of production the business incurs a total loss again.

A third point of interest is where the vertical distance between the total revenue and the total cost curves is at a maximum. It is at this point that maximum profits are achieved. The old concept that more sales are better holds true only until the quantity sold reaches the quantity at which profits are maximized.

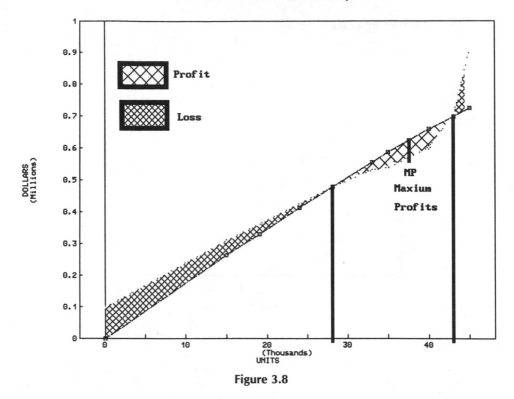

Figure 3.8

After the point MP is reached, the firm has diminishing returns for each additional unit of production (see Figure 3.8). When the firm reaches break-even point (BE2), it is no longer realizing any profits. It would be very interesting to know exactly where maximum profits exist. In the estimating process we can, if our curves are accurate, get a fairly good approximation of the point at which maximum profits occur.

There is good news and bad news relative to this point, MP. The good news is that the economic definition of the point MP is quite precise. It is that quantity of units sold where the additional cost to produce the last unit (marginal cost) is exactly equal to the additional revenue derived from selling that unit (marginal revenue). The bad news is that those numbers are normally difficult to attain in actual practice. Building the graph helps you to narrow your focus on this range, however.

USING COST-VOLUME-PROFIT RELATIONSHIPS FOR STRATEGIC PLANNING

Going through the analytical process of generating the cost and revenue curves necessary for a cost-volume-profit analysis is, in itself, a useful exercise. You will have been able to identify where on the cost curve you are probably operating. With this information, you can estimate whether you are above or below the maximum profit point. There may be situations where you are willing, in the short term, to forgo maximum profits now in order to ensure a better position in the future. This is where the use of the C-V-P model is helpful for strategic planning.

For example, you may believe that a competitor will fill the void if, rather than increasing production and selling at a lower marginal price, you choose to try to stay at the profit maximizing quantity. Therefore, to forestall that competition you may decide to produce and sell a higher quantity at a total profit lower than you could manage. However, you would probably do this only if you expected either to increase overall capacity or otherwise to alter the cost curve in such a way as to return toward optimal profitability in the longer term.

You might do this when you know that in the next year you will be opening a new plant with additional capacity. Once the plant opens, and you are meeting that additional demand from another facility, the cost curve will change beneficially and, with luck, return you toward the point of maximum profits. So you might take a lesser short-term profit to maintain market share from which you would later profit.

In order to evaluate where on the curve you should be operating, you simply use the discounted cash flow method or the internal rate of return method found in the capital budgeting chapter to ascertain the current costs of operating above the maximum profit point in terms of future cash flows.

SENSITIVITY ANALYSIS

People often banter around the expression "sensitivity analysis" as if it contains some mystique. In truth, sensitivity analysis is nothing more than an evaluation of how much change occurs in costs or revenue relative to changes in other variables. Sensitivity analysis is often used as a test of the underlying assumptions. For example, if we assume that the variable cost does, in fact, vary directly with the quantity produced, we could test the reasonableness of this assumption by looking at those variable costs associated with different production levels. One method of doing this is to look at historical variable costs actually incurred at different levels of production. (Remember, if the points are selected at too divergent periods, we may have a factor of inflation to take into consideration.) If the relationship is approximately linear, then the assumption is accurate. However, if the costs tend to fluctuate greatly on a per-unit basis, we can say that the cost relationship does not support the assumption.

The question is, How much variation can we accept before the assumption is rejected? In essence, that is the nature of sensitivity analysis: it tries to determine how sensitive an assumption is to variation.

OTHER PROBLEMS

The graphical curves we have constructed for both cost and revenue represent a relatively stable product or process configuration. The model assumes that production is equal to sales and policies, that the new product mix, technologies, and other factors are constant.

Realizing the weaknesses of some of these assumptions allows you to determine their relative impact on the model. For instance, one problem is the allocation of overhead to various products in the mix. You may use a burden or overhead rate to allocate these charges based on direct labor man-hours, in much the same way as labor rates are used directly to allocate labor costs. Changes in allocation affect the break-even point(s) significantly.

Sales need not be exactly equal to production. However, if production and sales are relatively constant, or there is a gradual building or reduction of inventory, the problem is not of such a nature to affect critically the reliability of the model. But there are other problems which must be considered:

Taxes. If the firm is only considering break-even, there may be no taxes. At break-even, total revenue equals total cost, and profits are equal to zero. Therefore, it is of only academic interest to operate in a break-even situation. The usual way to treat taxes in the C-V-P analysis is simply to ignore them. Taxes can be subtracted from the net profit picture later.

Fixed vs. Variable Cost. It is difficult to be really honest with ourselves concerning what or who is really a fixed expense. This is especially true when considering closing down a product or process line. What overhead do you *really* eliminate? Almost all costs that are considered fixed may in fact be variable. Assignment of costs to either the fixed or the variable category should at least be attempted. You should be careful to analyze and make distinctions between fixed and variable costs. This distinction is necessary in order to get an accurate picture of a total cost curve.

SUMMARY

Cost-Volume-Profit relationships (break-even analysis) have generally been used to determine the level of production above which the firm will operate profitably. The simple linear model has several limiting assumptions that tend to narrow the applicability of the model. However, as a model, it does have sound applications that should not be overlooked in favor of more flashy or sophisticated (and hence more costly) techniques.

The straight-line model has applications as a screen for making financial decisions. Its advantages are speed and low cost. The numbers are readily obtainable and the model is not difficult to manipulate. As a simple mathematical model, it has powerful applications in other areas where business decisions have to be made. It is a decision screen simple to use for advertising, credit policies, and comparability of alternative plans.

In the more complex configurations, the curved-line case has fewer limiting constraints and even more applications. With its power comes more difficulty in generating the cost and revenue lines. The curved lines are generated from cost and volume relationships estimated for varying prices and varying sales quantities. Properly done, however, these curves can give you a better understanding of where you are and of how pricing and selling decisions may affect your profitability.

One important application of the analysis is the determination of where on the cost curve you are operating or planning to operate. The curves can generate information relative to whether increasing or decreasing production will improve profitability.

APPENDIX: REGRESSION ANALYSIS FOR COST LINE CONSTRUCTION

The following data has been used for both example calculations in this Appendix:

Month	Units Produced	Total Costs
January	500	$1,200
February	200	700
March	300	1,100
April	600	1,500
May	100	600
June	400	1,100
July	500	1,500
August	200	500
September	400	1,000
October	450	1,200
November	300	800
December	550	1,700

EXAMPLE 1:
HEWLETT-PACKARD HP 12C™

Key Strokes	Display	Explanation
f clear Σ	0.00	
1200 Enter	1,200.00	
500 Σ+	1.00	
700 Enter	700.00	
200 Σ+	2.00	
1100 Enter	1,100.00	
300 Σ+	3.00	
1500 enter	1,500.00	
600 Σ+	4.00	
600 Enter	600.00	
100 Σ+	5.00	
1100 Enter	1,100.00	
400 Σ+	6.00	
1500 Enter	1,500.00	
500 Σ+	7.00	

Key Strokes	Display	Explanation
500 Enter	500.00	
200 Σ+	8.00	
1000 Enter	1,000.00	
400 Σ+	9.00	
1200 Enter	1,200.00	
450 Σ+	10.00	
800 Enter	800.00	
300 Σ+	11.00	
1700 Enter	1,700.00	
550 Σ+	12.00	
g s	155.94	Standard deviation units
X < > Y	376.89	Standard deviation costs
o g ŷ, r	237.38	y-intercept
1 g ŷ, r		
X < > y R↓ X <> Y −	2.23	slope of line
700 g ŷ, r	1,800.93	estimated costs of producing 700 units
550 g ŷ, r	1,465.89	estimated costs of producing 550 units

EXAMPLE 2:
LOTUS 1-2-3™ REGRESSION ANALYSIS

```
C17:                                                                    READY

        A       B       C       D       E       F       G       H
                    LOTUS 1-2-3 REGRESSION ANALYSIS EXAMPLE
                             A       B       C       D
                 MONTH       UNITS   COSTS   A*A     A*B
                 JANUARY     500     1200
                 FEBRUARY    200     700
                 MARCH       300     1100
                 APRIL       600     1500
                 MAY         100     600
                 JUNE        400     1100
                 JULY        500     1500
                 AUGUST      200     500
                 SEPTEMBER   400     1000
                 OCTOBER     450     1200
                 NOVEMBER    300     800
                 DECEMBER    550     1700
                   TOTAL


01-Jan-80  01:28 AM      UNDO                    CAPS
```

```
      A        B         C         D         E         F         G         H
                          LOTUS 1-2-3 REGRESSION ANALYSIS EXAMPLE
                                    A         B         C         D
                       MONTH      UNITS     COSTS     A*A       A*B
                       JANUARY    500       1200
                       FEBRUARY   200        700
                       MARCH      300       1100
                       APRIL      600       1500
                       MAY        100        600
                       JUNE       400       1100
                       JULY       500       1500
                       AUGUST     200        500
                       SEPTEMBER  400       1000
                       OCTOBER    450       1200
                       NOVEMBER   300        800
                       DECEMBER   550       1700
                          TOTAL
```

01-Jan-80 01:30 AM   CAPS

```
      A        B         C         D         E         F         G         H
                          LOTUS 1-2-3 REGRESSION ANALYSIS EXAMPLE
                                    A         B         C         D
                       MONTH      UNITS     COSTS     A*A       A*B
                       JANUARY    500       1200
                       FEBRUARY   200        700
                       MARCH      300       1100
                       APRIL      600       1500
                       MAY        100        600
                       JUNE       400       1100
                       JULY       500       1500
                       AUGUST     200        500
                       SEPTEMBER  400       1000
                       OCTOBER    450       1200
                       NOVEMBER   300        800
                       DECEMBER   550       1700
                          TOTAL   4500     12900
```

01-Jan-80 01:34 AM   CAPS

```
      A        B         C         D         E         F         G         H
                          LOTUS 1-2-3 REGRESSION ANALYSIS EXAMPLE
                                    A         B         C         D
                       MONTH      UNITS     COSTS     A*A       A*B
                       JANUARY    500       1200     250000
                       FEBRUARY   200        700      40000
                       MARCH      300       1100      90000
                       APRIL      600       1500     360000
                       MAY        100        600      10000
                       JUNE       400       1100     160000
                       JULY       500       1500     250000
                       AUGUST     200        500      40000
                       SEPTEMBER  400       1000     160000
                       OCTOBER    450       1200     202500
                       NOVEMBER   300        800      90000
                       DECEMBER   550       1700     302500
                          TOTAL   4500     12900
```

01-Jan-80 01:35 AM   UNDO   CAPS

VALUE

```
          A         B         C         D         E         F         G         H
                        LOTUS 1-2-3 REGRESSION ANALYSIS EXAMPLE
                                    A         B         C         D
                        MONTH       UNITS     COSTS     A * A     A * B
                        JANUARY     500       1200      250000
                        FEBRUARY    200       700        40000
                        MARCH       300       1100       90000
                        APRIL       600       1500      360000
                        MAY         100        600       10000
                        JUNE        400       1100      160000
                        JULY        500       1500      250000
                        AUGUST      200        500       40000
                        SEPTEMBER   400       1000      160000
                        OCTOBER     450       1200      202500
                        NOVEMBER    300        800       90000
                        DECEMBER    550       1700      302500
                          TOTAL     4500      12900
```

01-Jan-80 01:36 AM   CAPS

C5: +C5.C5   READY

```
          A         B         C         D         E         F         G         H
                        LOTUS 1-2-3 REGRESSION ANALYSIS EXAMPLE
                                    A         B         C         D
                        MONTH       UNITS     COSTS     A * A     A * B
                        JANUARY     500       1200      250000    600000
                        FEBRUARY    200       700        40000    140000
                        MARCH       300       1100       90000    330000
                        APRIL       600       1500      360000    900000
                        MAY         100        600       10000     60000
                        JUNE        400       1100      160000    440000
                        JULY        500       1500      250000    750000
                        AUGUST      200        500       40000    100000
                        SEPTEMBER   400       1000      160000    400000
                        OCTOBER     450       1200      202500    540000
                        NOVEMBER    300        800       90000    240000
                        DECEMBER    550       1700      302500    935000
                          TOTAL     4500      12900
```

01-Jan-80 01:37 AM   UNDO   CAPS

C17: @SUM(D5..D16)   READY

```
          A         B         C         D         E         F         G         H
                        LOTUS 1-2-3 REGRESSION ANALYSIS EXAMPLE
                                    A         B         C         D
                        MONTH       UNITS     COSTS     A * A     A * B
                        JANUARY     500       1200      250000    600000
                        FEBRUARY    200       700        40000    140000
                        MARCH       300       1100       90000    330000
                        APRIL       600       1500      360000    900000
                        MAY         100        600       10000     60000
                        JUNE        400       1100      160000    440000
                        JULY        500       1500      250000    750000
                        AUGUST      200        500       40000    100000
                        SEPTEMBER   400       1000      160000    400000
                        OCTOBER     450       1200      202500    540000
                        NOVEMBER    300        800       90000    240000
                        DECEMBER    550       1700      302500    935000
                          TOTAL     4500      12900    1955000   5435000
```

01-Jan-80 01:38 AM   UNDO   CAPS

```
C20:
Worksheet Range Copy Move File Print Graph Data System Add-In Quit
Global Insert Delete Column Erase Titles Window Status Page Learn
        A       B       C       D       E       F       G       H
```

LOTUS 1-2-3 REGRESSION ANALYSIS EXAMPLE

MONTH	A UNITS	B COSTS	C A*A	D A*B
JANUARY	500	1200	250000	600000
FEBRUARY	200	700	40000	140000
MARCH	300	1100	90000	330000
APRIL	600	1500	360000	900000
MAY	100	600	10000	60000
JUNE	400	1100	160000	440000
JULY	500	1500	250000	750000
AUGUST	200	500	40000	100000
SEPTEMBER	400	1000	160000	400000
OCTOBER	450	1200	202500	540000
NOVEMBER	300	800	90000	240000
DECEMBER	550	1700	302500	935000
TOTAL	4500	12900	1955000	5435000

01-Jan-80 01:39 AM   CAPS

```
C20:
Fill Table Sort Query Distribution Matrix Regression Parse
Calculate linear regression
        A       B       C       D       E       F       G       H
```

LOTUS 1-2-3 REGRESSION ANALYSIS EXAMPLE

MONTH	A UNITS	B COSTS	C A*A	D A*B
JANUARY	500	1200	250000	600000
FEBRUARY	200	700	40000	140000
MARCH	300	1100	90000	330000
APRIL	600	1500	360000	900000
MAY	100	600	10000	60000
JUNE	400	1100	160000	440000
JULY	500	1500	250000	750000
AUGUST	200	500	40000	100000
SEPTEMBER	400	1000	160000	400000
OCTOBER	450	1200	202500	540000
NOVEMBER	300	800	90000	240000
DECEMBER	550	1700	302500	935000
TOTAL	4500	12900	1955000	5435000

01-Jan-80 01:40 AM   CAPS

```
C20:
X-Range Y-Range Output-Range Intercept Reset Go Quit
Specify the output range
```

Regression Settings

```
X range:          C5..C16
Y range:          D5..D16
Output range:     B19..F29
Intercept:        Compute
```

MAY	100	600	10000	60000
JUNE	400	1100	160000	440000
JULY	500	1500	250000	750000
AUGUST	200	500	40000	100000
SEPTEMBER	400	1000	160000	400000
OCTOBER	450	1200	202500	540000
NOVEMBER	300	800	90000	240000
DECEMBER	550	1700	302500	935000
TOTAL	4500	12900	1955000	5435000

01-Jan-80 01:42 AM   CAPS

A	B	C	D	E	F	G	H
	MAY	100	600	10000	60000		
	JUNE	400	1100	160000	440000		
	JULY	500	1500	250000	750000		
	AUGUST	200	500	40000	100000		
	SEPTEMBER	400	1000	160000	400000		
	OCTOBER	450	1200	202500	540000		
	NOVEMBER	300	800	90000	240000		
	DECEMBER	550	1700	302500	935000		
	TOTAL	4500	12900	1955000	5435000		

Regression Output:

Constant   237.3831
Std Err of Y Est   150.9626
R Squared   0.854145

No. of Observations   12
Degrees of Freedom   10

X Coefficient(s) 2.233644
Std Err of Coef.   0.291882

01-Jan-80 01:43 AM   UNDO   CAPS

C19: (C19.$D$29)+$E$23   READY

A	B	C	D	E	F	G	H
JULY		500	1500	250000		750000	
AUGUST		200	500	40000		100000	
SEPTEMBER		400	1000	160000		400000	
OCTOBER		450	1200	202500		540000	
NOVEMBER		300	800	90000		240000	
DECEMBER		550	1700	302500		935000	
TOTAL		4500	12900	1955000		5435000	
							ESTIMATE
ESTIMATE		700					1800.934
ESTIMATE		550					

Regression Output:

Constant   237.3831
Std Err of Y Est   150.9626
R Squared   0.854145

No. of Observations   12
Degrees of Freedom   10

X Coefficient(s) 2.233644
Std Err of Coef.   0.291882

01-Jan-80 01:49 AM   UNDO   CAPS

C20: (C20.$D$29)+$E$23   READY

A	B	C	D	E	F	G	H
JULY		500	1500	250000		750000	
AUGUST		200	500	40000		100000	
SEPTEMBER		400	1000	160000		400000	
OCTOBER		450	1200	202500		540000	
NOVEMBER		300	800	90000		240000	
DECEMBER		550	1700	302500		935000	
TOTAL		4500	12900	1955000		5435000	
							ESTIMATE
ESTIMATE		700					1800.934
ESTIMATE		550					1465.887

Regression Output:

Constant   237.3831
Std Err of Y Est   150.9626
R Squared   0.854145

No. of Observations   12
Degrees of Freedom   10

X Coefficient(s) 2.233644
Std Err of Coef.   0.291882

01-Jan-80 01:51 AM   UNDO   CAPS

```
        A        B        C         D          E        F        G           H
             JULY           500      1500     250000        750000
             AUGUST         200       500      40000        100000
             SEPTEMBER      400      1000     160000        400000
             OCTOBER        450      1200     202500        540000
             NOVEMBER       300       800      90000        240000
             DECEMBER       550      1700     302500        935000
              TOTAL        4500     12900    1955000       5435000
                                                                         ESTIMATE
             ESTIMATE       700                                          1800.934
             ESTIMATE       550                                          1465.887
             ESTIMATE         0                                           237.3831
```

Regression Output:

```
             Constant                  237.3831
             Std Err of Y Est          150.9626
             R Squared                 0.854145

             No. of Observations            12
             Degrees of Freedom             10

             X Coefficient(s)  2.233644
             Std Err of Coef.  0.291882
```

01-Jan-80 01:53 AM   UNDO   CAPS

C21: (C21.$D$29)+$E$23   WAIT

Graph Settings

Type: XY   Titles: First REGRESSION ANALYSIS
                                                    Second EXAMPLE
X: C19..C21   X axis UNITS
A: G19..G21   Y axis COSTS
B:
C: Y scale: X scale:
D: Scaling   Manual   Automatic
E: Lower   0
F: Upper   2000
                                Format   (G)   (G)
Grid: None   Color: No   Indicator   Yes   Yes

Legend: Format: Data labels: Skip: 1
A   Both
B   Both
C   Both
D   Both
E   Both
F   Both
```

## REGRESSION ANALYSIS
### EXAMPLE
```

4

Investing in Long-Term Assets and Capital Budgeting

Most capital investment decisions should be made in two parts: first, the investment decision; then, the financing decision. You should first decide what facilities, equipment, or other capital assets you will acquire, when to acquire them and what to do with them. Then you should decide where and how to get the money. This chapter will consider only the investment decision; the financing issues are left to Chapter 10.

The term "capital budgeting" may be defined as planning for an expenditure or outlay of cash resources and a return from the anticipated flow of future cash benefits. The necessary elements to be considered for this decision are:

- Expected costs and their timing.
- The flow of anticipated benefits.
- The time over which those funds will flow.
- The risk involved in the realization of those benefits.

Each of these elements has distinct characteristics associated with your management philosophy. Tools have been developed that use the numbers generated by management to help answer questions and to make reasoned decisions among competing business opportunities for the use of scarce investment dollars. In this chapter we will look at the capital budgeting process as part of a cycle, not as an isolated exercise. We begin with an idea for a new product and proceed through to the discontinuance of that product and into the next generation. While we are using a specific example, you will note that the concepts have a general application.

Parenthetically, it is interesting to note that capital budgeting can also be defined in almost the same precise words as the definition of "economics": the study of the allocation of scarce resources to competing ends over time to maximize utility.

DEFINITIONS

Before attempting an explanation of the capital budgeting process, we need to be familiar with several terms. The common financial terms used in this chapter are:

Present Value. The present value of an item is the value *today* of an amount you expect to receive or to pay at some future date. For example, if you expect to receive $100 one year from today, and you can get 12 percent for your money, that stream of income has a *present* value of $89.29 because $89.29 invested today at 12 percent return *will be* $100.00 one year from today.

Annuity (regular or ordinary). The receipt or payment of a series of equal payments made at the end of each of a number of fixed periods. The receipt of $100 on December 31 of each year for ten years is an ordinary annuity. (An "annuity due" means payments are received at the beginning of each period rather than at the end.)

Payback Period. The payback period indicates how long it takes for you to get your money back. In other words, it is the time necessary for net cash in-flows to amortize an original investment. Interest or the time value of money is often not considered in simple payback calculations. However, a more appropriate form of payback calculation, called the discounted payback period, does consider the time value. In discounted payback, the present value of the inflows is considered in determining how long it takes to get the investment back.

Net Present Value (NPV). The present value of in-flows of cash minus the present value of the out-flows of cash. This is normally "after tax cash flows."

Present Value Index. The net present value divided by original investment (this index is useful only for positive net present values).

Internal Rate of Return (IRR). The discount (interest) rate, which when used in calculating NPV results in NPV being zero. This is sometimes called the true rate of return.

There are other accounting and financial tools and models you can use to analyze possible investments in a product or project. These models consider mostly the same information in different ways and can be found in investment or finance textbooks. The six mentioned above will be sufficient for our purposes.

OVERVIEW AND USE OF CAPITAL BUDGETING

Budgets, a frequently used tool, have been around for a long time. Operating budgets seem to be the most common. While seldom used to their potential, operating budgets are ordinarily among the first budgets attempted. The numbers for these budgets are not difficult to obtain and most managers will give at least some credence to their usefulness. Operating budgets are discussed in detail in the following chapter.

Cash budgets are not greatly different from operating budgets in their preparation and use. In cash budgeting, you focus attention on the receipt and expenditure of cash. However, cash budgets are often limited to use by fewer people within a business and often are not formalized until required by shortages of cash or the high cost of maintaining cash reserves. In periods of better financial conditions, the inefficiency of having too much cash is often overlooked. As a result, cash budgets sometimes fall into disuse during periods of prosperity.

Capital budgeting, on the other hand, does not fair well with many businessmen. This is due in part to the difficulties of preparing one. Estimates of cash flows must be pushed farther into the future and unfamiliar terms such as "weighted average cost of capital" and "internal rate of return" creep into the terminology. The calculations associated with these terms are often unfamiliar; many businessmen have learned to operate with no formal capital budget. However, used properly, a capital budgeting process can help to reduce your risk of making the wrong decision.

Capital budgeting is useful as a decision tool. Accountants, and some of your staff and some managers, have probably been trained to make the calculations necessary for determinations of present values, internal rates of return, and payback periods. These calculations are fairly simple and can be done using the forms provided in the Appendix to this chapter. Some inexpensive calculators can do most of the calculations with ease. The critical work is the gathering of the information necessary to make the capital budgeting process more understandable and useful to the business.

LIFE CYCLES

Products and projects, like people, have life cycles. They all go through similar stages: Conception, birth, growth, maturity, decline, and ultimately death. Each stage requires a certain degree of attention. The applicability of capital budgeting concepts to new projects or new products extends beyond application to new ventures. It can be used to consider the replacement of existing product lines and even to cost reductions in existing lines in the current or future periods.

THE CAPITAL BUDGETING SEQUENCE

There are four basic sets of actions that occur in a capital budgeting plan: proposal solicitation or generation, evaluation, implementation, and follow-up. We shall examine each in some detail.

Proposal Solicitation or Generation

1. The first step in proposal generation is evaluation of your present status. Many factors should be considered when making an evaluation of status. It is particularly important to pay attention to your position with respect to the availability of management talent, technological talent, financial and market positions, sources of labor, and the availability of markets for your product.

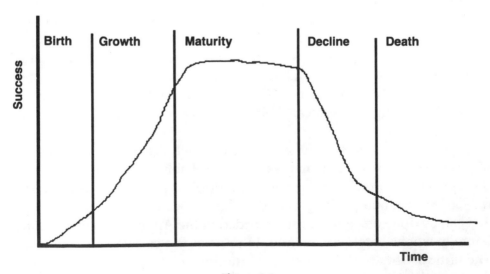

Figure 4.1

Example: Assume you manufacture heavy cast iron cylinders for which "the market" is located primarily in southeastern sunbelt states. Therefore, one particularly important factor is the cost of transportation of the product to the ultimate user. At least two alternatives are available: locate the plant in the area where the product is consumed, or acquire manufacturing facilities on low-cost transportation networks such as rail or water.

Another option may be to redesign the product. For example, assume you find that you can manufacture the cylinders out of aluminum with the installation of a tooled steel sleeve instead of the cast iron cylinder. The product now requires different raw materials, different processing and handling, and different packaging and shipping. The new product may change your marketing plans and a proposal for capital expenditures may result.

2. The questions that you should answer are standard business planning questions: "What do we do best?" and "Where are we going?" These require an evaluation of your business plan. The objectives formulated as a result of these questions may point out potential projects requiring capital expenditures.

Decisions relative to capital expenditures may be made at various levels within the organization depending on their size and significance. Rules for decision making should be consistently applied at whatever level of management you have established.

3. Cost reduction programs may be a rich source of capital budgeting projects. Cost reduction programs generally carry with them less risk than any other form of project. In most cases, cost reduction programs have obvious cost justifications. Potential payback periods and returns on investments can be readily calculated because the programs are intended to improve the cost efficiency of existing projects. Such programs, if adopted, help make employees feel they are a part of the decision-making process, as a large part of these proposals are usually generated from line employees.

4. Ideas from employees and customers are also often low-risk sources for increased profitability. Marketing or sales personnel meet with customers on a regular basis. They should be able to determine current market needs and may assess demands not being met. Often these opportunities can be exploited with little additional cost to you. By taking advantage of unmet market needs head-on, competition can be avoided and you may successfully expand your market presence. To encourage new ideas and market opportunities you may use either or both of the following avenues: 1) Encourage entrepreneurship by allowing self-interest to work for you. Monetary incentive programs for sales staff and other employees

are extremely effective in generating growth-producing ideas. 2) Surveys of customer needs can be made on a regular basis to inform you of potential growth possibilities.

5. Competitors are often a good source of potential growth-producing ideas. Sometimes it is beneficial to let competitors pioneer certain new products. Letting them take the risks often eliminates these products from your consideration as a result of their lack of profitability or outright product failure. Of course, this gives the competitor a head start on successful ventures.

6. Product matrix analysis will sometimes disclose holes in the market. A full discussion of product matrix analysis is given in the chapter on marketing.

7. Often new ideas are available through purchase from independent research and development firms or may be generated by your own R & D efforts.

8. Trade shows, conventions, seminars and publications are good sources of potential ideas. In this case, you are not paying for the development of ideas but instead are picking other people's brains.

9. You may decide on vertical growth—being your own supplier or marketer. Supplying yourself with components, services, or raw materials is a source of potential profit. Setting up your own distribution network outlets can be profitable as well. For example, some utilities have diversified into fields such as coal production and transportation in order to guarantee a source of supply and to reduce the risk associated with fuel cost variations. In this way, vertical integration provides them with additional revenue-producing sources of unregulated profit. Some natural gas utilities sell gas appliances. Being "the gas company" gives them an entry for marketing the appliances. Customers trust a company that provides gas to know which are the best gas appliances.

10. You may want to grow horizontally through product diversification or buying of competitors.

11. You can expand the use of present technologies. The question you should constantly ask is, "What can we do with what we know or what we do best?" How adaptable is the current technology to meet new product innovation or new processes? The opportunity here is to have growth-producing ideas with minimal risks. If you have learned to utilize your technologies efficiently, further endeavors with known technologies generally carry less risk than ventures into new and yet untried technologies.

12. Expand the use of your existing equipment. In-place equipment may not be fully utilized. Increased utilization through subcontracting

and selling of time on equipment or process capabilities will better utilize existing capital resources with little additional risk. More use of the fixed-cost base increases efficiency and at the same time produces additional cash flows.

Evaluation of Proposals

After proposals have been generated, you must evaluate competing proposals in a consistent manner to determine which proposals merit further consideration. There are basically four steps in the evaluation process:

1. The most critical step is a qualitative evaluation: Is this proposal consistent with the strategic plan of the business? If not, no future consideration is necessary. If yes, further analysis is indicated. Lots of time, effort, and money can be wasted on things that do not fit the direction you are determined to go in.

2. Define the evaluation process. Set up a system that will be applied consistently for all proposals.

- Estimate costs accurately and in the same way for all proposals.
- Estimate the benefits consistently.
- Use the same time constraints.
- Use the same method for calculating the net benefits.

3. Qualify your information sources. When gathering information you must evaluate the reliability and accuracy of the source of the information. For example:

- Engineers often underestimate the time (and costs) necessary.
- Salespeople frequently overestimate potential sales.

You should ask:

- Who is providing the information?
- How accurate were their last predictions?
- How often have I relied on this source before?
- Do my competitors use this same source?

4. Install the process. To install the process properly, all affected persons must understand how to use it.

- Develop appropriate forms to be used throughout the organization. (Appropriate does not have to mean complex or cumbersome.)
- Explain the forms and the evaluation methods to all affected persons.
- Use the system consistently to evaluate proposals made by members of the organization.
- Provide prompt response to members of the organization as to why their proposals were or were not accepted.

Implementation of a Proposal

In the implementation phase, effective project management requires a firm line of control. First, define responsibility. You need to know who will be responsible at various stages in the proposal's implementation to assure accountability and control. It is important to consider the time and the talent of the individuals involved and to match their abilities to the needs and responsibilities of each key position in the implementation process. Few things affect the failure or success of a product more than the match or mismatch of key personnel at critical steps in project implementation.

Next, establish check points by setting goals and objectives for milestones at successive stages in the process. You can review your decisions regularly, *before* the next costly step is taken and when progress can be compared with established standards. You may choose to terminate a proposal at some point short of completion if it appears that the project is exceeding cost projections or failing to meet benefit expectations.

It may be necessary to change the budget. This may seem a radical idea. However, if budgets are properly managed, changing a budget is nothing more than considering better data as it flows into the system. Budget changing should not become a self-fulfilling prophecy. Budgets are planning tools and, as such, comparisons between actual performance and projected performance will often show you how well or poorly your project is proceeding. Updating budgets for better control is useful in order to improve the quality of the decision making for the project.

When budgets are used for control, you need a regular feedback of information: the establishment of reports is another critical element in the implementation phase. The amount of reporting is a function of balancing the risk of ignorance against the cost of reporting. When reports are generated on a regular basis you can ensure maintenance of adequate control of the project.

Follow-Up

Neglect near the concluding stages of a project can result in unnecessary delays, increased risk, and higher costs for the discontinuation or normal termination of a product's life cycle. In the follow-up step, you should review the assumptions under which the original project was accepted, determine how well those assumptions have been met, review the evaluation systems that were in place, and, finally, evaluate the implementation of the project. It is at this point that an overall review of a project will show you how well it was planned, how well the budget projected reality, and the necessary areas where improvement in the system will help better evaluate future proposals.

There is really no doubt that all projects will eventually find themselves in the decline phase of Figure 4.1. Predicting when this will occur and planning appropriate actions for when it does can be time- and money-saving.

An important part of the follow-up step is the prediction of discontinuance or normal termination dates for the project. This allows for the timely introduction of proposals for the replacement project. Capital budgeting is cyclical, allowing you to control growth on a continuous basis. The follow-up stage naturally reverts back to proposal generation as each project approaches termination.

To review, the four steps in the capital budgeting cycle are proposal generation, evaluation of those proposals, implementation of selected projects, and follow-up.

PRODUCING NUMBERS TO GET DOLLARS, THE USE OF FORMS, AND CAPITAL BUDGETING MODEL

Risk/Return Relationship. It is axiomatic that the relationship between risk and return should be direct. High-risk ventures should have expectations of high returns; low-risk ventures will be expected to have a lower rate of return. Both must be made attractive to investors.

Figure 4.2 demonstrates the relationship between the risk and return expected for a new line, extending a current line, and the modification or change of a product line or cost reduction programs. From this relationship, a function can be derived to estimate the discount rate. The discount rate, or the necessary return for a project, is equal to the cost of capital plus the risk premium:

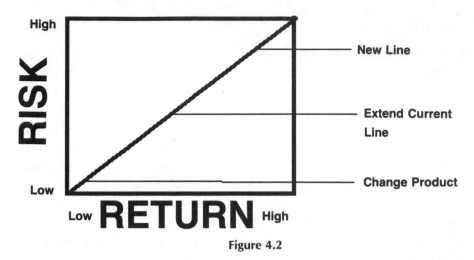

Figure 4.2

Required Return = Cost of Capital + Risk

The most important criterion in the calculation of a capital budgeting model is the required return. This number can be obtained by subjective estimation or by analytical methods that offer a means of estimating risk. But risk is mostly a perception in the mind of investors.

When considering the cost of capital to be used for the generation of net present-value numbers, you should be concerned more with the incremental cost of capital for the project than with the overall cost of obtaining funds. It is the incremental cost of capital—the cost of financing this deal (internally or externally)—with which you are concerned when determining whether a project is cost justified.

Producing Better Numbers for Dollars

Most capital budgeting models use after-tax cash flows as their basis. The following is a capital budgeting cash flow schedule, which will be used to help organize the numbers necessary for the capital budgeting model. Below are some helpful hints for getting the appropriate numbers into the columns of this schedule. The numbers correspond to the columns.

FILLING OUT THE CAPITAL BUDGETING WORKSHEET
1. Column 1 is used to list the estimated net annual cash inflows and outflows.

Misestimating or underestimating in early years is more damaging than incorrect estimates of amounts in the distant future as a result of the discount factor. Greater significance is placed on cash flows in the beginning

CAPITAL BUDGETING
CASH FLOW WORKSHEET

	1	2	3	4	5	6
YEAR	ANNUAL OPERATING CASH FLOW	ADJUSTMENTS	DEPRECIATION	NET BEFORE TAX 1 + 2 + 3	TAX	AFTER TAX 1 + 2 − 5
0						
1						
.2						
3						
4						
5						
6						
7						
8						
9						
10						

Figure 4.3

periods. The initial outflow will usually be in year zero, which means as of Day 1 of the project period. Therefore, the discount factor is 1.0000 because that is current dollars. (Remember that for most discounting tables, all cash flows are assumed to occur at the end of each year. Although this may be an unrealistic assumption in that carrying costs may be incurred throughout the year, these carrying costs can be calculated and added to the net cash outflows to predict more accurately the total first year cost.)

The initial investment includes not only the usual items, such as plant and equipment, but should also include investments in inventory, accounts receivable, training, product introduction, and the expenses for administrative changes and accounting. A more detailed list of cash flow items to check in the capital budgeting proposals is provided below.

For new products, annual inflows that stay level without fluctuations should usually be suspect because the actual patterns seldom occur this way.

2. In Column 2, adjustment to cash should include such items as build-ups of accounts receivable and inventories. This allows recognition of the actual cash flows in appropriate years. For example, a new product line may build up $500,000 in inventories in the first year and this investment may not be recovered in cash inflow until the end of the product's life cycle. Taxes and the treatment of expenses and income for tax purposes must be considered and adjusted for in the model. For example, increases

in receivables and inventories are examples of adjustments that affect current tax liabilities and must be considered in the calculation of estimated taxes. Inventories require cash in the year purchased but have tax effects when used or sold. Receivables may be taxable in the year sales are made, even though not collected until later periods.

Also, the effect of Investment Tax Credits (when and if Congress has them in place) and other project-related tax deductions should be included for the period in which the cash impact occurs.

3. Depreciation is included solely for the purpose of considering its effect on taxes. The model uses only cash flows and the items affecting cash flows. Depreciation expense is a non-cash item in the current period. If depreciation has already been "expensed" in the operating cash flows of Column 1, then an adjustment is necessary to assure that it is not double counted. In the model, the full cost of the investment is made in period -0-. Showing the allocation of that cost again through depreciation will count it twice.

4. Column 4 calculates the taxable portion of the inflows. Care must be taken to determine the appropriate tax consequences, as the goal of the model is to determine after-tax cash flows. Because tax consequences change at the whim of Congress, there are no "constant" rules.

5. Column 5 is used for the calculation of tax, which must be subtracted from cash flows. Note that the tax rate may be changed from year to year for sensitivity analysis.

6. Column 6 is the after-tax cash flow to be used in the various capital budgeting models for the evaluation of the proposals.

Ten Cash Flow Items to Check on Capital Budget Proposals

The following list of cash flow items to be considered in evaluating a capital budget proposal is not intended to be exhaustive. However, for every proposal these items should be carefully scrutinized so that a complete evaluation of appropriate costs can be made.

1. Plant and equipment items.
2. Installation and debugging of equipment and systems.
3. Inventories including consideration of:
   a) raw materials.
   b) work-in-process.
   c) finished goods.
   d) spare parts.

4. Market research and introduction.

5. Training.

6. System changes necessitated by engineering changes and product redesign.

7. Accounts receivable.

8. Accounts payable.

9. Taxes, to include:
   a) income.
   b) investment tax credits.
   c) property tax.
   d) credits.

10. Cash and requirements for cash working capital.

Inflation and Cash Flow Estimates

When you estimate cash flows, inflation should be anticipated and taken into account. Often there is a tendency to assume that the price for the product and the associated costs will remain constant throughout the life of the project. Occasionally, this assumption is made unknowingly and future cash flows are estimated simply on the basis of existing prices.

If anticipated inflation is embodied in the required return criteria, it is important that it also be reflected in the estimated cash flows from the product over the life of the project. To reflect cash flows properly in later periods, consider adjusting both the expected sales price and the expected costs by reasonable inflation numbers.

You may assume that if all proposals are evaluated without consideration of inflation, the decision matrix will be unchanged. This is not necessarily the case. As in the case for the generation of internal rates of return, inflation will change future cash flows relative to the year in which they occur by the inflation rate specific to that product or industry. Therefore, by not anticipating inflation and assigning values for particular future time periods, the decision model may be biased by not taking into account the different effects on cash inflows and outflows as a result of different rates of inflation. As a result, the project selection may not be optimal.

The Discounted Cash Flow

Since you are primarily concerned with discounted cash flow, we should begin our discussion with the required rate of return. This rate is called by many names, including the hurdle rate, the cost of capital, the interest rate, and the discount rate.

Actually, "hurdle rate" is probably best. It implies a barrier, in terms of the return on investment, which the proposal must clear in order to be considered. The other names arise from the mistaken idea that the cost of capital or interest, which is the cost of some of the capital, is the criterion for judging the investment. A weighted average cost of capital has been suggested; for small businesses, it may not be difficult to calculate because of the limited sources of capital employed. However, neither the marginal cost of capital, nor the weighted average cost of capital alone, take into account other factors that should be considered in deciding upon a required return or hurdle rate to be used, for instance:

- The relative risk of this proposal to other proposals.
- Other opportunities.
- Return on other investments already made.
- The company's loan limit.

There is no magic formula for the evaluation of all the relative factors used in arriving at a correct rate. However, you are encouraged to consider:

- How much return do you usually get?
- How much return can you reasonably expect to receive?
- How much does it cost you to borrow?
- How much should you penalize the proposal for the risk involved?

For many businesses, a simple formula for normal risk projects might be: discount rate = New York bank prime interest rate + 3 points (borrowing premium) + 4 to 6 points risk premium. This is, of course, a very rough rule of thumb and should be used with all appropriate caution.

Capital Budgeting Evaluation Worksheet

Once the cash flows have been determined from the Capital Budgeting *Cash Flow* Worksheet (see Figure 4.3), they are listed on the Capital Budgeting *Evaluation* Worksheet (Figure 4.4). Included at the bottom of the Capital Budgeting Evaluation Worksheet is an illustrative present value table for fifteen years, at rates varying from 10 percent to 40 percent. It is best to keep this table together with the capital budgeting worksheet so that later referral back to the worksheet will not result in questions concerning the origin of the numbers used in the calculation. The use of the Evaluation Worksheet is straightforward. The cash flows are taken

CAPITAL BUDGETING EVALUATION WORKSHEET

1	2	3	4	5	6	7	8
YEAR	RAW CASH FLOW	TRIAL % NO. 1	PV OF $1 FROM TABLE	PV OF CASH FLOW (2 × 4)	TRIAL % NO. 2	PV OF $1 FROM TABLE	PV OF CASH FLOW (2 × 7)
1	$			$			$
2	$	xxx		$	xxx		$
3	$	xxx		$	xxx		$
4	$	xxx		$	xxx		$
5	$	xxx		$	xxx		$
6	$	xxx		$	xxx		$
7	$	xxx	.	$	xxx	.	$
8	$	xxx	.	$	xxx	.	$
9	$	xxx	.	$	xxx	.	$
10	$	xxx		$	xxx	.	$
11	$	xxx	.	$	xxx		$
12	$	xxx	.	$	xxx	.	$
13	$	xxx	.	$	xxx	.	$
14	$	xxx	.	$	xxx	.	$
15	$	xxx	.	$	xxx	.	$
			TOTAL			TOTAL	$

PRESENT VALUE TABLE

YEAR	RATE .10−	.12−	.14−	.16−	.18−	.20−	.22−	.24−	.27−	.28−	.30−	.32−	.34−	.36−	.38−	.40−
1	.9091	.8929	.8772	.8621	.8475	.8333	.8197	.8065	.7937	.7812	.7692	.7576	.7463	.7353	.7246	.7143
2	.8264	.7972	.7695	.7432	.7182	.6944	.6719	.6504	.6299	.6104	.5917	.5739	.5569	.5407	.5251	.5102
3	.7513	.7118	.6750	.6407	.6086	.5787	.5507	.5245	.4999	.4768	.4552	.4348	.4156	.3975	.3805	.3644
4	.6830	.6355	.5921	.5523	.5158	.4823	.4514	.4230	.3968	.3725	.3501	.3294	.3102	.2923	.2757	.2603
5	.6209	.5674	.5194	.4761	.4371	.4019	.3700	.3411	.3149	.2910	.2693	.2495	.2315	.2149	.1998	.1859
6	.5645	.5066	.4556	.4104	.3704	.3349	.3033	.2751	.2499	.2274	.2072	.1890	.1727	.1580	.1448	.1328
7	.5132	.4523	.3996	.3538	.3139	.2791	.2486	.2218	.1983	.1776	.1594	.1432	.1289	.1162	.1049	.0949
8	.4665	.4039	.3506	.3050	.2660	.2326	.2038	.1789	.1574	.1388	.1226	.1085	.0962	.0854	.0760	.0678
9	.4241	.3606	.3075	.2630	.2255	.1938	.1670	.1443	.1249	.1084	.0943	.0822	.0718	.0628	.0551	.0484
10	.3855	.3220	.2697	.2267	.1911	.1615	.1369	.1164	.0992	.0847	.0725	.0623	.0536	.0462	.0399	.0346
11	.3505	.2875	.2366	.1954	.1619	.1346	.1122	.0938	.0787	.0662	.0558	.0472	.0400	.0340	.0289	.0247
12	.3136	.2567	.2076	.1685	.1372	.1122	.0920	.0757	.0625	.0517	.0429	.0357	.0298	.0250	.0210	.0176
13	.2897	.2292	.1821	.1452	.1163	.0935	.0754	.0610	.0496	.0404	.0330	.0271	.0223	.0184	.0152	.0126
14	.2633	.2046	.1597	.1252	.0985	.0779	.0618	.0492	.0393	.0316	.0254	.0205	.0166	.0135	.0110	.0090
15	.2394	.1827	.1401	.1079	.0835	.0649	.0507	.0397	.0312	.0247	.0195	.0155	.0124	.0099	.0080	.0064

Figure 4.4

from the Cash Flow Worksheet and are listed in Column 2. In Column 3, the first trial percentage rate is listed to generate the present value of income flow. Column 4 is read directly from the present value table for the first trial interest rate. Those numbers are filled into the form from the matrix. Column 5 is the multiplication of the cash flow from Column 2 by the present value factor from Column 4. Column 6 is used for a second trial percentage. Once again, the process is repeated and the present value rates are included in Column 7 for the second percentage selected. Column 8 is again calculated by the multiplication of the cash flows from Column 2 and, this time, the present value numbers in Column 7. In this manner, two trials can be made to evaluate the present values of a single cash flow estimate over two different discount rates. Using these worksheets, the cash flows for various proposals may be compared. Examples are included in the Appendix to this chapter.

Improving the Estimates

In most cases, the unfortunate truth is that things normally can get only a little bit better but a whole lot worse than expected. Therefore, if the distribution of possible outcomes is considered, it would probably be skewed to the left, in that there is a greater number of unfortunate outcomes than fortunate ones.

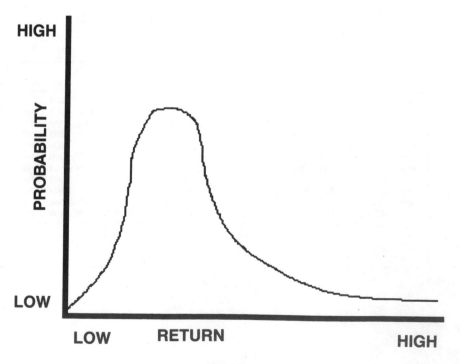

Figure 4.5

The possibility of improvement is also limited by the production capabilities. Therefore, the limiting factor on the right side may be plant capacity. Since capacity is normally added in significant increments as opposed to one or two units at a time, there is no continuum of outcome possibilities. Instead, production capacities occur in steps. Without getting into the problem of analyzing additional production quantities, consider the problem of improving the estimates from the standpoint of fixed or limited capacity.

The problem encountered in capital budgeting, as in all other planning, is that a "most likely" figure is normally offered. However, other alternatives should be considered. The following situation is not uncommon: "most likely" sales estimate is $300,000; "best case" (limited by capacity) is $400,000; "worst case" sales estimate is $100,000. One way to use this information is to multiply each by some estimated probability. For example, the probable outcome for "most likely" may be estimated as five chances out of ten; "best" is two chances out of ten; and "worst" is three chances out of ten. To calculate the expected outcome, we start by multiplying the "most likely" sales estimate by 5 and repeat this process for each outcome. So:

$$
\begin{array}{rcl}
\$3,000 \times 5 & = & \$1,500,000 \\
\$400,000 \times 2 & = & 800,000 \\
\$100,000 \times 3 & = & \underline{\$\ \ 300,000} \\
\underline{\underline{10}} & & \$2,600,000
\end{array}
$$

Sum up the probabilities of five, three, and two for a total of ten. Finally, divide the sum of the multiplications by the sum of the probabilities. The expected value is: $2,600,000/10 = $260,000.

The resulting expected value amount of $260,000 is less than the "most likely" figure of $300,000 and reflects the fact that the curve is skewed to the left. While $300,000 is still "most likely" a conservative estimate of $260,000 is also reasonable.

While not impressive statistically, this approach does make use of more information; this would usually justify its inclusion in cash flow projections. Understand that each of the figures—the sales figures and the probabilities associated with each of the three cases—is an estimate. In making these estimates you should take care to ask a lot of "what if" questions.

When trying to evaluate what is behind the numbers, it is also extremely important for you to evaluate the information sources. As was mentioned previously, engineers may tend to underestimate time to complete projects and thereby underestimate costs. Marketing and sales personnel may overestimate sales and sales potentials. Ask: "How good are the forecasts of the market, the economic conditions and the expectation of future cash flows?" It is often necessary to question where the numbers came from, who generated them, on what assumptions they were based, and what data were used. It is helpful to know the sources of data, the age of the data, and the method of generation.

Often, such sources as the following are used:

- Government publications, which give useful information on the trends in the economy, consumer spending, and other market information.
- Private company publications like Chase Econometric, Dow Jones, etc.
- Trade publications.
- Newspapers.

Experience in the industry usually helps provide an understanding about availability and reliability of certain information and data sources.

A major task in capital budgeting is estimating future cash flows. The quality of the final budget and plan is really only as good as the accuracy of the estimates. You should have efficient procedures set up to collect the information necessary for capital budgeting decisions. Try to standardize this information as much as possible for all investment proposals; otherwise, proposals cannot be compared objectively. One of the more difficult capital budgeting problems to evaluate concerns projects associated with environmental protection or safety. It is difficult in those projects to quantify the net cash flows because in most cases the benefit to you is more in the nature of a cost avoidance.

The reason the expected benefits from a particular project are expressed in terms of cash flows rather than in terms of income is that cash is central to all your decisions. You invest cash now in the hopes of receiving cash returns of a greater amount in the future. Only cash receipts can be reinvested or paid to stockholders in the form of dividends. Thus cash, not income, is what is important in capital budgeting.

MISCELLANEOUS CONSIDERATIONS

Another aspect of estimating future cash flows is that the information must be provided on an incremental basis so that the difference between your cash flows may be analyzed with and without the project. This is important in that, if you are contemplating a new product that is likely to compete with existing products, it is not appropriate to express cash flows in terms of estimated sales of the new product without consideration of the effect the new product may have on existing products. You must consider that there probably will be some cannibalization of existing products.

Another assumption often made is that the risk or quality of all investment proposals under consideration is the same as the risk of existing investment projects. Therefore, the acceptance of any proposal or group of investment proposals does not change the relative business risk of the firm. This isn't necessarily true; each proposal should be looked at individually relative to its riskiness.

Depreciation. Ordinarily, after-tax cash flows are used for capital budgeting calculations. Usually, depreciation at the maximum allowable method is used for tax purposes. Remember, however, that if depreciation is subtracted other than for calculating taxable income, you are double counting. This occurs because you have already "expensed" (treated the cost as a cash outflow) the investment in year zero. The only reason for being interested in depreciation is for the calculation of expected tax.

Lease-Purchase. Internal rate of return cannot be used for making a decision as to whether to lease or purchase a piece of equipment because a true lease requires no investment. The rate of return, therefore, would be infinite. It is, however, often more profitable to buy. Leasing is usually done because of a lack of, or an attempt to conserve, cash. It is a method of financing and therefore is a part of the second-stage financing decision mentioned at the beginning of this chapter.

Interest. Interest costs on borrowed money should not be included in the calculation of cash flows because the method of financing should not determine the decision as to whether the project is a good deal. Besides, the cash flows will be multiplied by the discount rate, which already includes interest as part of the cost of capital considerations.

Uncertainty. Uncertainty should be included in the discount rate. When trying to quantify uncertainty, you should question the sources of the information: "How old is the information?" and "How reliable is the information?" And always search for alternative sources of information as well as means to accomplish the ends.

There is rarely only one way to accomplish a project. Find other methods and evaluate them. Be suspicious if it appears there is only one way to do the project. Your people may be reluctant to consider alternatives.

Ask such questions as: "Are there less expensive ways?" "Are there less risky ways?" "Are there ways that retain more options?"

PRODUCT DISCONTINUANCE

One of the often overlooked uses of the capital budgeting process is for the determination of product discontinuance. In a highly diversified business, where you manufacture large numbers of similar or related products, reevaluation of existing product lines should be undertaken on a regular basis using capital budgeting techniques. This is useful to determine whether existing products are optimally utilizing the company's resources.

Checklist of Data

The following is a checklist of the data required to make a decision about maintaining or eliminating a product.

1. An estimate of the variable expenses directly applicable to the production of specific products, including the costs of production and marketing.
2. An indication of the number of units of the product sold during past periods.
3. Total sales revenues generated by each product within each time period.
4. Estimates of sales revenues for competitive products and the price per unit, units sold, and market share of each competitor.
5. Current and past pricing structures for all products including price discount policies and the distribution of order quantities.
6. Inventory turnover ratio for each period of time.
7. Competitive pricing policies, including the average price obtained for a competitor's product.
8. The total company sales volume for past periods.
9. A projection of future sales for each product carried.
10. Estimation of the total overhead costs devoted to each product.

This checklist can be used to detect a warning signal indicating whether a product needs help or should be considered for elimination. The discontinuation of products can result in increased profits through the elimination of marginally profitable or high-cost products and by reducing over-diversification in a business's product mix. Elimination of over-diversification can increase production and marketing efficiencies by concentrating your efforts and resource utilization.

It should be noted, however, that the indications of candidacy for elimination of a product is not simply a go/no-go test established from quantification of the checklist items. Sometimes healthy products should be eliminated if an analysis shows that your overall goals are better met by product elimination and concentration of efforts. An evaluation of the contributions products make to your objectives will often reveal that the assets dedicated to production of a particular product, if expended on the production of a more profitable item, will create greater returns.

List of Warning Signals Indicating Product Difficulties

1. A decline in absolute sales volume.
2. Sales volume decreasing as a percentage of the firm's total sales.
3. A decrease in a market share.
4. Sales volumes not up to projected amounts.
5. Unfavorable future market potential of products.
6. Return on investment below minimally acceptable levels.
6. Variable cost in excess of actual revenues.
8. Costs, as a percentage of sales, consistently increasing.
9. An increasingly greater percentage of managerial and executive oversight necessary for the product.
10. Price must be lowered repeatedly in order to maintain current or projected sales levels.
11. Promotional budgets must be increased in order to maintain sales.

For most of these indicators, a simple graph on a month-by-month basis can quickly show trends. The graph then becomes a simple budget-tracking device.

The key to a successful elimination program is the availability of timely and pertinent information. This is true of all major business decisions. Accounting sources provide the requisite raw data upon which you may decide which products to discontinue, which to retain, and which products should be expanded or contracted in your business plan.

BAILOUT

This is where you ask a question that few people want to think about: "What happens if things go sour?" While the answers do not always yield clear-cut decisions, they do provide input to the go/no-go decision. Furthermore, the use of the bailout consideration forces some planning.

To consider bailout, start by asking questions. For example: "What can we bail out with if the project must be shut down after two years?" Then, look at cash flows, discounted of course, through that period, including salvage. Because a likely reason to bail out may be lack of sales, lowered sales estimates should be substituted for original estimates. All this can be done in the same format previously used to estimate net present value.

An important value of the bailout consideration is that it reminds you that things do not always go as planned. Many people are eternally optimistic and will resist looking at "the dark side." But such considerations can result in much more protection for the remainder of your business should projections not come to pass.

SUMMARY

The necessary steps in the evaluation of capital budgeting decisions include:

1. Use a discounted payback screen. A screen is in essence nothing more than a go/no-go test. Think of the device used to screen gravel for size: At each successive stage a keep or reject decision is made and the process continues. Ultimately the process narrows down the alternatives so that an educated choice can be made.

2. Use net present value index. A little more conservative than the net present value in its assumptions, the index therefore will act as a more critical go/no-go decision. The index is the net present value divided by the going-in cost. As an example, if for an initial investment of $300,000 the net present value is $150,000, the NPV index would be .5. For an initial investment of $600,000 and a net present value of $200,000 the NPV index would be .33. If one looked just at the NPV, the $600,000 investment would appear to be the better option, as its NPV is $200,000 instead of $150,000. However, for an investment of $300,000, the NPV index of .5 indicates a better return than does the .33 for the larger investment. Thus the NPV index may give a relative go/no-go test and a better indication than a "NPV only" test. Rank proposals by their Internal Rate of Return (IRR).

3. Use break-even in examining alternatives. It is often helpful in assessing risks as a result of misestimations in sales levels. The break-even analysis, although a very simple test, shows how varying sales forecasts will affect the period over which we can expect to break even.

4. Ask "What if" questions and apply some calculations using the bailout consideration. Bailout is simply an attempt to determine the minimum amount for break-even on operations.

5. Relate the size of the decision to the decision maker. This is merely a reminder that the level in management at which the decision should ultimately be made relates to the significance of that project to your overall objectives.

6. Keep records. It is difficult to learn from mistakes if no records exist. Feedback is necessary for improvements. It is a good idea for records be kept from the inception. In order fully to use this information, records should be indexed and retained for future analysis or review. Often estimates generated for other projects may be very useful in evaluating future projects.

7. Plan for retirement—not just yours, but the end of each project. Periodic discontinuance is part of the process. Remember that as each product is discontinued, another product should be ready to take its place to ensure that your growth and prosperity continue. Planning is a cyclical process and the element of discontinuance should herald the introduction of new products.

APPENDIX: EXAMPLES AND COMPARISON OF CALCULATIONS

The facts are:
A project with an initial cost of $55,000 will return:

	Inflows	Depreciation
Year 1	$ 5,000	$ 5,000
Year 2	25,000	10,000
Year 3	35,000	10,000
Year 4	15,000	10,000
Year 5	20,000	10,000
Year 6	15,000	-0-

The tax rate is 20 percent.

The first calculation example uses the forms developed in the chapter. The second example shows the calculation on an HP12C™ calculator. The third example uses computer spread sheets.

	18%	20%
Present value of inflows	$58,572.00	$55,480.00
Present value of outflows	55,000.00	55,000.00
Net present value	$ 3,572.00	$ 480.00

The Interest Rate of Return (IRR) (the discount rate, which causes the NPV to be zero) is very close to 20 percent.

CAPITAL BUDGETING
CASH FLOW WORKSHEET

YEAR	1 ANNUAL OPERATING CASH FLOW	2 ADJUSTMENTS	3 DEPRECIATION	4 NET BEFORE TAX 1 + 2 + 3	5 TAX	6 AFTER TAX 1 + 2 − 5
0	<55,000>	∅	∅	<55,000>	∅	<55,000>
1	5,000	∅	5,000	∅	∅	5,000
2	25,000	∅	10,000	15,000	3,000	22,000
3	35,000	∅	10,000	25,000	5,000	30,000
4	15,000	∅	10,000	5,000	1,000	14,000
5	20,000	∅	10,000	10,000	2,000	18,000
6	15,000	∅	10,000	5,000	1,000	14,000
7						
8						
9						
10						

CAPITAL BUDGETING EVALUATION WORKSHEET

1	2	3	4	5	6	7	8
YEAR	RAW CASH FLOW	TRIAL % NO. 1	PV OF $1 FROM TABLE	PV OF CASH FLOW (2 × 4)	TRIAL % NO. 2	PV OF $1 FROM TABLE	PV OF CASH FLOW (2 × 7)
1	$5000	18%	.8475	$4238	20%	.8333	$4167
2	$22000	xxx	.7182	$15801	xxx	.6944	$15277
3	$30,000	xxx	.6086	$18258	xxx	.5787	$17361
4	$14000	xxx	.5158	$7221	xxx	.4823	$6752
5	$18000	xxx	.4371	$7868	xxx	.4019	$7234
6	$14000	xxx	.3704	$5186	xxx	.3349	$4689
7	$	xxx	.	$	xxx	.	$
8	$	xxx	.	$	xxx	.	$
9	$	xxx	.	$	xxx	.	$
10	$	xxx	.	$	xxx	.	$
11	$	xxx	.	$	xxx	.	$
12	$	xxx	.	$	xxx	.	$
13	$	xxx	.	$	xxx	.	$
14	$	xxx	.	$	xxx	.	$
15	$	xxx	.	$	xxx	.	$
			TOTAL	58572		TOTAL	$55480

PRESENT VALUE TABLE

YEAR	.10−	.12−	.14−	.16−	.18−	.20−	.22−	.24−	.27−	.28−	.30−	.32−	.34−	.36−	.38−	.40−
1	.9091	.8929	.8772	.8621	.8475	.8333	.8197	.8065	.7937	.7812	.7692	.7576	.7463	.7353	.7246	.7143
2	.8264	.7972	.7695	.7432	.7182	.6944	.6719	.6504	.6299	.6104	.5917	.5739	.5569	.5407	.5251	.5102
3	.7513	.7118	.6750	.6407	.6086	.5787	.5507	.5245	.4999	.4768	.4552	.4348	.4156	.3975	.3805	.3644
4	.6830	.6355	.5921	.5523	.5158	.4823	.4514	.4230	.3968	.3725	.3501	.3294	.3102	.2923	.2757	.2603
5	.6209	.5674	.5194	.4761	.4371	.4019	.3700	.3411	.3149	.2910	.2693	.2495	.2315	.2149	.1998	.1859
6	.5645	.5066	.4556	.4104	.3704	.3349	.3033	.2751	.2499	.2274	.2072	.1890	.1727	.1580	.1448	.1328
7	.5132	.4523	.3996	.3538	.3139	.2791	.2486	.2218	.1983	.1776	.1594	.1432	.1289	.1162	.1049	.0949
8	.4665	.4039	.3506	.3050	.2660	.2326	.2038	.1789	.1574	.1388	.1226	.1085	.0962	.0854	.0760	.0678
9	.4241	.3606	.3075	.2630	.2255	.1938	.1670	.1443	.1249	.1084	.0943	.0822	.0718	.0628	.0551	.0484
10	.3855	.3220	.2697	.2267	.1911	.1615	.1369	.1164	.0992	.0847	.0725	.0623	.0536	.0462	.0399	.0346
11	.3505	.2875	.2366	.1954	.1619	.1346	.1122	.0938	.0787	.0662	.0558	.0472	.0400	.0340	.0289	.0247
12	.3136	.2567	.2076	.1685	.1372	.1122	.0920	.0757	.0625	.0517	.0429	.0357	.0298	.0250	.0210	.0176
13	.2897	.2292	.1821	.1452	.1163	.0935	.0754	.0610	.0496	.0404	.0330	.0271	.0223	.0184	.0152	.0126
14	.2633	.2046	.1597	.1252	.0985	.0779	.0618	.0492	.0393	.0316	.0254	.0205	.0166	.0135	.0110	.0090
15	.2394	.1827	.1401	.1079	.0835	.0649	.0507	.0397	.0312	.0247	.0195	.0155	.0124	.0099	.0080	.0064

RATE

EXAMPLE 1:
HEWLETT-PACKARD HP 12C™

Key Strokes			Display
f clear	clx		
55,000	CHS	g CFo	−55,000.00
5,000	g	CFj	5,000.00
22,000	g	CFj	22,000.00
30,000	g	CFj	30,000.00
14,000	g	CFj	14,000.00
18,000	g	CFj	18,000.00
14,000	g	CFj	14,000.00
18	i		18.00
f	NPV		3,571.32
f	IRR		20.33
20	i		20.00
f	NPV		479.47

EXAMPLE 2:
LOTUS 1-2-3™ REGRESSION ANALYSIS

```
E3:  +B3+C3-D3                                                    READY

        A         B         C         D         E         F         G         H
                                    LOTUS 1-2-3 EXAMPLE
        CASH FLOW      ADJUST.    DEPREC.      NET B/T      TAX      A/T CASH
        -55000         0          0          -55000
         5000          0          5000
        25000          0         10000
        35000          0         10000
        15000          0         10000
        20000          0         10000
        15000          0          0

01-Jan-80 01:10 AM        UNDO                          CAPS
```

E11:   READY

        A   B   C   D   E   F   G   H

                          LOTUS 1-2-3 Example Chapter 4 Appendix
        CASH FLOW   ADJUST.   DEPREC.   NET B/T   TAX   A/T CASH
        -55000   0   0   -55000
         5000   0   5000   0
        25000   0   10000   15000
        35000   0   10000   25000
        15000   0   10000   5000
        20000   0   10000   10000
        15000   0   10000   5000

28-Mar-90 02:53 PM   UNDO   CAPS

F5: +E5.0.2   READY

        A   B   C   D   E   F   G   H

                          LOTUS 1-2-3 Example Chapter 4 Appendix
        CASH FLOW   ADJUST.   DEPREC.   NET B/T   TAX   A/T CASH
        -55000   0   0   -55000
         5000   0   5000   0   0
        25000   0   10000   15000   3000
        35000   0   10000   25000   5000
        15000   0   10000   5000   1000
         1000   0   10000   10000   2000
        15000   0   10000   5000   1000

28-Mar-90 02:56 PM   UNDO   CAPS

G4: +B4+C4-F4   READY

        A   B   C   D   E   F   G   H

                          LOTUS 1-2-3 Example Chapter 4 Appendix
        CASH FLOW   ADJUST.   DEPREC.   NET B/T   TAX   A/T CASH
        -55000   0   0   -55000   -55000
         5000   0   5000   0   0   5000
        25000   0   10000   15000   3000   22000
        35000   0   10000   25000   5000   30000
        15000   0   10000   5000   1000   14000
         1000   0   10000   10000   2000   18000
        15000   0   10000   5000   1000   14000

28-Mar-90 02:58 PM   UNDO   CAPS

```
        A        B        C        D        E        F        G        H
                         LOTUS 1-2-3 Example Chapter 4 Appendix
        CASH FLOW       ADJUST.    DEPREC.        NET B/T      TAX      A/T CASH
        -55000          0          0             -55000                -55000
         5000           0          5000               0        0         5000
        25000           0         10000          15000       3000       22000
        35000           0         10000          25000       5000       30000
        15000           0         10000           5000       1000       14000
         1000           0         10000          10000       2000       18000
        15000           0         10000           5000       1000       14000
```

NPV of Inflows 58571.32

```
        A        B        C        D        E        F        G        H
                         LOTUS 1-2-3 Example Chapter 4 Appendix
        CASH FLOW       ADJUST.    DEPREC.        NET B/T      TAX      A/T CASH
        -55000          0          0             -55000                -55000
         5000           0          5000               0        0         5000
        25000           0         10000          15000       3000       22000
        35000           0         10000          25000       5000       30000
        15000           0         10000           5000       1000       14000
         1000           0         10000          10000       2000       18000
        15000           0         10000           5000       1000       14000
```

NPV of Inflows   58571.32
Net Present Value   3571.32

```
        A        B        C        D        E        F        G        H
                         LOTUS 1-2-3 Example Chapter 4 Appendix
        CASH FLOW       ADJUST.    DEPREC.        NET B/T      TAX      A/T CASH
        -55000          0          0             -55000                -55000
         5000           0          5000               0        0         5000
        25000           0         10000          15000       3000       22000
        35000           0         10000          25000       5000       30000
        15000           0         10000           5000       1000       14000
         1000           0         10000          10000       2000       18000
        15000           0         10000           5000       1000       14000
```

NPV of Inflows   58571.32
Net Present Value   3571.32
Int. Rate Return   0.203251

COMPARISON OF THE INTERNAL RATE OF RETURN METHOD AND THE NET PRESENT VALUE METHOD

When comparing two mutually exclusive proposals using both the net present value method and the internal rate of return method, you will find cases where one project is preferable to the other using one method, and the reverse is true using the other method. It is important to understand how and why this happens. The result is obtained because the two projects will have differing cash flows in different periods. Therefore, the compounding effect of the discount rate and the time value of money will produce different results.

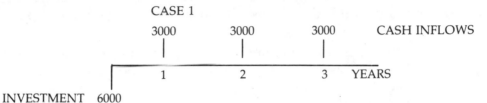

The NPV at 15% discount rate is $849.68.
The IRR is 23.5%.
The project returns $9,000 total and an undiscounted break-
  even in 2 years.

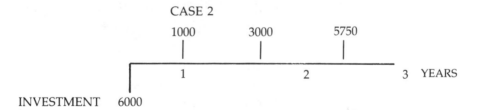

The NPV at 15% discount rate is $918.71.
The IRR is 22%.
The project returns $9,750 total and a break-even in 2 years
  and 4 months.

Which project is a better investment?
  This example readily points up how similar cash flows in different periods will affect your decision-making process. Reliance upon any one method, therefore, without understanding how it works, may result in a distorted decision-making process.

Some people prefer the net present value method as superior to the internal rate of return on a theoretical basis. The reason for this is that the internal rate of return method implies reinvestment rates that will differ depending upon the cash flow stream for each investment proposal under consideration. With the net present value method, however, the implied reinvestment rate, namely the required rate of return or hurdle rate, is the same for each proposal. In essence, this reinvestment rate presents the minimum return on opportunities available to you. You must employ judgment in evaluating what each model generates as a decision. In order to determine which method is preferable, factors other than the rate of return may alter the decision from one proposal to the other. For instance, long-term tax planning may favor one cash flow projection over the other in order to optimize long-term tax liabilities. Do not accept the decision blindly. Evaluate the expected cash flows and their timing. Question everything!

Capital budgeting in the ongoing system of planning, evaluation, and execution of the business is itself a process. It starts with a determination of where you are, then where you want to be, then how you intend to get there. Even if you do not institute capital budgeting as an ongoing process, simply going through the exercise of trying to set up a process is a valuable endeavor of self-examination. It gets people to think through how prudent investments in capital-intensive projects may help the business grow, diversify, or replace existing plant and equipment.

Capital budgeting is a four-step process of proposal solicitation or generation, evaluation, implementation, and follow-up. In the evaluation step, various alternative proposals have various related returns associated with the investment. With this expected return is a probable risk of loss of all or some part of the invested funds. In any endeavor, the decision must be based upon balancing the return against the associated risk. The problem, of course, is that no certainty, even in the estimates of risk and return, exists. In order to minimize the risk, you should consider the method by which estimates, projections, and other numbers are generated.

You should be cautious when only one solution is proposed because there is seldom a problem without several. When preparing a capital budgeting plan, develop contingency plans and scenarios after asking many "What if" questions. As part of your contingency planning, do not put your "head in the sand." Consider the dark side of the project— "What if it goes sour?" For such a proposition, you should be ready for bailout as a planned withdrawal; you should not be forced into mindless panic in the event that the project faces immediate failure.

5

Budgeting for Operations

Operating budgets, sometimes called operating plans, are used by many manufacturing firms, retail stores, service companies, and governmental agencies for planning, operating, and control functions. To improve your probability of success, you should engage in not only long-range but also operational budgeting/planning. The fulfillment of the planning process requires marketing planning, product planning, capital planning, and financial planning. We want to emphasize that your plans should drive the budget and not the reverse. However, the process isn't complete until it is quantified—that is, until budgets, as an outcome of the plan, have been prepared.

DEFINITION OR PURPOSE OF AN OPERATING BUDGET

An operating budget is a quantification of your business plan. It is a projected, and hopefully realistic, number picture of your income and cost objectives for a period.

Usually, operating budgets are constructed for a year, by months. Some people construct five-year operating budgets with varying reporting periods. Such budgets are often constructed monthly for the first two years, quarterly for the next two years and annually or semiannually for

115

the remaining year. However, a one year budget that is extended quarterly so that it again projects a full year is probably adequate for most uses.

As with any plan, the ensuing actual performance can be compared with the operating budget to detect "off-target" performances and to direct attention to troubled areas. In this way the operating budget serves both as a planning tool and a control device. All functions of the business should be included when structuring the operating budget. By including all of your operating costs, more performance measures and controls are possible. The costs you incur to increase the level of preparation detail will relate favorably to your realization of cost savings through better control.

Since measurements of performance many be devised according to an operating budget, there is a natural tendency for people to "adjust" the budget process. The potential consequences should be considered: Sales managers may make overly optimistic assessments of the market, thus reducing the reliability of the cash allocations and expenses anticipated for that level of production and sales. Some manufacturing managers may "pad" a budget to build in a safety margin or premium. In a tight market or competitive sales conditions this pad could make a product look less attractive than competing products. Your concern should be to get the budget as realistic and accurate as possible because a reasonable budget based upon a reasonable plan encourages reasonable performance.

SIGNS OF BUDGET INEFFECTIVENESS

Some signs that the budget or budget process are less than optimally effective are:

- *Management or supervisory inattention to the budget.* Since a budget is, or can be used as, a measurement tool, accountability and review are necessary for control. Without review, there can be little corrective action and thus there is a loss of control. If management is not using the budget as a control tool, you will want to determine whether the problem is with the budget or with the management.

- *A lack of complete participation by all levels of management within the firm.* Budgets dictated from upper management without input from the accountable people may have negative effects on the psychology of the employees and lower management. An attitude of "It's their budget, let's see them make it!" may develop.

- *Uncorrected large variances between planned performance and budget objectives.* Large budget variances may indicate one of several weaknesses:
  1) Poor estimates.
  2) Poor feedback and lack of timely, corrective action.
  3) Ineffective management policies concerning budget maintenance.
- *Lack of participation in the operation of the business by those who actively prepare the budgets.* Without a working knowledge of the dynamics of the operations of the business, it is difficult to maintain a working knowledge of current operational status. The amount or frequency of contact with operating departments is usually directly related to the stability of processes. The greater the variability in the operations of the business the more frequently those who prepare the budget should observe and experience the operating environment.
- *Supervisors or first line managers do not know how their budgets were determined nor what is contained within their budget.* In such cases, the department manager does not know how performance is being evaluated, how well s/he is performing to expectations, where s/he may be doing well and where s/he is experiencing unplanned difficulties.

Budgets of all types are good planning tools and can also serve a very valuable control function. In order to be used for control, other systems have to be built to supplement the budget process.

- Creating the budget itself does not cause programs to be installed to implement the budget. A feedback loop is necessary to direct attention to areas where difficulties may be encountered in meeting the business plan. Periodic budget reports should generate feedback on performance against budget. These reports should trigger action. If the budget and related performance against budget reports do not flag attention to problem areas, you are missing the opportunity for needed improvements.
- The feedback loop requires continuous measurement of performance to budget estimates. For feedback to work properly, it should be regular, expected, and consistently reported. Comparisons are most effective when they are done regularly, consistently, and timely. Trend analysis of budget performance is a good early warning device. Of course, benefits of the budget reporting process must outweigh the costs. However, the ongoing evaluation process is one of the places where you should realize substantial savings.

RESPONSIBILITY ACCOUNTING

Responsibility accounting means structuring systems and reports to highlight on the accountability of specific people. The process involves assigning accountability to departments or functions where the responsibility for performance lies.

Specific responsibility is a necessary concept of management control. Accounting has grown to encompass at least three purposes: financial reporting, product or service cost reporting, and performance evaluation reporting. The third function of accounting, the performance measurement function, is closely related to the operational function of the business. Since many businesses now evaluate and manage employees by objectives, the need for more sophisticated performance measurement tools has increased.

In a Management by Objectives (MBO) system, one critical element is to ensure that the individual has the authority necessary to carry out the responsibility s/he is asked to execute. Without the necessary authority, a person cannot, and should not, be expected to meet the responsibilities imposed. Since this is not intended to be an argument for an MBO system, we will assume that the manager has an appropriate balance of authority and responsibility.

Within this level of responsibility, a person can be evaluated only when the performance reporting system is tied to the expected level of performance. A person's actual performance is keyed to this budget expression of expected performance.

Responsibility accounting should not be restricted to any one level but should measure expected performance throughout the hierarchy of the business. Key indicators can be built into the system to evaluate performance and to trigger reactions to unanticipated results. In this way, management at each level is called upon to intervene only when it is necessary to correct problems or substandard performance. This management by exception system frees up significant time for managers to plan and coordinate other essential business functions.

Contrasted with financial accounting, responsibility accounting does not simply group like costs, but instead segments the business into distinct responsibility centers. A measurement process is established to compare results obtained against objectives established for the segment prior to the end of a plan/budget period. These objectives are part of the operating budget and comprise the targets of operation for every segment of the business.

To be effective, responsibility accounting must be tailored to each individual business. The accounting system must be adjusted to conform with the responsibility centers established. The revenue and expense categories must be designed to fit the functions or operations management feels are important to monitor and evaluate. For example, the use of electricity by a particular machine may be significant, and excessive use may be an early warning sign of a process problem. Management would want to meter electricity consumption and have the expense reported as a line item to be measured against standard consumption rates by machine or by department.

In a service business, it may be important to accumulate and evaluate costs for "expedited" mailings as a distinct item not included in the "postage expense" numbers. Such costs might indicate inefficient operations in the mail room.

Another function of the responsibility accounting system is to compile the individual centers' performance reports into successively aggregated collective reports to identify broader categories of responsibility. Behind these groupings is still a great deal of detailed information available for analysis.

Developing Responsibility Centers

A responsibility center has no standard size. It can be as small as a single operation or machine or as large as the entire business. The business is, after all, the responsibility center of the chief executive of the business. Typically, the business is broken down into a large number of centers or segments which, when plotted in successive layers or groupings, appear as a pyramid. This pyramiding represents the hierarchy of authority and responsibility of the business. Various types of responsibility centers may be established for various purposes. The nature of the centers or segments can also vary.

1) If a person is charged with only the responsibility for the costs incurred in a process or operation, you have established a *cost center*. Cost centers can be line operations (such as painting) or staff functions (such as recruiting). The emphasis of a cost center is on producing goods or providing specific services in conjunction with other physical measures of performance. Usually, there is no direct revenue production measurement by that center because the center does not produce final product.

2) Another segment is a unit held responsible for the profit contribution it makes. This responsibility center is aptly named a *profit center*. Profit centers are often larger units than cost centers because a profit center

requires the production of a complete product or service to make a contribution to the profit. (However, a salesman could be considered a profit center.) The establishment of a profit center should be based upon established managerial criteria of revenues and costs.

3) Other divisions can be established such as *revenue centers* and *investment centers*. Revenue centers, for instance, are segments of the larger profit centers charged with the responsibility of producing revenue. Sales departments are a typical example. An investment center is a profit center that also has the responsibility of raising and making the necessary investment required to produce the profit. This added investment step would require the use of some rate-of-return test as an objective measure of the center's performance.

The appropriate establishment of cost centers, profit centers, etc. is a critical element of the responsibility reporting system, and as such must be performed carefully and accurately.

Establishing Costs

Another important aspect of responsibility accounting is the accumulation of costs. Accountants have labeled the standard types of costs typically encountered: fixed, variable, and semivariable. Within these classifications, some costs may be incurred at the discretion of specific levels of management while others are nondiscretionary at given levels of management. Sometimes, costs relate to more than one center and must be allocated between them. The most effective system will probably result when responsible management has been an active participant in the determination of the allocation of costs and the maintenance of the reporting system.

One complication of accumulating costs is the problem of transfer pricing. In manufacturing businesses a cost center's performance is a function of the added costs and the intracompany movements of raw materials, work-in-progress, finished goods, and services performed. A market price may not be available or may be too uncertain, because of fluctuations, to use as an objective measure of performance. Some compromise is often necessary to establish transfer prices among departments.

Fixed Costs. A fixed cost is one that does not vary directly with volume. Some costs are really fixed, such as interest on debt. Other typically identified fixed costs, such as depreciation expense, may vary under some circumstances. Generally, over a broad range of operations, total fixed costs are represented as step functions because they are incurred in increments as production or the number of services increases.

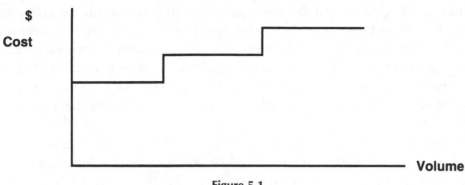

Figure 5.1

This characteristic of fixed costs should not present any great difficulty. Since production or sales is predicted for a budget period, the level of fixed costs can be established from graphs such as that in Figure 5.1. Unfortunately, fixed costs, because of their apparent static behavior, are not always reviewed regularly and critically to determine reasonableness. Like all other costs, the larger the amount of individual fixed costs the more frequently they should be reviewed. Insurance premiums are a good example. From year to year insurance premiums may vary little, if at all, and be paid without reconsideration, particularly in good times. A schedule of review should be set up based upon a two-factor analysis.

Figure 5.2 represents the relationship between the magnitude of a particular fixed cost and the frequency with which it should be reviewed.

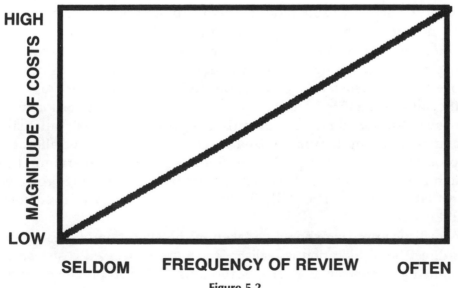

Figure 5.2

When making such an assessment for yourself, you should be aware of such factors as the cost of reconsideration in setting the time periods for "seldom" through "often." The process of reevaluating your insurance coverage may be a significant task, requiring a major allocation of time and resources. However, the returns could be equally significant if you realize substantial savings resulting from a renegotiation of the insurance policy and rates.

Another concern with fixed costs is the method of allocation of those costs among your different products or services. Fixed costs are often assigned in an arbitrary manner, creating an unrealistic profit or loss statement for each product. Otherwise nonprofitable products are some-times carried by an "average fixed cost" allocation, which may not accurately depict costs associated with the product. Accurate decisions are unlikely without correct information concerning a product's costs. You should undertake to allocate fixed costs properly through the preparation of an operating budget. Your accountant should have a reasonable understanding of the magnitude of the costs and which products or services are affecting the amount. Also, you should determine how varying activity levels influence the costs you incur for different products and services.

When analyzing fixed costs, you should determine what causes that cost to be incurred and what causes it to change in amount. This analysis will go a long way toward identifying to which product(s) or service(s) the cost should be assigned and in what manner that allocation should be made.

For some fixed costs, this will be a very difficult process. Some ad-ministrative costs may simply not be identifiable with any one product or service. Successive allocations through your costing hierarchy may be needed to arrive finally at a "product attributable" status.

You may treat such costs as variable and determine a rate at which to assign these costs against labor hours. In determining this burden or overhead rate, such fixed costs are divided by an estimate or projection of the anticipated direct labor hours and are allocated proportionately. However, this method may unfairly assign costs to labor intensive products, ignoring that more fixed costs should perhaps be allocated to products with large capital or fixed investments. Furthermore, this assignment could under-recover fixed costs by misestimating projected direct labor hours. Or, equally likely, an over-recovery of fixed costs could occur.

A realistic approach should be taken in the allocation of these costs. If a direct hour allocation is realistic, then use it. If fixed costs can be identified to particular product(s) or service(s), it is appropriate to do so.

Variable Costs. In order to be properly classified as variable, a cost should meet two distinct criteria: no cost should be incurred until an activity begins and a direct relationship should exist between the amount of the cost and the level of activity. An example of a purely variable cost is a sales commission. As sales increase or decrease, the amount of commission varies in a direct relationship to the level of sales.

The relationship between the cost and the level of production may be a straight-line relationship or the cost rate may increase as the level of output increases. When plotted, this increasing cost relationship will appear as a curvilinear (or curved shape) graph.

While this relationship is common to variable costs, Figure 5.3 is not the usual way it is shown. The more usual case is the straight-line relationship. Often set-up costs are spread over production, in which case there is a curvilinear relationship; but that is not the same case. In the set-up cost allocation, a fixed cost is spread over varying units of output, decreasing as the length of the production run increases. The earlier example is an increasing cost per unit as the number of units produced increases.

Typically, costs such as direct labor, scrap costs, packaging, and shipping are treated as variable costs. However, direct labor and other costs may not be purely variable. For example, the assumption that direct labor varies directly with the number of units produced relies upon the divisibility

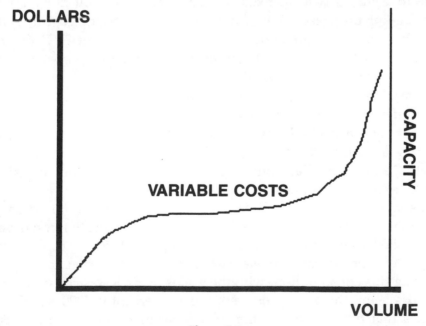

Figure 5.3

assumption. But labor is not infinitely divisible. If an employee can produce 1,600 units in a standard eight-hour workday but only 1,200 units are required, unless that employee can be used in another operation he has been used at a 75 percent utilization level. Either this idle-time labor can be effectively used in other places or 25 percent of these (unutilized) efforts are assigned to fewer units produced. In most cases, direct labor and direct materals are treated as variable costs for budget purposes even if they are not perfectly divisible.

If you have established labor standards for your operations, these can be used for budgeting purposes. By accumulating data and establishing labor standards, you can begin to target costs. The difficulty is establishing objective labor-hour targets for the planning period. Reliance solely upon historical data may bias projections, ignore the effects of the learning curve on efficiency and avoid consideration of past inefficiencies.

For planning purposes, remember that the graph of these fixed and variable costs appear reversed *when they are assigned on a per unit basis*. When variable costs are assigned on a per unit basis, they are constant and fixed per unit. When fixed costs are assigned on a per-unit basis, they vary as production levels change.

Mixed Costs. Mixed costs are those that behave as if they have fixed and variable components. Many items of cost fall into this category. Some people treat mixed costs as fixed costs. If you do so, you must assume an average or projected level of output and allocate the cost over that level. This may over- or under-recover that component of fixed cost. Some might say that it is not important because the over- or under-recovery will be insignificant.

A consistent bias toward under-recovery of the fixed component of one mixed cost may be equally true about an under-recovery of the fixed component of every mixed cost, allocated on the basis of that misestimated output level. If this biased data is used to make capital investment decisions, marketing and pricing decisions, and expansion or contraction decisions, you may experience serious problems.

It is sometimes difficult to determine what portion of a mixed cost is fixed and what portion is variable. Fortunately, this allocation can usually be established from historical data. As an example, data for the consumption of electricity in one department were tabulated for the previous six months.

Plotting this consumption, with the Y axis being KWH consumed and the X axis being the units produced, the Y intercept is 5000 KWH. This indicates that for zero production the department still consumes 5000 KWH of electricity each month, the fixed component of cost.

	KWH USED	UNITS PRODUCED
JAN	7500	400
FEB	8000	480
MAR	8250	520
APR	8750	600
MAY	9500	720
JUNE	8750	600

Figure 5.4

The variable component can then be determined by using the formula:

$$Y = MX + B$$

Because (b), the Y intercept, is 5000:

$$Y = MX + 5000$$

Substituting any set of values from the table into the equation:

$$7500 = M(400) + 5000$$

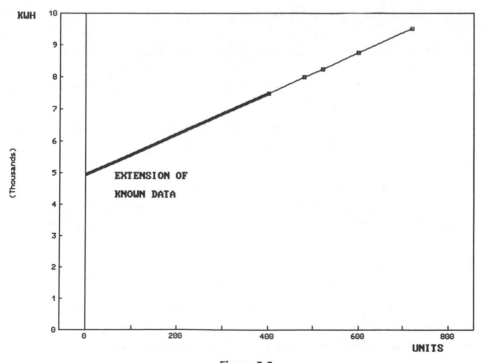

Figure 5.5

and solving for (M), $M = 6.25$. Therefore each unit of production has a variable component of 6.25 KWH in electrical consumption. By applying the electric rate to each component of electrical usage, the fixed and variable cost components of the mixed cost are determined. Sometimes the equation is not so straightforward and linear regression may have to be used to project the line. This can be done using the linear regression "least squares" model found in Chapter 3.

Historical Data. One major concern of using historical data as a basis for future prediction is that the firm may be perpetuating past inefficiencies. However, historical data may be the best or even the only data available. When using historical data, you should be sure that:

- Historical data accurately state the past. An examination must be made of the conditions under which data were collected, and what is and is not contained in the data.
- Historical data are relevant to what it is the firm is trying to predict. To the extent current conditions are not the same as past conditions, historical data become more difficult to use in projecting the future.
- The use of the data encourages performance that improves upon the past performance.
- The effects of inflation are properly considered.

Further *practical points* in the use of historical data:

1. Avoid using historical data more than 12 months old in periods of high inflation or deflation.
2. Be consistently objective. Do not bias the data by summarily rejecting data that seem to be out of line. There may be a reason for unusual numbers.
3. Be creative; try not to be bound by traditional thinking. Some of the relationships between costs and activities may not seem direct and quantifiable. This could be the result of delayed billings or nontraditional billings.
4. Consider and try using moving averages for data that tend to be nonlinear or scattered.
5. Use extrapolation to project data for future estimated production or service levels.
6. Never use tools past the point that common sense tells you is meaningful.

Projecting Revenues

Often firms want a forecast of earnings for the entire enterprise to compare with the operating budgets. This forecast of revenues should be reconciled with the operating budget.

The basis of all revenue projections is a sales forecast. Many companies start the operating budget process by first generating this sales forecast. The sales forecast is exploded with lead and lag times added so that departmental schedules are created. This departmental scheduling of activities is then used to create the operating budget. For example, Fruit Crate Manufacturing Co., Inc., has a maximum production capacity of 1000 crates per week and expects the following sales forecast.

	July	Aug
Type A crate	2000	3000

To produce a type A crate the firm's process breaks down into three steps: sawing, curing or drying, and assembly. The sawing and curing is done in batches of 1000 crates and the rate of production is:

sawing	1000 crates/ 1 week
drying	1000 crates/ 3 weeks
assembly	1000 crates/ 1 week

Since all sales are shipped on the first of each month, the exploded production schedule shown in Figure 5.6 is used for budgeting.

Armed with this operating schedule, the company can plan its equipment, labor, and materals scheduling, and a budget of expenses can be generated. Without carrying the example too much farther, it is easy to see how much of each operation must be done and when. For example, in May, two weeks of sawing and one week of drying must be budgeted; in June, three weeks of sawing, eight weeks of drying and two weeks of assembly, and so forth.

As manufacturing and related costs are pushed back in time, the receipt of payments (cash flows) are pushed forward in time. If Fruit Crate Manufacturing Co., Inc., offers a 2/10; N/30 payment schedule, it will ship on July 1, having incurred expenses in May and June but not expect payment until July 10 or August 1. The timing of cash flows, the revenue portion, and the expense portion of the plan, must be coordinated to ensure that adequate funds are on hand (cash flow budget) to meet

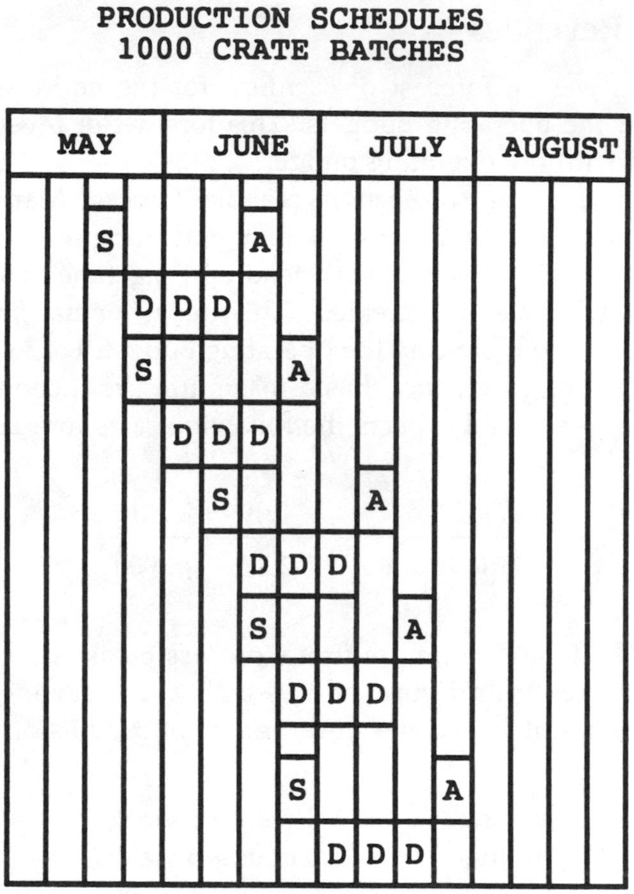

PRODUCTION SCHEDULES
1000 CRATE BATCHES

Figure 5.6

expected operations. For this example, there is a negative cash flow for at least two and a half months.

BUDGET TRACKING AND MAINTENANCE

So far this chapter has emphasized establishing responsibility and developing a budget and accounting system that conforms to an allocation of responsibility. The cardinal principle behind this system is that those who are to be measured by the system understand how it works and agree that the objectives are attainable *through their efforts*.

The first requirement should be an integration of your objectives, goals, and tactics to the managerial level involved. One method for integration is to have each manager participate in establishing and maintaining the objectives and goals. The test of reasonableness should apply. That is, there should be a reasonable likelihood of obtaining the objective in order to motivate compliance.

An element that often impedes effective budgeting and attainability is the inability to identify controllable and uncontrollable costs or expenses. Controllable costs should be identified and targeted. If elements of uncontrollable costs are included in a responsibility-based budget they may have a negative motivation factor. Practically, all revenue and expense factors are controllable by some manager at some point. However, such expenses as property taxes may influence profits yet be beyond the control of an operations manager. Such items as administrative overhead allocation are uncontrollable within departments of the firm. As a general rule, these items should be assigned and accounted for separately, so as not to indicate responsibility of the manager (e.g., heating, lighting, janitorial).

The final element in the budget tracking plan is variance analysis and reporting. Variance reporting can take many forms but the most common is to compare monthly actuals to monthly projections with year-to-date comparisons as well. Often the report will contain space for an explanation of the variance from budget. The report can be generated in many forms, including by product; by operation or group; by labor; and by materals. A typical report could look like:

	MONTH			YEAR-TO-DATE			EXPLANATIONS
	Budget	Actual	% Var	Budget	Actual	% Var	
A. Controllable							
Direct Labor							
Operating Supplies							
Repair Labor							
Repair Supplies							
Heat, Light, Power							
Subtotal							
B. Raw Materials							
Subtotal							
C. Overhead							
Supervisory Salaries							
Corporate Overhead							
Taxes							
Insurance							
Depreciation Expense							
Subtotal							
TOTAL							

Figure 5.7

This form of reporting consistently shows management the variations from budget, with an explanation of causes and circumstances. It thus meets the second and third objectives of a budget, to keep score and direct attention.

PARTS OF AN OPERATING BUDGET

Budgets are what you make of them. There are no hard and fast rules for what budgets must look like. To assist you in better operating the business, budgets should be devised specifically. Some typical elements of operating budgets are discussed below.

Sales Forecast. Providing for all potential service(s) or sales may determine the amount of product to have on hand or the personnel needed for the provision of services. Thus, the foundation of operational planning is an estimate of how much you expect to sell and when. A sales forecast provides data for these two questions. Since it is the basis of a forecast of earnings, many people first develop a sales budget. These budgets are scrutinized to ensure that the volume is attainable under economic conditions expected in the budget year. Marketing experts or personnel may be called in to compare their budgets with forecasts prepared by sales personnel, since the latter are sometimes unrealistic in the evaluation of economic and market conditions.

The sales forecast is then exploded to include major product lines so as to consider production planning requirements and manufacturing capacity. The forecast may be refined to:

- Separate forecasts of physical units and price per unit (in lieu of total sales dollars).
- Recognition of seasonal variation.
- Utilization of daily or weekly averages.

Cost of Goods Sold Budget. For a specified level of production, a budget can be prepared if two pieces of data are assembled: a complete bill of materials and an objective set of labor-hour standards. If subassemblies or parts are received from a vendor, a market price must be established. This will probably include a component for in-house receipt, storage, and handling. For example, Fruit Crate Mfg. Co., Inc., for a projected *manufacturing* cost estimate, has established the following costs, labor

Fruit Crate Mfg. Co., Inc.
Manufacturing Cost Estimate, Type A Crate, May–July

Labor	May	June	July
Trimming slats/Finishing	.04 hrs.	.04 hrs.	.03[a]
Slats to nailing frame	.025	.025	.025
Cutting and nailing	.033	.030[b]	.025[b]
Attached stiffeners	.020	.018[b]	.017[b]
Attach label and move to storage	.040	.040	.040
Total direct labor hours	.158	.153	.137
Labor rate	$4.25/hr	$4.25/hr	$4.50/hr[c]
Total Labor Cost	$.672	$.650	$.617
Materials			
Slats 3 board feet @ $200/1000	$0.600	$0.600	$0.600
Wire/nails	0.060	0.065[d]	0.065
Labels	0.025	0.025	0.025
Total Materials Cost	$0.685	$0.690	$0.690
Overhead			
Plant & equipment	$0.15	0.15	0.15
Supervisory salaries	0.03	0.03	0.03
Taxes and insurance	0.010	0.010	0.015[e]
Utilities and maintenance	0.015	0.015	0.015
Total Overhead	$0.205	0.205	0.210
Total Manufacturing Cost	$1.562	$1.545	$1.517

[a] High speed sander becomes operational.
[b] Effects of learning.
[c] New labor contract goes into effect.
[d] Projected cost increase of steel impacting fabricated steel parts.
[e] New taxes due to become effective as a result of change in state's budget year.

Figure 5.8

components, transfer prices, and overhead for the assembly of a type A crate for a projected three-month period (see Figure 5.8).

Variable Manufacturing Budgets. As seen above, the manufacturing cost element provides a useful cost evaluation tool to manufacturing managers but it should also relate the manufacturing activity to the profit forecast. The variable manufacturing budget relates the various costs in a department or cost center to ranges of possible production. These budgets use a probabilistic or statistical method for establishing costs. This can be compared with the fixed operating expense budget shown in the Fruit Crate example above.

NEED FOR BUDGET UPDATING

Flexible or variable budgets should be kept current so that targets are realistic and accurately reflect deviations from expected costs. Budgets, however, may lose their effectiveness as a measuring and control device if they are adjusted for every small change in operating costs. There is no rule of thumb for triggering a budget adjustment. However, budgets should be adjusted for changes in product mix, major changes in cost levels, and schedule variations that significantly alter cost relationships.

On a departmental level, budget performance reflects actual departmental cost behavior and budget gains or savings directly result in improvements in profits. The budget becomes an individual department's profit and loss expectation based on responsibility accounting. The key is to ensure that, in emphasizing profit, quality output, good service, and employee morale are maintained.

One area in which you may not recognize potential problems is deferred maintenance. When increased output or profit is being emphasized, periodic maintenance is often deferred to "keep the wheels turning." This may be short-sighted, resulting instead in deferred costs when breakdowns occur.

SUMMARY

The operating budget is a tool that can be integrated into your overall operations. It can give you an indication about the delays between cash outlays for manufacturing and sales receipts. This delay can be quantified in the budget and thereby permit you to plan for carrying or acquiring additional cash for predictable periods.

As with any good planning tool, the operating plan and related budget points up the opportunity for capital expenditures or the need for tightening capital investments. Because sales predictions are the driving force behind budget numbers, you will plan sales forces, marketing objectives, advertising budgets, sales quotas, credit policies, and many other factors as parts of operational budgeting/planning.

Finally, manpower planning and allocation can be computed straightforwardly from the production schedule and direct labor rates. The formula is simply a direct allocation of hours per operation per product, times the number of units of product scheduled for production, summed over all operations. For example, in the Fruit Crate case:

- The total labor hours per crate was .158 hours in May.
- In May the firm scheduled 2300 crates (equivalent) for production.
- That represents 363.4 direct labor hours.
- There were 176 hours (gross) per worker available in the month. The firm planned for 81 percent utilization in hours as a result of breaks, sickness, leave, and fatigue.
- The firm calculates 142.6 hours per man per month effective work time.
- Dividing 363.4 by 142.6, the firm arrives at 2.5 direct laborers necessary to produce the crates.

Using such an analysis, the firm can also break out, by operation, the number of employees needed for each task.

As a control device, an operating plan or budget can provide needed information and direct attention where variances have occurred.

II

OPERATING THE BUSINESS

Section I was largely devoted to tasks that can and should be accomplished prior to the start of the business (or of the fiscal period for an ongoing business). It focused on planning what you want and intend to make happen.

The five chapters of Section II discuss those areas you must manage when the business period is under way:

Cash Flow Concerns

Managing Inventories

Pricing

Marketing Analysis

Financing

Obviously, these also require planning. But they are, to a greater degree, day-to-day management functions, which require constant attention, willingness and ability to adapt, and control.

Day-to-day management should be based upon the overall planning discussed in Section I; but changes to the plan may be necessitated by unanticipated occurrences. Therefore, the concepts presented in the following chapters offer a system for adjusting the implementation of the plan in response to new information without changing the basic and underlying desired accomplishments.

6

Cash Flow Concerns

Managing working capital is an important function of the business. Contained within working capital are four major elements that you must plan for and consider in order to maintain viability:

- Cash
- Accounts Receivable
- Accounts Payable
- Inventory

Inventory constitutes such a significant portion of the assets of many businesses that we have treated it separately in Chapter 7. The intent of this chapter is to discuss the management of cash, accounts receivable, and accounts payable.

CASH

Cash is the most liquid of all assets and serves many purposes within the business:

- *Transactions*. Cash is used as a medium for transactional payments. Regardless of the form or nature of the payments, in the final analysis there is normally a transfer of cash.

- *Investment*. Whether made by outside individuals, businesses, banks, or the business investing in itself (reinvestment of excess cash), the transactions ultimately involve cash.
- *Security*. A reasonable level of cash in a liquid account is a measure of security to the business. Depending upon the nature and size of the business, the amount of cash necessary may be significant.

When considering the investment of cash, there are four factors most investors consider in determining whether to invest, and if so, how much:

- *Yield*. Yield is in itself composed of two elements: growth and dividends. The *growth* of a business is represented in the market by the market price of its stock or an increase in its valuation, indicating an increase in the equity worth. For example, if your stock is increasing in value in the market at a rate of 12–15 percent per year, this could be an adequate expected return, sufficient to attract investors even without cash dividends. If your stock is valued at a relatively constant $10 per share in the market but pays an average annual *dividend* of $1.20–$1.50, it too is yielding 12–15 percent on the investment. In the small or closely-held business, the yield is often taken out in the form of higher compensation or "perks" by the owners.
- *Risk*. This element of investing is intangible. Different investors will make different assessments of risk, for example, institutional investors and individual ones looking at the same business. A constant growth business and a steady earnings business, although both have the same return, may be seen as having different risks. If your business demonstrates steady growth and reinvestment of excess earning, it may be seen by bankers as less risky than a business that earns a steady amount and "throws off dividends" to its owners.
- *Liquidity*. Here the investor is concerned with how quickly the investment can be converted to cash. Liquidity is essentially a timing issue; risk and return will affect liquidity. Real estate may be more risky and have higher returns than treasury bills but an investor who wants a liquid asset will prefer T-bills because they can be traded with little or no delay. Real estate may tie up the investor's funds for months while he tries to find a buyer, or he may have to discount the price in order to convert the asset quickly.
- *Transactional Costs*. Whatever gross yield an investment shows, transactional costs have to be deducted. For the above example, the steadily growing business shows a gross yield of 12–15 percent per year but the investor realizes no gain until he sells the stock and pays brokerage fees and appropriate taxes. In the steady dividend business, the

investor realizes his yield periodically through direct payments with no transactional costs except taxes. The transactional costs associated with a real estate sale can be quite significant. Brokerage fees may amount to 6 percent or more. Attorney's fees, recordings, documentary stamps, title search, title insurance, and other factors may amount to an appreciable portion of the gain.

Cash becomes of critical concern to you when there is too little to meet the immediate needs of the business. However, it is equally important for you to consider cash when there is an ample supply available. When there is a surplus of cash many people ignore the significance of this circumstance. Many businesses leave excess cash idle in non-interest bearing accounts. Optimal cash management requires the investment of idle cash in profitable endeavors. It is easier to earn an income on cash than any other commodity you have. Since it is liquid, cash may be managed or converted without the delay that inhibits the liquidity of other assets.

WHAT TO DO WITH EXCESS CASH

There are many profitable means available to invest excess cash. Some of the more prominent, convenient, and well-known opportunities will be discussed here.

Interest Accounts. Cash flows into and out of the business on a daily basis. Unfortunately for most businesses, large and small, the inflows and outflows are neither steady nor all predictable within an acceptable degree of certainty. The business may be cash rich or poor at different times during the month.

Because of this uncertainty, you must always have adequate cash on hand or in liquid accounts to meet the demands as they are returned for payment. You should be equally concerned that no idle excess cash is sitting in a non-interest bearing checking account. If the buffer of cash is excessive, you are losing the opportunity to earn on that money.

Investigate the options available at your bank for earning interest on checking or for keeping cash in an interest bearing account, with provisions for automatic transfers when checking balances are below a certain level.

Another option is the deposit of cash in money market accounts. This is a liquid, higher-yield form of savings account. Often these accounts may be used in conjunction with a form of checking, with restrictions as to minimum balances in the accounts and as to the maximum number of transactions per period.

Idle cash represents an opportunity easy to capture; the returns can be worth the effort expended in finding a solution.

Treasury Securities. U.S. Treasury obligations constitute the largest segment of the money market. The principle securities issued are bills, tax anticipation bills, notes, and bonds. Treasury bills are auctioned weekly by the Treasury Department, with maturities of 91 days and 182 days. In addition, nine-month and one-year bills are sold periodically. Treasury bills carry no coupon but are sold on a discount basis. These securities are extremely popular with companies, large or small, as short-term investments. In part because of the large amount outstanding, the market is very active and the transaction costs involved in the sale of treasury bills in the secondary market are small. Very often, in some of the more sophisticated financial models treasury bills are considered risk-free, interest bearing notes. They are used as the basis on which to place risk premiums in such financial models as the capital asset pricing model taught in most business schools.

Agency Securities. Obligations of various agencies of the federal government are guaranteed by the agency issuing the security and not usually by the Treasury. The principal agencies issuing securities are the Federal Housing Administration and the Government National Mortgage Association. These obligations are not guaranteed by the Treasury; however, there is an implied backing of the government. It would be hard to imagine the federal Treasury allowing an agency to fail. Major government-sponsored agencies that issue securities include the Federal Home Loan Banks, Federal Land Banks, and the Federal National Mortgage Association. The securities provided by these agencies return a modest yield advantage over treasury securities of the same maturity. These securities have a high degree of marketability and are sold in the secondary market through the same security dealers as the treasury securities.

Banker's Acceptances. Banker's acceptances are drafts accepted by banks and used in financing foreign and domestic trade. The creditworthiness of banker's acceptances is judged relative to the bank accepting the draft rather than the drawer. Acceptances generally have maturities of less than 180 days and are of very high quality. They are traded in an over-the-counter market dominated by a few dealers. The rates on banker's acceptances tend to be slightly higher than rates on treasury bills of similar maturity.

Commercial Paper. Commercial paper consists of short-term unsecured promissory notes issued by finance companies and certain industrial concerns. Commercial paper can be purchased either directly or through dealers. Among the companies selling commercial paper on this basis are CIT Financial Corporation, Ford Motor Credit Company, General Motors Acceptance Corporation, and Sears-Roebuck Acceptance Corporation.

Negotiable Certificates of Deposit. Negotiable time certificates of deposit are time-certain investments. The certificate (CD) is evidence of the deposit of funds at a commercial bank for a specified period of time and a specified rate of interest. Money-market banks quote rates on CDs that are changed periodically in keeping with changes in other money-market rates. Yields on CDs are greater than on T-bills but are about the same as on banker's acceptances and commercial paper.

CASH FLOWS

Before dealing with the problem of insufficient cash, we should consider the sources of cash inflow. There are four sources of cash inflow to the business:

- New investment.
- New debt.
- Sale of fixed assets.
- Operating revenues (including collection of accounts receivable).

Each of these sources has important limitations on it; there are, in fact, no other sources of cash. The only source that can be depended upon in an ongoing way is operating profits. That is what makes profit planning such an important activity for any business. When the business experiences continued profitable operations, *accompanied by a positive cash inflow*, it can grow most efficiently.

Inflows

The inflows, or the receipt of payment from customers for product or services, is the lifeblood of any business. The obvious rule with inflows is to get customers to pay as promptly as possible. For example, many doctors and lawyers now demand cash on receipt of service for routine office visits.

It is obvious that the efficiency of cash management improves with the acceleration of customers' payments. The fast-food industry illustrates how, by sticking strictly to a cash-only business, an extremely low current ratio can be maintained. Contrasted to cash payments, payments by check have an inherent delay associated with the time it takes for a check to clear the bank. During this period the funds are not available for use by the business. The objective should be to reduce the delay in receiving payment and the clearing time necessary for the transfers of funds. In addition to the recent federal legislation concerning maximum times for banks to clear checks, several methods have been developed to decrease the float (i.e., the speed of realizing actual cash receipt).

- *Concentration banking.* If your business is large enough to have broad market coverage, you may consider using banks at various locations within your market areas to speed the clearance of checks. Using banks in areas where sales occur allows for the processing of local checks. These generally clear faster and funds can be more quickly concentrated for wire transfer to a central bank.

- *Lock boxes.* Businesses may use a lock-box system for collections. To do so, you rent a post office box, centrally located in a market, and authorize your bank to open the box and directly credit payments to your account, similar to direct deposit for Social Security. This has advantages and disadvantages. The obvious disadvantage is the loss of control over the physical receipt of funds and the direct monitoring of clients' payment habits. You do not have the ability to process receipts before the bank gets them. This elimination of handling saves you time but the bank does charge a fee for the service.

- *Elimination of unnecessary accounts.* Having an account in each local bank where you do business or have some operations creates goodwill and a sense of presence. However, by maintaining many separate and diverse accounts, you are dispersing money that could be used more effectively if it was concentrated. By concentrating cash you can probably reduce cash reserves and still function efficiently.

Outflows

The largest volume of cash outflows is generally referred to on the income statement as expenses, although some "accrued" expenses may not yet have been paid in cash. Other non-cash flow expenses shown on income statements are such things as depreciation. Another item to be added to "other expenses" is the principal portion of loan payments, which, while not an expense item, is still a use of cash.

The business must be concerned with the timing and nature of the demands made on its cash. Earlier we discussed the timing of cash inflows and the importance of shortening the "float." For cash outflows, the corollary is that you want to ride the float or use the delay in cash transfers to your advantage. Some businesses capitalize on the float by writing checks on accounts without sufficient funds available to cover those checks. They may in fact have adequate reserves of cash maintained in high-yield accounts until needed to meet a draw. In this way the business is maximizing its return by using the float to its advantage. Extreme care must be exercised to avoid "kiting," an illegal act.

How does one plan for the use of float? A reasonable float pattern to study is that of paychecks. Some employees have automatic deposits to credit unions; others deposit their checks immediately, some even in the employer's bank; some employees will hold their checks for several days; and a few hardy souls may hold their checks for a week or more. To determine the necessary balances you should gather some data:

- Collect the number of checks and the amount presented for payment on each day after the pay day.
- Calculate the amount presented by day.
- Repeat the process for successive pay periods.
- Construct a frequency distribution of funds demanded by day.

From this frequency distribution, you can plan for having the appropriate amount of cash in your account at the right time. In order to ensure that you are not embarrassed by insufficient funds, maintain a safety margin in the account. (Even this safety margin can be determined statistically if there is sufficient data to determine variations in returned checks.) If the payroll is significant, holding portions of that payroll even for a day or two in a high-yield account amounts to significant returns. In the case of automatic deposits, you can determine with certainty the delay in funds transfer and can earn extra interest on this systematic float. You should probably have an agreement with your bank either to notify you if your account is underfunded, to make automatic transfers from another account, or to "cover" you with a line of credit.

INTRODUCTION TO CASH FLOW BUDGETS

Before you attempt a cash flow budget for the business, it is useful to do a cash flow analysis. Preparing a cash flow analysis often gives managers a much better understanding of the operation of their business. It is particularly important for some small businesses to get an understanding of cash flows because they are especially vulnerable to problems dealing with cash. Smaller businesses tend to operate with inadequate cash reserves or none at all.

Perhaps the most critical element to be considered is the timing of cash flows. If all of the cash outflows occur in the first six months and most of the cash inflows occur during the second six-month period, the business may fail before it has an opportunity to receive sufficient cash inflows to sustain itself. Timing of flows is critical.

INDICATIONS OF CASH FLOW PROBLEMS

Many businesses never achieve cash flow control. These businesses are always in trouble, chronically overdrawn and slow in paying bills. Many eventually fail. Some could survive if managers would take the necessary planning steps to create a cash flow budget and manage their cash flows as they manage other portions of the business.

1. *Decreased liquidity.* Running out of working capital. Some symptoms include too little inventory to meet demand and stretching payables.

2. *Excessive turning.* Turning inventories over more than other businesses of comparable size in the industry. This can be an indication of good management, but in extreme cases may be caused by too little working capital to support adequate inventories.

3. *Excess reliance on short-term debt.* Here you may be rolling over short-term debt to raise needed working capital. Contrary to popular belief and most finance books, not all working capital is short-term. In most businesses there is a level of working capital required for the reasonable operation and growth of the business. We call this "fixed working capital."

4. *Dropped discounts.* Past term payments and failure to take advantage of timely payment discounts could indicate poor management of payables or the lack of cash necessary to pay in a timely way.

5. *Slow collections.* A high percentage of old receivables probably indicates poor management of receivables. It certainly indicates a potential cash problem.

These problems may be caused by insufficient cash or the insufficient cash may be the result of poor management. In some cases, low cash balances might even indicate a planned result. For example, rapid inventory turns may be advantageous. In the grocery business, with a low margin per sale, the more frequently sales are made and inventory is turned over the more profit is earned. Indicators of cash flow problems may signal nothing more than that further investigation may be necessary; but they always show that at least investigation is warranted.

MANAGING CASH

The control of cash is not mysterious, nor is the process itself complex. What is required is a systematic and organized approach. A few simple guidelines, set out in the following eight steps, help organize the process and make for an efficient handling of cash.

1. Identify all your sources of cash inflows: operations, debt, sale of assets, and investment.
2. List the uses to which you put the cash.
3. Identify the timing of cash flows, both in and out.
4. Calculate the difference between cash inflows and cash outflows. It is important here to identify time delays in receiving cash.
5. Identify any bottlenecks to getting cash in quickly and determine how to open up the inflow.
6. Enumerate any constraints on the use of cash, such as bank loan covenants.
7. Identify those cash inflows and outflows that can be rescheduled or whose timings may be changed.
8. Most important, establish a plan for positive cash flows. This step cannot be accomplished until the other seven steps have been completed and analyzed. Each of these steps will require your time and effort to complete. However, like most planning, the rewards in the long run significantly outweigh the costs to gather and analyze the information. It may save your business.

In order effectively to carry out the design and implementation of a cash flow analysis, a flowchart of how cash flows through the business is helpful. For the development of a cash flow budget we have constructed the following flowchart as an aid, with an analysis of each step contained in it.

CASH BUDGETING FLOW CHART

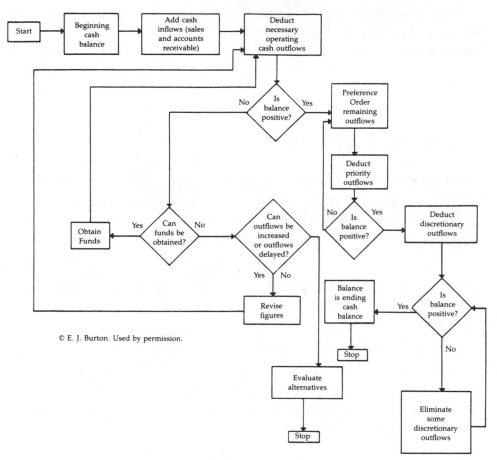

© E. J. Burton. Used by permission.

Figure 6.1

Step 1. Identify all sources of cash inflow.

- New investments and debt are sources of cash. However, they are infrequent and cannot be relied upon as continuing sources of cash.

- The sales of fixed assets are like new investments. The sale of fixed assets is not a source of recurring cash. You can sell the asset only once legally. While these sources cannot be ignored, they are secondary to operating profits. Consequently, it is important to focus on operating profits as your main source of cash. It should be noted, however, that operating profits will probably not be the source of capital for major plant expansions.

- Operating profits, unlike new investments or debt, are ongoing and also harder to track. They must be constantly monitored and controlled. Even growing businesses, with increasingly larger amounts of cash inflows, must review the budget and related variances periodically

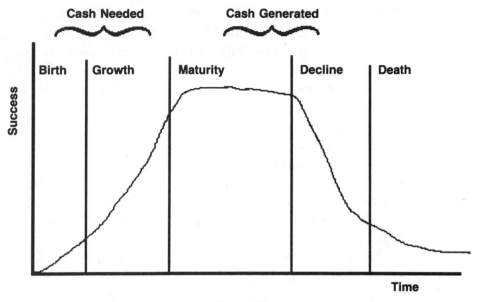

Figure 6.2

and maintain control or they may suffer from shortages of cash. As your business grows, you will often suffer from liquidity problems. Such problems may cause your business to fail to meet its short-term obligations even when it is quite viable and profitable.

As you advance through the business or product life cycle, cash demands will vary with the stages of the cycle. Typically a company's life-cycle graph will look like that in Figure 6.2.

For example, in periods of fast growth, the business will probably need growing inventories, receivables, and transactions cash. These inventory growth periods demand the commitment of large amounts of working capital, much as would be the case for adding to a building. This we call the "fixed working capital" problem.

The following example may help explain this unusual (at least as far as calling it "fixed") problem.

Typical Growth Company

Sales Level	Inventory Turn	Inventory Amount	Receivables Turn	Receivables Amount	Transactions Cash	Working Capital
$1,000,000	6.0	$100,000	10	$100,000	$10,000	$210,000
1,250,000	6.2	121,000	9	139,000	12,500	272,500
1,500,000	6.5	138,500	8	187,500	15,000	341,000
1,750,000	7.0	161,500	7	250,000	17,500	429,000
2,000,000	7.0	185,000	7	285,000	20,000	490,000

Figure 6.3

Notice that inventory turn is shown as improving as more sales produce faster turn. Also notice that receivables turn degenerates as sales are made to marginal customers and staff is not available to perform proper credit checks and follow-up. Unfortunately, these are typical scenarios.

Assume these numbers are indicative of trends in many businesses and could apply to you.

On sales of $1,000,000 with profits at, say, 15 percent of sales, you generate $150,000 to contribute to your working capital needs. On sales of $2,000,000 (assuming you have to "deal" to get the other sales) your average profit percentage drops to 13 percent, so you generate $260,000. Your working capital needs increased by $280,000 ($490,000 − 210,000) while your profit contribution increased by only $110,000. How do you finance this growth?

The "fixed" working capital issue is that there is some minimum amount of investment in working capital that is required and should be financed as a long-term asset, not on a short-term basis. In our illustration, if base sales stay around $1,500,000 with peaks and valleys, then the "fixed" component of working capital is about $340,000.

The period of rapid growth, rather than being a source of net cash inflow, may be a problem period. In periods of fast growth, inventory, receivables, and so on might not only consume all of your profits but might also require debt financing.

Part of the problem might result from offering extended payment terms to customers while at the same time being required to pay material suppliers on short terms. This difference between the time when you must pay suppliers and when you receive payment from your purchasers could mean the difference between continuing to operate and having the business fail.

Step 2. List cash outflows or uses.

A good place to start considering cash outflows is the cash journal or, if you don't have one, the checkbook. The important activity for this step in the process is to determine where the cash is going.

Many businesses experience lengthy delays between the time they pay for goods for resale and when they actually receive cash from the sale. To some extent, the delay is unavoidable. By analyzing the delay, however, you can plan for the amount of cash necessary to sustain this short-term investment in inventory and receivables. A representative (but hypothetical) example of the analysis of delay might look like:

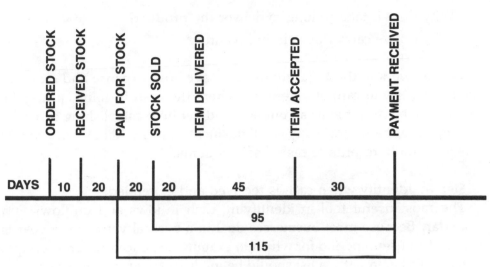

Figure 6.4

In this example, you paid for the item of inventory but do not receive payment from the customer until 95 days later. Built into the system is some unavoidable delay. But the problem can become worse. In this example, you sold the item before you had to pay for it. If the item sat on the shelf for a month or more the problem gets worse.

All expenditures of cash should be listed and carefully considered. Then, the effort must be made to determine whether all of those cash expenditures are necessary. Pertinent questions are:

- Can we get along without it?
- Can we postpone this expenditure?
- Is the timing proper?
- Would it make more sense to pay for it earlier or later?
- Can it be done less expensively?

We often get into the rut of believing there are only two ways of doing something: our way and the wrong way. People typically act according to habit simply because it takes less mental effort than to think out every action in the day. The way to be innovative is to ask *why*.

When addressed to business activities, probing questions might uncover areas where significant savings can be realized. For the computer system dealer in Figure 6.4 above, several questions can be asked:

- Why do we have a 45-day acceptance period?
- Why do we have a 30-day credit period after acceptance?

- Why does it take so long to deliver the product?
- Why do we carry this item in inventory?

The answers to these questions may save both expense and cash immediately. If you cannot determine where the cash is going, it may be necessary to consult your accountant and get help establishing controls. On the other hand, for many small businesses, a checkbook can provide adequate daily records of cash disbursements.

Step 3. Identify when cash is received and expended.

The most useful tool in identifying cash inflows and outflows is a calendar. Because most businesses deal in a cyclical variation, a year is generally a useful period for which to examine expenditures and receipts of cash. To begin with, a list should be made of those outflows that have fixed dates:

- Paydays
- Tax deposits
- Bank debt repayments
- Insurance payments
- Other periodic obligations

Continue to list those items where cash is expended until you are sure that you have accounted for all of the periodic expenditures that occur in an annual period.

Once the cash outflows are listed you may begin listing inflows. In doing so, you must consider the delays in receiving accounts receivable payments and your seasonal and periodic sales fluctuations. It may be necessary to consider mean or average receipt times for some of these items.

Step 4. Examine the timing of cash inflows minus cash outflows.

A positive cash flow period is one in which the inflows of cash exceed the outflows of cash. This may not happen in all circumstances. However, it should average out over the year. In the event that the business is experiencing a negative cash flow period, then, for any operating period in which this occurs, funds must be obtained from some other source.

Negative cash flow periods will occasionally occur—for example, during growth spurts. Many businesses experience sales rhythms. If you are experiencing such a rhythm, look to see if it is typical for the industry.

In such cases, you must understand the rhythm and time-discretionary cash inflows so as to properly plan for those periods where you may experience a negative cash flow period. Understanding the phenomenon of delayed cash inflow as a result of growth will help to determine how fast the business can afford to grow. It may be better to sustain a slower growth rate in order to avoid significant negative cash flow problems.

By looking at the timing of cash inflows and cash outflows, you may find ways to improve profitability by both cutting costs and increasing your opportunities.

Step 5. What effect does the current cash flow have on the business?

Plan payments so as to maximize the utilization of cash. That is, consider extending payments for as long as practical without incurring adverse consequences from the creditors.

Everyone in business knows that the way to improve cash flow is to slow down the outflow of cash while speeding up the inflow. This is particularly true in a tightening economy. However, before blindly following this path you should consider the consequences of slowing down payment to vendors. In business, terms for payment are still commonplace. In fact, 2/10; N/30 is a commonly offered discount. In order to monitor discounts taken and discounts missed, you should establish a regular reporting mechanism to control this process.

The chart in Figure 6.5 can be expanded or redesigned to meet the specific discounts available and the payment schedules you use. In this way, you can effectively monitor performance.

The intent of discounts is to encourage early payment. But what are the consequences of not taking the discount? Let's assume a 2/10; N/30 discount. For one thing, if you wait the full 30 days to pay, you are still incurring, in essence, a 36.9 percent annualized interest rate on that money. Even if the payment period is extended for a full 50 days without

ANNUALIZED INTEREST
EQUIVALENT COST OF NOT
TAKING A CASH DISCOUNT

If paid in:	1/10; N/30	2/10; N/30
Day 10	0%	0%
Day 20	36.9%	73.8%
Day 30	18.5%	36.9%
Day 40	12.3%	24.6%

Figure 6.5

adverse consequences from the vendor, you have merely cut the interest rate to 18 percent. This is derived from the following relationship: Under the 2/10; N/30, you receive a 2 percent discount on the money due if you pay within the first 10 days. However, in the event you wait the full 30 days to pay the bill you incur interest of 2 percent of the amount due for holding the money for an additional 20 days. As there are approximately 18 such 20-day periods per year, the annualized interest rate of 2 percent per 20 days amounts to an annual interest rate of 36 percent. This is hardly an equitable interest rate to incur for borrowing money for such a short period. Even if you extend the period for a full 50 days, you are, in a sense, borrowing at 2 percent for 40 days. Since there are approximately 9 such 40-day periods per year, the 2 percent for each of the 9–40 days amounts to 18 percent per annum. Most businesses can afford to borrow from a bank at less than 18 percent interest rate.

Other consequences may result from delaying payment for up to 50 days. The creditor may institute proceedings for collection. But even if it doesn't, you will not become a favored customer by holding the vendor's money for a 50 day period. In times of tightening economics or shortage of the materials provided by this vendor, the slow-paying customer will not sit high on the list of "most favored customers." You may find shortages of necessary materials or none at all coming from that vendor, if you are more costly to do business with than other customers.

In managing accounts payable, there are four rules to be considered:

1. Do not buy necessary material too early; buy no unnecessary materials at all. Manage your purchases using the procedures set forth in the chapter on inventories.

2. Plan buying so as to balance needs with some measure of safety stock.

3. Pay so that unnecessary costs are not incurred. In doing so, consider vendor relationships and the interest rates associated with early payment discounts.

4. Set up an accounting system to monitor discounts lost or not taken. Most accounting systems list discounts taken. While this has some benefits, you will fail to take advantage of the opportunity costs. These lost opportunities may, in the long run, be more important than those discounts taken. Since it should be policy to take discounts, exception reporting would dictate capturing discounts lost.

Step 6. Identify which cash inflows or outflows cannot be changed. Many payments made periodically by the business may not be re-scheduled. In addition, collection policies might fail to achieve their objectives. Identify the extent to which payments and receipts are inflexible. Consider methods intended to speed up cash inflows. It is possible to identify particular clients who are for the most part reliable in payment and others who are dilatory. It may prove to be true that it is more profitable to discontinue sales to purchasers with late payment records than to continue to provide them with goods. Remember, in shipping goods to a purchaser, you are in effect loaning that purchaser money. Those goods represent a cash investment by you and can be considered a loan to that purchaser.

An important consideration here is to establish a credit policy. Having a credit policy and exercising that policy consistently is a major point of control. Before extending credit, you have the maximum leverage upon a particular purchaser. Once credit has been extended, much of that leverage is lost. Although there is legal recourse against the purchaser, that will not improve the cash flow in the short run.

The following are four rules for credit extensions:

1. Have a written credit policy.
2. Have a business collection policy that everyone understands.
3. Know your legal rights when it comes to collections.
4. Know the legal restraints and conditions when offering credit.

It is important to maintain an aged accounts receivable file. Knowing which accounts either to collect or receive payment from and in what period of time is very important for estimating cash inflows. Remember the following points about aged accounts receivables:

- The older the account gets without payment or collection, the less likely you are to receive payment or make collection. The age of the account has a direct effect on the efforts that must be made in collecting.
- You may want to establish rules for termination of further shipments based upon the age of receivables.

When establishing a collection policy, consider the following:

1. Know the steps you wish to take in making a collection. This may include "first letters," first phone calls, referral of the collection to the legal department, etc.
2. Set the steps. Make a conscious effort to determine the order in which they will be taken.

3. Do not establish fixed time frames for advancing from step to step. If the time frames are known, many customers will wait to pay until the last possible moment before you move on to the next collection step.

4. Don't be predictable in collection efforts. Once your collection efforts become normalized, debtors will behave accordingly.

Step 7. Identify those cash inflows and cash outflows that can be rescheduled.

By identifying those cash inflows and outflows that can be rescheduled, you may be able to balance payments and receipts so as to avoid unnecessary negative cash flow situations. Sometimes talking with your creditors and working out payment schedules that meet your needs and theirs can be an effective compromise. A surprising number of banks and large companies are willing to work out such payment schedules, because a smaller payment that can be expected with some degree of certainty is preferable to uncertainty or no payment at all. Also, creditors, if they know that there may be a nonpayment period, are able to work out their own cash flow requirements so as not to be adversely affected.

Very often businesses get into trouble with their accounts payable. You may end up spending more time talking with the people to whom you owe money than you spend in producing the money to pay your bills. This can become a cycle that gets you deeper into trouble. The solution to this problem may be to sort through all the creditors and identify all the small bills under some particular cut-off. Creditors of less than the cut-off can prompt as many phone calls as the large creditors. Often it is less expensive to borrow an amount of money and pay off all of the small creditors than to try to pay off each one separately. In this way, time becomes available to get back to the business of earning money. The bank may be able to help you out of short-term financial problems. Often grouping together many small bills into one large bill with a fixed payment period may resolve some of the intermediate cash flow problems. Be careful about lumping nonrevolving payments (due upon billing) into revolving or longer-term, periodic payments so as to avoid the following:

- Building in an interest payment (perhaps lower than the penalty or interest due on all the small bills).
- Paying off many nonrevolving accounts. This may encourage the incurring of further liabilities on these accounts. In doing so you simply restart the cycle.

Trade associations and trade organizations may be good sources of information on how to improve the business's cash outflow and inflow picture. Other businesses in the same industry may have had similar experience with collections and have ready advice on how to improve collections.

Step 8. Plan for positive cash flow.

A major tool available for planning cash flow is a cash budget. Cash budgets involve projections of future cash needs as well as cash receipts. This budget reveals the timing and amount of expected cash inflows and outflows over a particular period. For example, most businesses use a one-year business cycle. You may want to consider a two-year cash budget with modifications to the second year's budget after significant experience in the first year. The cash flow budget should take into account seasonal variations in sales and cash outflows. If cash flows are extremely volatile, short time period increments should be used in the budgeting process. If the budgeting shows a more stable period, the time periods may be longer depending upon the stability of the data. Remember that the farther into the future you try to predict cash flows, the more uncertain the forecast is. The cash budget is only as useful as the accuracy of the forecast that is used to make the predictions. If your cash flows are subject to high levels of uncertainty you should provide for either a cash cushion, ready borrowing, or both.

PREPARATION OF THE CASH BUDGET

Receipts

A key to the accuracy of most cash budgeting is a forecast of sales. When using an internal approach for the generation of a sales forecast, the salesmen must be asked to project sales for the forthcoming periods. The product sales manager or other appropriate person gathers these estimates and consolidates them into a sales estimate for a particular product line, thereby building up data into useful information. Often, however, internally generated sales forecasts may be too narrow in scope and overly optimistic. They may miss important trends in the economy and the industry generally. For these reasons, many companies use externally generated sales forecasts. Advisory or consulting businesses are available that use econometric modeling techniques to approximate future industry and economy conditions. These businesses may be helpful only to larger, multioperational, multiproduct, multisectional companies.

Given the basic predictions of business conditions and industrial sales, the next step is to estimate market share by individual product, price, and the expected customer reception of the new products. These estimates should be made in conjunction with the business's marketing managers. By using a consolidated approach with the sales forecast generated in conjunction with internal and external marketing personnel, a more accurate projection may be realized. The importance of the accuracy of sales forecasts cannot be overstated, as most of the other budgets, projections, and forecasts are based upon expected sales.

The next step in generating a cash budget is to determine the cash receipts from the expected sales. Consider your past history of cash and credit sales to determine offsetting factors and time delays associated with each. Some probabilities may be applied to projected sales in order to generate expected receipts. In this way, you are considering the credit terms used and offsetting the timing of receipt of those sales dollars.

DISBURSEMENTS

Given a sales forecast, another important body of information to be generated is a production schedule. Decisions must be made whether to gear production closely to sales or to produce at a relatively constant rate over time, ignoring the periodic fluctuations in demand. Remember that with a level production schedule, inventory carrying costs are generally higher than when the business tends to match production to sales. However, level production is generally more efficient than fluctuating production. Therefore, it is important to consider the trade-off in inventory carrying costs versus the efficiencies that can be realized in various production schedules.

Another important consideration is whether you intend to produce just enough to meet demand or to commit the resources to build inventory levels. The sales forecast is a valuable tool in determining expected future production needs. You should consider the generation of a production forecast based upon some strategy for meeting this expected need. Almost all strategies will require a commitment of resources. Even production tailored to meet demand exactly requires a commitment of cash and other resources before you expect to receive cash inflows. If you plan to build a buffer inventory, you must expect an even greater delay in receipt of compensating cash inflows.

Once a production schedule has been established, estimates can be made concerning the necessary materials to be purchased, the labor required for that production, and any additional fixed assets you may need to meet the demand. From the production schedule you can evaluate the expected cash outflows and even the timing of those outflows. There is a lag between the time a sale is made and the time of actual cash payment.

Wages are assumed to increase with the amount of production. Another factor of wages is the trade-off of overtime versus increased production staff. Very often production peaks can be taken care of more cost effectively by using overtime rather than incurring the cost of hiring new employees. You should establish a policy concerning the amount of overtime you will tolerate before hiring additional employees. This can be calculated on a cost basis. For example, if the cost to the business for overtime is 2.5 times the cost of regular time (adding in overtime benefits, wages, premiums, and the like), how many hours of additional labor justify the addition of another employee?

$$\text{Break-even for new employee} = \frac{40 \text{ hrs/wk}}{2.5} = 16 \text{ hours of overtime}$$

If your business *sustains* more than 16 hours of overtime for a particular function, it may be cheaper to hire another employee.

In calculating the trade-off between overtime hours and the decision to hire additional labor we have simplified the problem for example purposes only. The problem is more complex. In the example we have considered only the variable cost component of adding an additional employee. There are still fixed and semivariable components. When you decide to add a new employee, you will incur additional costs associated with recruitment, training, insurance, administrative processing, health examinations, and other factors. In making the overtime versus hire decision, consider the costs of additional overtime hours against these fixed and semivariable cost components as well. Obviously, this is only a first approximation. You must also consider the duration of the need and the learning time for new employees to become productive.

In addition, you will have other demands on cash. Included in other expenses are general, administrative and selling expenses, property taxes, interest expenses, power, light, and heat expenses, and maintenance expenses. These expenses tend to be reasonably predictable over the short run.

You must also take into account capital expenditures, dividends, federal taxes, and other cash outflows. As shown in the capital budgeting chapter, a business should plan as far in advance as possible for its capital expenditures. These forecasted expenditures should be predictable for the short-termed cash budget. Dividend payments, if appropriate, for most companies are discretionary and are paid on specific dates. Estimation of federal income taxes can be based upon projected profits, which a cost accountant or bookkeeper can readily generate. These cash outlays must be combined with the total cash expenditures in order to obtain a schedule of total cash disbursements. The four most critical categories to be included in the schedule of cash disbursements are :

- Total cash expenses
- Capital expenditures
- Dividend payments
- Income taxes

These should be listed on a month-by-month basis for the fiscal year.

NET CASH FLOW AND CASH BALANCES

An enterprise must carefully review its schedules in order to ensure that it has taken into account all foreseeable cash inflows and cash outflows. By combining the cash receipts and the cash disbursements schedules, you can obtain the net cash inflow or outflow for each period. Once you have identified the months in which you will have difficulty in meeting your cash needs, means must be found to address the cash deficiencies and to plan for them. This is further discussed in Chapter 10. Before seeking additional cash to meet these demands, you may be able to delay your capital expenditures or your payments for purchases so as to prevent the negative cash flow months from occurring. Knowing what the cash position will be in each month allows you to consider such options as when to make capital investments, investments of excess funds in marketable securities, and other forms of cash planning.

EXCEPTIONS TO EXPECTED CASH FLOWS

A cash budget merely represents an estimate of future cash flows. Depending upon the care devoted to preparing the budget, the volatility of the market, and the accuracy of the data used, there may be considerable deviation between the actual cash flows and the expected cash flows. When considering such uncertainty, it is necessary to provide information about the range of possible outcomes. Considering cash flows using only one set of assumptions may result in a faulty perspective of the future and misinformation for planning purposes.

In order to consider deviations from expected cash flows, it may be important to work out additional cash budgets using different forecasted sales levels. Such cash budget scenarios help you plan for contingencies. In addition, you may want to generate budgets for best case, most likely, and worst case scenarios.

One of the benefits of discussing the cash budget within the business is that management is better able to plan contingencies for possible consequences and probable events. These discussions tend to sharpen the perspective of management on the future. Finally, management will be encouraged to realize the magnitude and impact of various occurrences on the profitability of the business.

Computers may be of some assistance in evaluating different scenarios. An example of such a computer-generated budget is included in the Appendix to this chapter. Very often the cash budget can be designed in such a manner that you may substitute different probabilities for outcomes, thus generating a probable cash budget more rapidly and with more flexibility than by trying to adjust by hand for all the alternatives. In addition, you may change the assumptions dealing with some occurrences. In this manner, cases may be rerun on a computer allowing extensive analysis of the sensitivity of your decisions. Using this information, you can more accurately gauge minimum cash balances, the maturity structure of needed debt, the borrowing power of the business, and the ability of the business to adjust to deviations in expected outcome. For example, questions such as the following may be asked:

1. How flexible are expenses?
2. What can be cut or eliminated?
3. How much can be eliminated?
4. How quickly can we respond?
5. How much effort should be devoted to the collection of receivables?
6. What additional purchases will be required for unexpected increases in business?
7. Can labor be expanded and at what cost?
8. Can the present plant handle the additional demand?
9. How much money will be needed in order to finance build-up?

The answers to these and other questions will show the efficiency and flexibility of the business under varying conditions. By relying on numerous budgets with different ranges of possible outcomes, you have the option to consider and be prepared for many more contingencies. It is important to be truthful to yourself in the preparation of these budgets. Do not fall prey to extreme optimism or pessimism but rather examine numerous possibilities.

SUMMARY

Your working capital is principally composed of cash, accounts receivable inventory, accounts payable, and other short-term payables. Inventory, constituting such a major portion of the investment, is treated in Chapter 7.

Cash serves many functions within the business and actually is the medium of exchange for all transactions. The investment of excess or temporarily idle cash should be made with a consideration for the expected yield, the associated risk, the liquidity of the investment, and the transactional costs associated with the exchange of investment with cash. There are many ways you can invest excess cash, each one of which has a risk and return relationship and other conditions and constraints. Many of the constraints deal with liquidity and transactional cost considerations.

A business selling its product in a large geographic area has to be concerned with the time delays associated with the physical transfers of payment (cash). This delay, or float, costs you money. Many methods have been developed to minimize the delay and to speed up the receipt of cash—concentration banking, lock boxes, and others. The other side of the coin, of course, is the delay in making cash outflows. You can analyze these cash flows and take advantage of them for earning interest.

You should have a cash flow budget. Determining how cash flows within the business may best be envisioned as an actual flow of dollars for each transaction. Cash management should consider how things are being done and question all cash expenditures: can we get along without it; can we postpone it; can it be done more cheaply; and so on.

As with cash, you can profit from managing your accounts receivable. One of the easiest methods of gaining an understanding of how well collections are being made is to establish a frequency distribution of the age of the receivables. It may be more profitable to discontinue sales to delinquent customers than to continue to advance credit, tying up valuable assets. An unpaid account receivable is an outstanding loan.

The other side is your policy about paying your bills. Another simple tool is a chart showing discounts taken and, more important, discounts not taken. A common discount, 2/10; N/30, means that it costs you 2 percent of the invoice amount to extend payment for 20 days. This can be equated to a 37 percent per annum interest rate. Discounts lost can have serious cost implications.

Timing is all-important in transactions. Many businesses experience cycles that impact the cash status. Planning for these timing variations may allow you to earn during periods of excess cash while having enough cash available in times of poor cash flow to avoid cash borrowing.

APPENDIX: CASH FLOW EXAMPLE

SHEET 1.1

		DEC	JAN	FEB	MAR	APR	MAY	JUN	JUL	AUG	SEP	OCT	NOV	DEC
TOTAL DOLLAR SALES		110000	120000	140000	180000	240000	242000	187000	154000	121000	110000	110000	110000	121000
COLLECTIONS	CASH SALES	10	10	10	10	10	10	10	10	10	10	10	10	10
AS PERCENT	COLLECT IN 30 DAYS	40	40	40	40	40	40	40	40	40	40	40	40	40
OF SALES	COLLECT IN 60 DAYS	50	50	50	50	50	50	50	50	50	50	50	50	50
COLLECTIONS ON NOVEMBER SALES		40000	50000											
AVERAGE GROSS MARGIN PERCENTAGE		70	70	70	70	70	70	70	70	70	70	70	70	70

ASSUMPTIONS   SHEET 1.2

	DEC	JAN	FEB	MAR	APR	MAY	JUN	JUL	AUG	SEP	OCT	NOV	DEC
TOTAL PURCHASES ON CREDIT	112000	144000	192000	198000	153000	126000	99000	90000	81000	90000	90000	90000	117000
LINE-OF-CREDIT INTEREST RATE:	14	14	15	17	18	16	16	16	16	16	15	14	12
LINE-OF-CREDIT BALANCE IN DECEMBER:	0												
LONG TERM DEBT INTEREST RATE:	14												
LONG TERM DEBT BALANCE IN DECEMBER:	100000												
LONG TERM DEBT PAYMENT SCHEDULE:	2500	2500	2500	2500	2500	2500	2500	2500	2500	2500	2500	2500	2500
MINIMUM ACCEPTABLE CASH BALANCE:	20000	20000	20000	20000	20000	20000	20000	20000	20000	20000	20000	20000	20000

CASH RECEIPTS DETAIL   SHEET 2.1

	JAN	FEB	MAR	APR	MAY	JUN	JUL	AUG	SEP	OCT	NOV	DEC
CASH SALES	12000	14000	18000	24000	24200	18700	15400	12100	11000	11000	11000	12100
COLLECTIONS OF RECEIVABLES	44500	103000	116000	142000	186000	216800	195800	155100	125400	104500	99000	99000
OTHER												
TOTAL CASH RECEIPTS	56500	117000	134000	166000	210200	235500	211200	167200	136400	115500	110000	111100

CASH DISBURSEMENTS DETAIL

	JAN	FEB	MAR	APR	MAY	JUN	JUL	AUG	SEP	OCT	NOV	DEC
PAYMENT FOR PURCHASES ON CREDIT	112000	144000	192000	198000	153000	126000	99000	90000	81000	90000	90000	90000
OPERATING EXPENSES	12250	12250	12250	12250	12250	12250	12250	12250	12250	12250	12250	12250
LONG TERM DEBT INTEREST	1167	1151	1135	1119	1103	1087	1071	1054	1037	1020	1003	985
PRINCIPAL	1333	1349	1365	1381	1397	1413	1429	1446	1463	1480	1497	1515
INTEREST PAYMENT ON LINE OF CREDIT	0	728	1498	2700	3099	2601	1372	198	0	0	0	0
INCOME TAXES	3000	0	0	3000	0	0	3000	0	0	3000	0	0
OTHER	0	5000	0	0	2000	0	5000	0	2000	0	25000	0
TOTAL CASH DISBURSEMENTS	129750	164478	208248	218450	172849	143351	123122	104948	97750	107750	129750	104750

ANALYSIS OF CASH REQUIREMENTS

	DEC	JAN	FEB	MAR	APR	MAY	JUN	JUL	AUG	SEP	OCT	NOV	DEC
NET CASH GENERATED THIS PERIOD		-73250	-47478	-74248	-52450	37351	92149	88078	62252	38650	7750	-19750	6350
BEGINNING CASH BALANCE		35000	20000	20000	20000	20000	20000	20000	20000	67404	106054	113804	94054
CASH BALANCE BEFORE BORROWINGS		-38250	-27478	-54248	-32450	57351	112149	108078	82252	106054	113804	94054	100404
CASH NEEDS COMPARISON		-58250	-47478	-74248	-52450	37351	92149	88078	62252	86054	93804	74054	80404
CURRENT PERIOD SHORT TERM BORROWINGS	0	58250	47478	74248	52450	-37351	-92149	-88078	-14848	0	0	0	0
TOTAL SHORT TERM BORROWINGS	0	58250	105728	179976	232426	195075	102926	14848	0	0	0	0	0
ENDING CASH BALANCE	35000	20000	20000	20000	20000	20000	20000	20000	67404	106054	113804	94054	100404

BALANCES IN KEY ACCOUNTS

	DEC	JAN	FEB	MAR	APR	MAY	JUN	JUL	AUG	SEP	OCT	NOV	DEC
CASH	35000	20000	20000	20000	20000	20000	20000	20000	67404	106054	113804	94054	100404
ACCOUNTS RECEIVABLE	99500	152000	174000	218000	288000	313800	265100	213400	170500	147400	143000	143000	152900
INVENTORY	35000	95000	189000	261000	246000	202600	170700	152900	149200	162200	175200	188200	220500
ACCOUNTS PAYABLE		144000	192000	198000	153000	126000	99000	90000	81000	90000	90000	90000	117000
LINE OF CREDIT	0	58250	105728	179976	232426	195075	102926	14848	0	0	0	0	0
		64750	85272	121024	168574	215325	253874	281452	306104	325654	342004	335254	356804

7

Managing Inventories

Inventories represent a significant portion of many businesses' assets, and accordingly, require substantial investments. In order to keep this investment from becoming unnecessarily large, inventories must be managed efficiently.

Inventories are a very important link in the production and sale of a product. Often when people talk of inventories they envision finished products. However, inventories include such items as work-in-process, subassemblies, office supplies, raw materials, spare parts, and equipment. A business may need to maintain hundreds of items in inventory to assure the reliability of delivering its product or service on time.

Businesses with complex product manufacturing facilities must often maintain significant amounts of each component in the product line as well as inventories for each machine in the manufacturing process. This may be necessitated by the complexity of the equipment used at the various work stations the product passes through as it moves down the line. Equipment malfunctions can cause the entire line to stop operating if there are inadequate work-in-process stocks available at that station to keep the line going while necessary repairs are made.

If costs were not a concern, it would be advantageous to manage the inventory level of every single commodity, product, or subassembly. However, costs become a real constraint in determining which products, supplies, or materials are to be monitored.

Because a particular product, supply or material may be insignificant in the overall business plan does not mean that you should ignore the

constant (not a variable), we need not treat the unit cost as one of the important variables in calculating order size. Those cases where quantity discounts are available will be considered later.

ORDERING COSTS

The costs of placing an order include all those costs that begin to accumulate when you check inventory levels and find that it is time to place an order and end when an accounting entry has been completed to record the transaction. These costs may include:

- Checking inventory levels.
- Requisitioning new inventory.
- Approving the requisition.
- Checking quotes.
- Preparing the purchase order.
- Approving the purchase order.
- Distributing the purchase order.
- Receiving the new inventory.
- Stocking.
- Accounting.

All of the above, mostly clerical in nature, require someone's time. Additionally, paperwork and mailing costs must be included. Many companies find that the sum of all the costs associated with this process is in the neighborhood of $50 per order.

Some will argue that the costs of the people should be ignored since they are already on the payroll and will be there whether or not they prepare another purchase order. The difficulty with this argument is that it assumes that we are dealing with only one purchase order more or less than is already being done. In fact, the decision to use a given method of deciding on order size may very well make a considerable difference in the number of orders to be placed. The effect of this policy decision may affect staffing levels. Even when it does not affect staffing levels, the policy may free up a person to assume other duties or, conversely, result in overtime.

For a given level of demand in a period and for a known fixed cost of placing an order, as the order size increases the number of orders will decrease. As the number of orders decreases, the total cost of placing

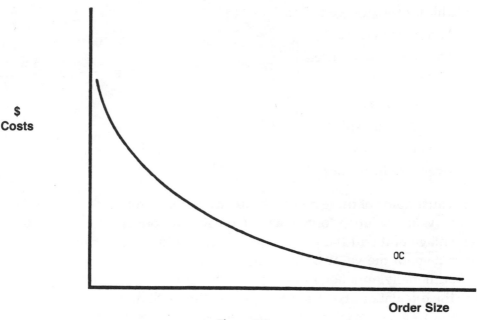

$ Costs

OC

Order Size

Figure 7.2

orders (ordering costs or OC) decreases. The effect of this is shown in Figure 7.2.

To calculate OC at any given level of order size, proceed as follows:

1. Determine the cost of placing an order.
2. Determine the number of orders that would be placed if a particular order size is used. This is done by dividing the demand for the period by the order size.
3. Multiply the cost of placing an order by the number of orders to be placed.

The equation for ordering costs, then, is: $OC = (D \times O)/OS$ where D equals demand, O equals the cost of placing an order, and OS equals the size of the order placed.

HOLDING COSTS

The costs of holding inventory are usually not as easily calculated as those of ordering inventory. Holding costs include:

• Cost of money.
• Cost of storage space.

- Utilities for storage space.
- Warehouse labor.
- Warehouse insurance.
- Spoilage.
- Obsolescence.
- Theft and unexplained losses.
- Ad valorum taxes.
- Inventory insurance.

Because some of these items are already stated in terms of a percentage of the value of inventory, it is customary to convert the others to a percentage and add the percentages to determine the storage costs as a percentage of the value of the item.

Additionally, inflation or deflation in the price paid for the item enters into the calculation. For example, if you estimate that the price of holding an item in inventory for one year is equal to 15 percent of the value of the item and you expect that the price paid for the item will inflate by 5 percent during the year, then subtract the inflation from the costs and the total cost of holding would be 10 percent due to the "holding gain." Conversely, if you expect the price to go down (as in the case of many high tech components), then the deflation percentage would be added to the cost of holding the item in inventory ("holding loss"). Of the elements comprising holding costs, ordinarily the three largest are warehousing, interest, and changes in price levels. Special care must be taken in determining warehousing costs, since the amount of space taken up by an object is not always related to the value of the object. The actual cost of space may be negligible for small-size, higher-priced items.

If the order is so small that we have very few items in inventory, then holding costs would also be small. As the order size increases so does the average inventory. In fact, for a non-varying level of usage, the average inventory would be one-half the order size. Figure 7.3 shows the total costs of holding inventory (holding costs, or HC) beginning at zero and growing on a straight line as order size grows.

Demand for a period can be estimated by looking at the starting inventory, plus the amount ordered in a period, minus the ending inventory. If the results obtained for a representative number of periods are examined, you can calculate a reasonably accurate average demand.

Safety Stock

In considering safety stock, you should look at the historical records to determine how frequently you run out of the particular commodity.

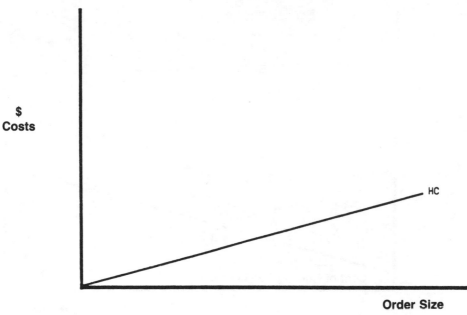

Figure 7.3

If you have never run out of the commodity, then it is safe to assume that you have more than adequate supply of safety stock. Try to use up part of the safety stock and in this way reduce your inventory levels. Since safety stock represents invested capital, this more than adequate level of safety stock would be a likely candidate for reduction.

If in looking at the inventory for a particular product you determine that, on an infrequent but acceptable basis, you have had shortages, then it might be safe to assume that the safety stock is at, or near, an appropriate level. If you have been experiencing repeated shortages of a particular commodity or product, then you may assume that the safety stock level is too low and that you should consider buying or building to increase the amount of safety stock on hand.

It cannot be stressed too often that safety stock represents embedded investment in inventory. The amount of safety stock should represent a balance between the risk of shortages or outages and the cost of carrying that safety stock. As noted earlier, businesses that *must* minimize the risk of outages should have on hand sufficient safety stock to meet the demand if there is an interruption in supply. This will be the case when the cost of an outage far outweighs the carrying cost of additional inventory.

Holding Costs with Safety Stock

In some cases, a choice is made to hold safety stock—a level of stock below which we do not expect to fall except in periods of unusually high

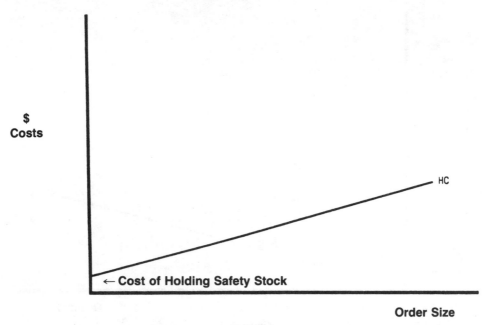

Figure 7.4

demand or unusually late deliveries. When this choice is made, the holding costs of the safety stock (which presumably does not vary) must be added to the holding costs of the rest of the inventory. The resulting graph is shown in Figure 7.4.

Notice that the slope of the line has not changed from that shown in Figure 7.3. The starting point for the line has merely been moved up to reflect the cost of holding safety stock.

To calculate the holding costs (HC) at any given order size, proceed as follows:

1. Determine the average level of inventory. If there is no safety stock and the usage rate of inventory stays constant, the average inventory level will be half the order size. If safety stock is carried, the amount should be added to the previous figure. The equation for average inventory level is: $AI = (OS/2) + SS$ where AI = Average Inventory, OS = Order Size, and SS = Safety Stock.

2. Determine the percentage holding costs to be used. This percentage is usually calculated on an annualized basis. If the demand is not stated in terms of annual usage, then the holding costs percentage must be converted to a number appropriate to the period to which the demand applies. For example, if the annualized holding costs are calculated to be 20 percent, and the demand is stated in terms of a quarter, then you would use only one-fourth of the calculated

annualized percentage (or 5 percent) to calculate holding costs for the period.

3. Determine the cost per unit (CU) of the item in inventory. Usually, the expected cost of the next purchase is used here.

4. Calculate the costs of holding inventory for the period. We will refer to this number as H; the equation is $H = AI \times HC\% \times CU$ where AI = Average Inventory, HC% = the holding cost percentage per period, and CU is the cost of a unit of inventory.

ECONOMIC ORDER QUANTITY

As can be seen in the above graphs, holding costs and ordering costs operate in opposite directions as order size increases. While ordering costs are constantly declining, holding costs are constantly increasing. To be influenced by one of these and not the other would be a mistake. The best solution is to add the two costs and seek the point at which the sum of these is minimized. We can refer to this sum as Inventory Costs (shown in Figure 7.5 as IC).

As you can see from Figure 7.5, total inventory costs begin declining as order size grows, reach a minimum, and then begin to climb. The

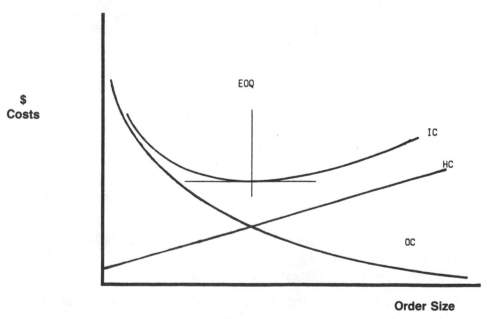

Figure 7.5

point we seek is the point at which it reaches its minimum. This is the point we refer to as the Economic Order Quantity (EOQ).

The equation for the EOQ is (we will not burden the reader with its derivation):

$$EOQ = \sqrt{\frac{(2 \times D \times O)}{H}}$$

where D = the expected demand for the period, O = the cost of placing an order, and H = the cost of holding one unit in inventory for the period.

Since the time period used occurs both in the numerator and the denominator these will cancel each other out; therefore the period of time is not particularly important (but you must use the same period in both numerator and denominator). This is the manner by which you can handle seasonal variations and demands that occur during a short period of time. It is not necessary to consider only annual demands. Any period you may wish to define can be used. Therefore, if you wish to calculate an Economic Order Quantity for ice, you can recognize the expected demand in the summer as being higher than that in the winter and use different order quantities during different seasons.

DOING THE MATH FOR EOQ—A "CASE STUDY"

To demonstrate the use of the foregoing information, let's build an example and see how the calculations might work in a "real life" situation. For this, we transport ourselves to a nearby campus and to the fraternity house of a group of scholars well known for their devotion to mathematical models and beer and commonly known as the DUI house. One of its members, having achieved the status of junior in the local business school, has recently been exposed to some concepts of inventory management. Ever watchful for topics suitable for term papers, this scholar has gathered the following information concerning some items of inventory moving through the rather large cooler attached to the kitchen of the house.

- The house purchases "industrial strength" beer shipped directly from the brewery in the Rocky Mountains to the house in 50 gallon drums. Delivery time is usually one week.

- Average purchases for the last three years have been 100 drums, or 5,000 gallons per year.

- The house usually orders 10 drums at a time, placing the order when they have 10 drums on hand.

- The price paid is $5.00 per gallon, including transportation from the Rocky Mountains. The cost of placing each order averages about $25.00. This cost includes the time spent each week checking the level in the barrels, notifying the chef, who sends a requisition to the fraternity president, letters and phone calls by the president to place the order, reassure himself that the order will be shipped, and expediting when necessary (due to his forgetfulness in placing orders on time), unloading the beer truck by the kitchen staff, testing for quality (usually accomplished by the same staff with the assistance of any members who happen to have seen the truck arrive), and the usual costs associated with writing checks and getting them approved by the faculty adviser, who must be reconvinced each time that the expenditure really is a necessity.

- Warehousing costs include $200 per month, the amount necessary to cover building and maintaining a 20,000 cubic-foot walk-in refrigerator, $100 per month for electricity to operate the refrigeration unit, and $100 per month for kitchen labor assigned to taking care of things that may be placed in the cooler.

- The house has received its insurance bill for the coming year and the company has noted the addition of the cooler and responded by raising their rate on the house by $50 per month plus 1 percent of the value of items kept in the cooler.

- At present the house seldom finds itself with more than 15 drums of beer on hand and the amount of storage space in the cooler used by these drums is approximately 750 cubic feet.

- The brewery has so far been able to hold the line on prices, but has informed the house that it should expect an annual price increase of approximately 3 percent for the foreseeable future.

- Although its account is negligible, the house is a member of the campus credit union and is eligible to receive interest at the rate of 7 percent on money deposited with the credit union.

- A member of the house majoring in physics is still running tests, but despite all theory offered to date, the chef assures the president that a shrinkage rate of $\frac{1}{4}$ of 1 percent of the inventory per month is entirely normal. Another member (a pre-med major) has offered the suggestion that blood tests on the chef might be more revealing than any test run to date.

- A spring snow storm once delayed the delivery truck causing the supply to be exhausted before new supplies arrived. This disaster resulted in a change of leadership in the fraternity and since that day 5 drums have been kept with locked spigots and chained to the wall as safety stock.

Now let's look over the shoulder of our scholar from the business school as he calculates EOQ for beer for the DUI house.

1. We know the equation for EOQ: $EOQ = \sqrt{(2 \times D \times O)/H}$ where D = demand, O is the cost of placing an order, and H is the cost of holding one unit in inventory for the period. The units that we have been using are gallons and the period we have been discussing is a year.

2. Records indicate that the amount used during the year is 5,000 gallons.

3. He has established the cost of placing an order at $25. This was done by adding the times necessary to perform all the functions associated with ordering from the initial recognition that supplies were low to the final accounting functions associated with paying for the order. A cost per hour (including overhead) was multiplied by the time taken for all these functions. To this were added other out-of-pocket costs for phone calls, mailing, and miscellaneous paper work.

4. Now he must calculate the costs of holding one gallon in stock for one year. This should be stated as a percentage of the value of one gallon. Several of our costs (such as cost of money, insurance, and shrinkage) are charged in terms of a percentage of value. However, others must be determined. Most important of these is the cost of storage space. This is done as follows:

Cost of the cooler:	$2,400	per year
Cost of utilities:	$1,200	per year
Cost of labor:	$1,200	per year
Cost of insurance:	$ 600	per year
TOTAL	$5,400	per year

As there are 20,000 cubic feet of space in the cooler, this works out to $.27 per cubic foot. As it takes approximately 1½ cubic feet to store 1 gallon, storage costs per year, per gallon, are approximately $.40. This number is then divided by the cost per gallon of $5. The number thus obtained (.08) is the annual storage cost stated as a percentage of the cost per gallon.

5. We now add the other percentages for other costs such as insurance and shrinkage.

6. Now he must deal with inflation. Since the cost of beer is expected to rise, there may be some advantage to having it in inventory. He therefore subtracts the expected inflation from the other percentages. (Of course, if the price of beer had been expected to fall, the effect would have been detrimental, and the expected deflation rate would be added to the other costs). Now he adds up all the percentages:

Cost of money:	7%
Cost of warehouse:	8%
Cost of insurance:	1%
Cost of shrinkage:	3%
Cost of inflation:	3% (minus)
TOTAL	16%

7. The cost, then, of holding one gallon in inventory for one year (although we might hesitate to drink that particular gallon) is the percentage we have calculated multiplied by the cost of one gallon. This works out to be 16 percent of $5 or $.80.

8. Now he has the numbers to feed into the equation. Demand is 5,000 gallons, cost of placing an order is $25 and the cost of holding one gallon in inventory for one year is $.80. Therefore:

$$\text{EOQ} = \sqrt{\frac{(2 \times D \times O)}{H}} = \sqrt{\frac{(2 \times 5,000 \times 25)}{.8}} = 559$$

According to his calculations, the amount to order is 559 gallons per order.

PROBLEMS

But wait. All is not well. The house buys beer in 50-gallon drums and 559 gallons is not evenly divisible by 50. This leaves the choice of rounding up to 12 or down to 11 drums per order. While the choice could be made arbitrarily, it could also be made mathematically. The objective would be to calculate the sum of ordering costs and holding costs under each of these options and choose the one that is the least. We'll see how to do that later when we consider quantity discounts.

The second problem is that although the school operates four quarters in a year, the house is open only three of these quarters. The house closes for the summer quarter and is not used. Additionally, a rather extensive social season occasioned by rush parties and football parties in the fall results in approximately 3,000 gallons of the annual quantity being consumed in that quarter, the balance of the demand being spread rather evenly over the spring and winter quarters. This means that if the house orders based on an annual demand there will probably be excessive ordering costs in the fall quarter, excessive holding costs in the spring and winter quarters, and inventories left over in the summer.

Of course, if demand is then stated in terms of quarterly demand, holding costs must also be stated quarterly (or one-quarter of the annual holding costs). Now the calculations must be repeated.

For the fall quarter:

$$EOQ = \sqrt{\frac{(2 \times D \times O)}{H}} = \sqrt{\frac{(2 \times 3,000 \times 25)}{.2}} = 866 \text{ gallons}$$

For spring and winter quarters:

$$EOQ = \sqrt{\frac{(2 \times D \times O)}{H}} = \sqrt{\frac{(2 \times 1,000 \times 25)}{.2}} = 500 \text{ gallons}$$

We again see the necessity to round up or down. Notice that, as expected, when the demand was higher the orders were larger.

Adding Quantity Discounts to EOQ Calculations

Gathering the information and doing the calculations for economic order quantity under the conditions described above is a relatively simple process and has been used for over 50 years. The catch in the system is that most users do not know how to make it work under conditions where quantity discounts are offered. There is even a generation of very expensive software for tracking inventory and making purchasing decisions that cannot calculate for conditions of quantity discounts. If you have software that makes purchasing recommendations, a very easy test will determine whether or not it has this capability. If the software has no provisions for accepting information about quantity discounts, it stands to reason that such information cannot and is not being used in making the purchase recommendations. If this is the case, understanding and using a model that does take into account quantity discounts may result in considerable savings.

Unit Costs

Previously, it was not necessary to consider unit cost as part of the decision process because there was no change in unit cost with respect to order size. However, when quantity discounts are offered, the effect is to change the price per unit depending on the size of the order placed—with prices decreasing as order size grows. The graph shown in Figure 7.6 shows the effect of order size on unit cost (UC). For order sizes less than quantity A, the first price (UC_1) prevails.

For order sizes larger than A and smaller than B, the second, cheaper price (UC_2) prevails, and for orders larger than quantity B, the third (and cheapest) price (UC_3) prevails.

Holding Costs Revisited. Because one of the components of holding costs was the cost of money used to buy the inventory, you should expect

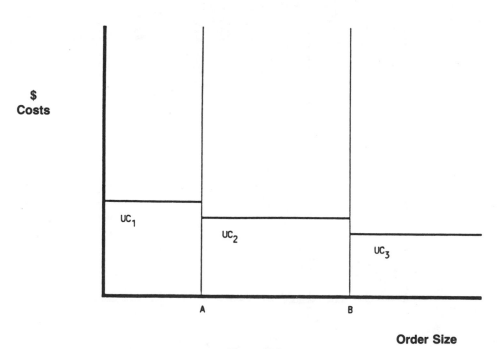

Figure 7.6

that as the cost of the units changes, the holding costs will change with it. The effect is shown in Figure 7.7. Notice that you began with an assumption of safety stock as in Figure 7.4, but this time you have three lines—each of them depicting holding costs. Only the solid portion of each line should be considered because the unit costs that comprised part of the calculation of holding cost is different for each quantity range.

Notice that the three lines do not have the same point of origin: although the same level of safety stock is applicable to all three, varying unit costs attach to that safety stock depending on the size of the order. Since the holding cost is in part related to the cost of the units, the same level of safety stock will have a variable holding cost depending on the price paid for the units in that safety stock. The three holding cost lines are referred to as HC_1, HC_2, and HC_3.

Ordering Costs Revisited. It is not necessary to construct a new graph for ordering costs because the costs of placing an order does not vary when the price of the unit ordered varies. This graph will remain the same.

Summation of the Graphs Revisited. If you graph the cost of the units, add to that the graph for order cost (unchanged), and add to that your

Figure 7.7

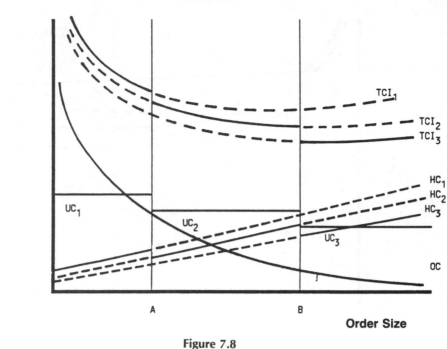

Figure 7.8

new graph for holding costs, the graph summing these three really turns out to be three graphs (curves). This is shown in Figure 7.8.

This is a rather messy looking graph and with all the dotted lines (which are irrelevant) is not very helpful. Let's remove the extra lines and look at only those relevant portions of the curves. This gives us Figure 7.9. Once again, the task is to find the point at which each curve reaches its minimum and then select the one that is the least of the three.

Notice that in the case depicted in this graph, the price breaks were sufficiently large, the ordering costs sufficiently high, and the holding costs sufficiently low so that the curve for TCI_3 is always the lowest and the purchaser is driven to buy at the lower price. *This is not always the case.* For example, it is possible for the lowest point of curve TCI_1, to be lower than some portions of either TCI_2 or TCI_3. Therefore, you should not assume from looking at the graph in Figure 7.9 that it will always be cheaper to buy at the high quantity/low price option.

This is where the calculations start to get a bit complicated. First calculate the lowest point (or indicated EOQ) for each of the curves. Next, make comparisons.

1. The lowest point on a curve may fall within the quantity range relevant to that curve. If this is the case, then that indicated EOQ is used for subsequent calculations.

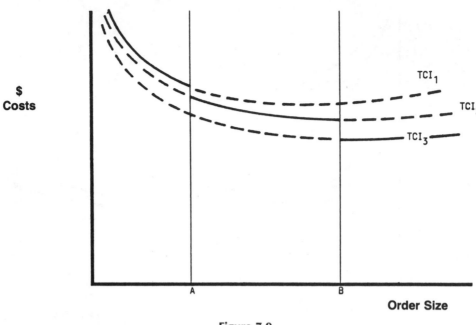

Figure 7.9

2. The indicated EOQ may fall in the next higher range. If this is the case this quantity is considered "infeasible" and is not used. After all, if you are buying in that next-higher range, you would expect to pay a lower price and thereby be on the curve for that range.

3. The indicated EOQ may be in the range below the minimum quantity necessary to obtain the price used in the calculation. If this is the case, then the program needs to throw out the number calculated and use the lowest number that would get that price (the lowest number in that quantity range).

Completing the Calculations. Having calculated the indicated EOQs and made the above checks, you then test to see which of these numbers gives the lowest *overall* costs of inventory. For each case, calculate the total costs of the units purchased, add to that the total holding costs, and add to that the total ordering costs. These totals are compared and the order size resulting in the lowest total costs selected. This is the number finally referred to as "EOQ Under Conditions of Quantity Discounts."

COMPLETING THE EXAMPLE

To see how these calculations work, let's return to the DUI house where the president is somewhat concerned over a letter he has recently received from the brewery. In the letter, the brewery states that it is changing its pricing structure. An examination of its records indicate a rather high cost in processing small orders, necessitating some changes in pricing. To begin with, it will no longer sell in quantities under 250 gallons.

The prices above 250 gallons are as follows:

LOWER LIMIT	UPPER LIMIT	PRICE PER GALLON
250	600	$6.00
650	1000	$5.00
1050	none	$4.75

Now let's go through the calculations as described above.

1) Calculate an EOQ for each of these prices. We will refer to these as EOQ_1, EOQ_2, EOQ_3 for these prices of $6.00, $5.00, and $4.75 respectively.

$$EOQ_1 = \sqrt{\frac{(2 \times 3000 \times 25)}{(.04 \times 6.00)}} = \sqrt{\frac{150{,}000}{.24}} = 790$$

$$EOQ_2 = \sqrt{\frac{(2 \times 3000 \times 25)}{(.04 \times 5.00)}} = \sqrt{\frac{150{,}000}{.20}} = 866$$

$$EOQ_3 = \sqrt{\frac{(2 \times 3000 \times 25)}{.04 \times 4.75)}} = \sqrt{\frac{150{,}000}{.19}} = 888$$

Having calculated the EOQ at each of these prices, notice that the only change in each of these equations was that of price. There was no change in the constant (2), the demand level, the ordering costs, or the holding cost percentage. The only change was in price.

Now put the calculated EOQs to the test previously indicated.

(A) The EOQ calculated for the $6.00 price was 790 units. However, as you check the pricing table you see that if you were to order at that level, you would be eligible for the $5.00 price, because the quantity indicated is above 650 gallons. It stands to reason that you would not order at this level and still expect to pay the $6.00 price. Therefore, discard this number and do not consider it any more. In other words, you have now made a decision that whatever your order quantity, it will be more than 600 gallons. The 780 gallon purchase at $5.00 is considered "infeasible."

(B) The EOQ calculated using the $5.00 price was 866 units. This falls in the quantity range applicable to the $5.00 price and, therefore, you can consider the number. However, since you must order in multiples of 50 gallons, round this number to 850 for your further calculations.

(C) The EOQ calculated using the $4.75 price was 888 units. This is not a sufficient quantity to gain the $4.75 price. If you want that price, you must order a minimum of 1050 gallons. Since you fell below that quantity, discard the 888 gallon calculation and use the lowest number which would gain the $4.75 price. That number is 1050 gallons per order.

You now have two options remaining. You can either order 850 gallons per order at the $5.00 price or 1050 gallons per order at the $4.75 price. To make this decision, calculate the cost of the beer, the cost of storage, and the cost of ordering for both options, sum these for each option, and choose the lesser of the two.

(2) In both cases you expect consumption to be 3,000 gallons. The cost of 3,000 gallons at $5.00 per gallon is $15,000 and the cost at $4.75 a gallon is $14,220.

(3) Now calculate holding cost. At $5.00 a gallon, your holding costs are 4 percent of $5.00 or $.20 per gallon per quarter. For the $4.75 price, the cost will be 4 percent of that price or $.19 per gallon per quarter. Now calculate the average inventory. Since this is equal to half the ordered quantity plus the safety stock, this will vary depending on the order size. For an order size of 850 gallons the average inventory will be half that, or 425 gallons + the 250 gallons held for safety stock, the total being 675 gallons. At an order level of 1,050 units, half that is added to 250 gallons for safety stock yielding a total of 775 gallons of average inventory. At the $5.00 price, then, multiply 675 gallons of average inventory by $.20 per gallon per quarter and you obtain a cost of $135 per quarter for storage. At the $4.75 price level, we multiply 775 gallons by $.19 per gallon, obtaining $147 per quarter storage costs.

(4) Now calculate ordering costs. You know that the cost of placing an order is $25.00. The number of orders placed is equal to the demand for the period divided by the amount ordered. For the lower order quantity, the number of orders placed is 3000/850, which you multiply by $25.00 giving an ordering cost for the period of $88.00. At the higher order level, divide 3,000 by 1,050 and multiply that by $25.00, giving an ordering cost of $71.00. Notice that in both these cases the division yielded a whole number and a fraction. Since we are assuming that the DUI house is an

ongoing operation, we can deal with fractional orders using the assumption that orders will also be placed in subsequent quarters. However, during spring quarter this assumption is not valid because you don't want beer left during the summer. Therefore, the last order placed in the spring quarter will probably be for an amount in excess of 1050 gallons.

(5) Now calculate the Total Cost of Inventory (TCI) for each of the two order quantities under consideration. Refer to these as TCI_2 and TCI_3.

$$TCI = \text{Unit Costs} + \text{Holding Costs} + \text{Ordering Costs}$$

$$TCI_1 = \text{Infeasible}$$

$$TCI_2 = 15,000 + 135 + 88 = \$15,233$$

$$TCI_3 = 14,220 + 147 + 71 = \$14,438$$

(6) Comparing the total costs of inventory under each of the two potential order quantities, you see that the house can save $785 during the fall quarter by choosing the 1,050 order quantity over the next most preferable quantity of 850 gallons. While these savings are considerable, we should not forget other considerations that may have an affect on the decision. If the house continues to keep 250 gallons of safety stock, the receipt of an order for 1,050 gallons will use almost all of the available cooler space, leaving little for other purposes. Of course, the savings of $785 realized during the fall quarter could be used to purchase a refrigerator. (This is an example of how some of the calculations used in inventory management can also be used to assist in justifications for capital purchases.) The house must also be aware that as the amount of inventory stored rises, the opportunity for undetected pilfering also rises. The house should probably consider purchasing additional locks for drums.

REORDER POINT

When is the proper time to place an order? If you order too soon, the order will probably be received before you need it and the overall average level of your inventory therefore goes up. If you order too late, you may run out of inventory before the order is received. Ideally, you should place the order when inventory has been depleted to the point where you will use the remainder (except, of course, for safety stock) during the waiting period for the receipt of the order. To calculate the reorder point, then, you need only three pieces of information. Establish the lead time (usually in weeks) and multiply that by the usage rate (usually stated in units used per week). This establishes the amount of inventory that will be used during the lead time. To this add the amount held as safety stock. The sum of these is the reorder point.

In the case of the scholars at the DUI house, their lead time is one week and their consumption rate during the fall quarter is five drums per week or 250 gallons per week (3,000 gallons divided by 12 weeks). The reorder point then, is the amount used during lead time (five drums) plus safety stock (five drums), or ten drums. However, this reorder point is too high for the spring and winter quarters, a time in which the consumption rate drops. Just as the economic order quantity should be recalculated for those quarters, so should the reorder point be recalculated. It should be remembered that in some cases the reorder point may be an amount less than the amount ordered. This does not mean that the house will run out of inventory before the order is received. It merely means that more than one order may be outstanding at any given time. For example, you may place an order on February 15 for delivery on March 15. During the period between February 15 and March 15 you could receive a previously placed order and also place yet another order. Then you could have a situation where an order is placed on February 15, a previously placed order is received on March 1, and the February 15 order is received on March 15. If you check the order file on February 25, you would find two orders outstanding. Thus, with long lead times and relatively small order quantities, you may find situations where there are multiple orders outstanding.

SAFETY STOCK DETERMINATION

Two of the variables to be dealt with in managing inventory are lead times and usage rates. If you could forecast these with accuracy, it would certainly make life simpler. Unfortunately, you seldom can. Since either or both of these are subject to variation, you usually hold some inventory aside to take up the slack in case use is at a greater rate than you had forecasted or lead time is longer than you had expected. This extra inventory, as previously stated, is usually referred to as safety stock.

Calculating the correct amount to hold in safety stock is not difficult. Unfortunately, supplying the numbers for those calculations is usually very difficult. It usually involves probability distributions related to usage rates and sometimes with respect to lead times. Most businesses (especially smaller businesses) have difficulty in supplying probability distributions for use in such a model. Consequently, they find other ways to determine the correct amount of safety stock to hold. Unfortunately, these other methods sometimes lead to holding excess safety stock and thereby increasing the cost to the company.

One of the more common methods employed involves treating stock-outs as a major disaster and adding to the level of safety stock any time a stock-out is encountered. This implicitly states the purpose of safety stock as trying to insure that *no* stock-outs will occur. For most items of inventory, an occasional stock-out is not a major disaster and this method of establishing safety stocks can lead to holding costs much higher than can be justified by the stock-out costs avoided. The real purpose of safety stocks should be to attempt a balance between additional holding costs and stock-out costs somewhat similar to the balance attempted between ordering costs and holding costs in establishing order quantities.

For most businesses, this balancing of stock-out and holding costs is done not with a mathematical model but more often by gut feeling. You can accept this as a starting point and attempt to improve the quality of the decision by giving the decision maker more information. At a minimum this information should consist of stock-out costs and holding costs. Information necessary to the determination of holding costs should have been gathered to assist in calculating order quantities. Determining stock-out costs is more difficult.

To assist in determining the costs of stock-outs, the following questions might be asked:

- What is the cost of a stock-out in terms of a lost sale?
- Is a lost sale likely to result in a lost customer as well?
- Where might costs be incurred in the event of a stock-out: Expediting? Production shut downs or dislocations? Extra price paid for temporary inventory?
- What is the longest lead time we have ever encountered with this item?
- How many stock-outs have we encountered in the past year with our present level of safety stock?

In our example of the DUI house, safety stock at present is five drums. This is the amount consumed during the average lead time during the period of high use (the fall quarter). During the fall quarter, if the president forgot to place an order and realized it only when all other stocks ran out, safety stock would probably still be sufficient to carry the house until receipt of an order. During the other quarters, it would be more than sufficient. We have no indication that any recent order has ever been so late that the entire safety stock has been used up. Additionally, if safety stock was used up, the house could probably supplement their supply from local sources. Overall, it seems that the safety stock is certainly high for the spring and winter quarters and is probably more than necessary for the fall quarter as well. The house should consider reducing the amount of safety stock.

Any safety stock requires periodic justification. Raising the level of safety stock also requires justification. In many cases, inventory to cover the period of a stock-out may be available (although at a higher cost) from an immediately available source. It may be that this occasional extra cost is less than the cost of carrying safety stock. In some cases, it may be troublesome but not costly to have a stock-out. In these cases, it may be more worthwhile to simply tolerate the stock-out than to carry safety stock. In other cases, a stock-out can be disastrous (as when a scuba diver runs out of air); safety stock is at times essential.

Because many business owners delegate responsibility for inventory management, you should establish some guidelines:

- Calculation of holding costs and description of expected benefits of maintaining a given level of safety stock.
- Required justification for raising safety stock on any item.
- Required justification for establishing any item of inventory as one for which safety stock will be held.
- A periodic listing of all items of inventory that have safety stock and have not had a stock-out within the past 12 months.
- Be cautious about accepting arguments that safety stock should be carried for an item or raised for an item. Consider forcing a reduction in safety stock for any item that has not encountered a stock-out in the last 12 months unless a stock-out for that item is very critical or demand has increased.

OTHER USES OF EOQ CALCULATIONS

Calculation and use of Economic Order Quantities can be a significant help in reducing the cost of ordering and carrying inventories. However, this is not the only situation in which EOQ calculations can be useful. Following are several other situations where a calculation of Economic Order Quantity may help in making managerial decisions.

Determination of Reasonable Inventory Levels

The calculation of EOQ when using quantity discounts required a calculation of average inventory level. The average inventory level was defined as safety stock plus one-half of the quantity ordered (see Figure 7.10). With this knowledge, you have a quick method to determine actual safety stocks being held and thereby gain the opportunity to reconsider whether those safety stocks are appropriate in size. This is done by subtracting one-half the recommended order quantity from the average amount held in inventory. The remainder is the safety stock. Care should be taken to insure that the amount used for average inventory really is average. Using the high point of inventory and subtracting half the order quantity would yield an unrealistically high indication of safety stock held. Using the low point of inventory would likewise give an unrealistic indication.

A use of the knowledge of amount of safety stock for various items of inventory being held can be useful in determining what items might be reduced in inventory and converted to cash or other assets. This can be very helpful to a company experiencing cash flow problems or for those trying to improve return on invested capital.

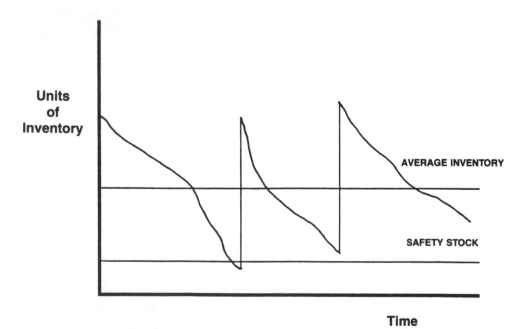

Figure 7.10

Sub-Optimizing Inventory Levels and Order Quantities

In some cases, managers are subjected to pressure from above to increase inventory turn ratios and/or to squeeze dollars out of inventory by reducing inventory levels. In these cases the manager is sometimes forced to forgo profitability in order to reach the objectives. This is not always a bad thing to do, because profitability sometimes must take a second position to other objectives (such as survival). In these cases the usual result is purchasing in quantities less than that suggested by an EOQ calculation. While this will not result in the optimum with respect to minimizing costs, you can still use the calculation to sub-optimize (select the *next* best quantity at which to buy).

- If the EOQ selected is the lowest quantity in its price range, then a lesser quantity will obviously fall in another price group. Recall that the examples had calculated an EOQ for each price group and had then calculated the total cost of inventory (TCI) at that order quantity. Select the TCI that is second best and the order quantity that produces this number.

- If the suggested order quantity is an amount in a price group that is not the smallest number in that price group, then a reduction in ordered quantity may be made without a resulting higher price per unit. In this situation, one quantity that should always be checked is the lowest quantity that will qualify for that price group.

Capital Planning

In some cases, the calculation of EOQ may yield suggested ordering quantities, which result in inventory levels being higher than can be contained within the present warehouse space available. When this is the case, if additional warehouse space can be acquired for a price consistent with that used in calculating holding costs, the indication is that it might be wise to consider acquiring the warehouse space. While this may be offered as partial justification for the acquisition of more warehouse space, it should not be substituted for normal capital budgeting procedures, which should include the discounting of the savings and comparison to initial expense for the space.

In some cases the calculations may indicate that present order quantities (and therefore inventoried quantities) are higher than optimal. If this happens in a sufficient number of cases, it may be that the company presently possesses too much warehouse space for its optimum inventories and should consider divesting this space or using it in other ways.

Data Entry Forms

The following three Data Entry Forms are furnished so that users can accumulate information required for data entry into the calculation. You may wish to make copies of these forms, fill in the appropriate information, and save copies of the completed forms.

Notice that the product ID code is requested for EOQ Calculation and Holding Cost Calculation but is not included on the Ordering Cost Calculation form. In general, ordering costs should not be expected to vary

---

**DATA ENTRY FORM
FOR ORDERING COSTS CALCULATION**

	MINUTES		MINUTES
CHECK INVENTORY LEVEL	_____	PURCHASE ORDER APPROVAL	_____
REQUISITION COMPLETION	_____	DISTRIBUTION	_____
REQUISITION APPROVAL	_____	RECEIVING & INSPECTION	_____
CHECK QUOTES	_____	STOCKING	_____
PURCHASE ORDER COMPLETION	_____	ACCOUNTING	_____

CLERICAL RATE $ _____ /HR

OVERHEAD RATE $ _____ /HR
MAILING & PAPER COSTS $ _____

Figure 7.11

**DATA ENTRY FORM
FOR HOLDING COSTS CALCULATION**

PRODUCT ID CODE _____

LEASING OR PURCHASING SPACE	$ _____ /MO	SIZE OF INVENTORIED ITEM	
UTILITIES FOR WAREHOUSE	$ _____ /MO	(IN INCHES)	
WAREHOUSE LABOR COSTS	$ _____ /MO	LENGTH _____	
WAREHOUSE INS. PREMIUM	$ _____ /MO	WIDTH _____	
SPACE AVAILABLE (CUBIC FT.)	$ _____	HEIGHT _____	

EXPECTED COST/UNIT OF INVENTORIED ITEM $ _____
   ANNUALIZED %
LOSS DUE TO SPOILAGE   _____
LOSS DUE TO OBSOLESCENCE   _____
UNEXPLAINED LOSSES   _____
AD VALORUM TAX RATE   _____

INS. PREM. INV. VALUE   _____
INTEREST RATE   _____
RATE OF PRICE CHANGE   _____   PRICE CHANGE DIRECTION (UP) (DOWN) (NONE)

Figure 7.12

DATA ENTRY FORM
FOR EOQ CALCULATION

PRODUCT ID CODE _____

MONTHS IN PERIOD CONSIDERED _____   VENDOR'S LEAD TIME (WEEKS) _____

DEMAND DURING THE PERIOD _____   DESIRED SAFETY STOCK LEVEL _____

NUMBER OF PRICE GROUPS _____

MINIMUM PURCHASE QUANTITY _____   UNIT PRICE (GROUP 1) $ _____

LOWEST QUANTITY (GROUP 2) _____   UNIT PRICE (GROUP 2) $ _____

LOWEST QUANTITY (GROUP 3) _____   UNIT PRICE (GROUP 3) $ _____

LOWEST QUANTITY (GROUP 4) _____   UNIT PRICE (GROUP 4) $ _____

ORDERING COST $ _____   ANNUALIZED HOLDING COST _____

PRESENT PURCHASED QUANTITY _____

Figure 7.13

for different products and therefore it will usually be necessary to complete this form only once. On the other forms, you will notice items such as price and size, which usually vary from product to product; this makes it necessary to have different sheets completed for different products.

Manufacturing Quantity Levels. In determining lot sizes for manufacturing, the same problem arises as for the economic order quantities. Instead of ordering cost, the associated cost for manufacturing is the set-up cost. The cost relationships are the same for manufacturing lot sizes as for the order cost in that, as the run size or quantity produced (Q) increases, the set-up cost associated per item decreases. Additionally, the relationship for the holding cost is precisely the same linear relationship as for the holding cost of inventory. The total cost of manufacturing looks the same as the economic order quantity relationship we saw in Figure 7.5.

The 80/20 Rule. A good rule of thumb for the use of the EOQ models and other inventory control systems is to remember that 80 percent of the quantity of inventories will probably be worth only about 20 percent of the total value of inventories. The converse is also true; the remaining 20 percent of inventories may account for 80 percent of the total value of inventories. As a rule, in implementing an inventory control system it is wise to work with the "big bucks" inventory items first. Getting control of the 20 percent of the inventory that accounts for 80 percent of the inventory dollars would mean that one out of every five commodities in inventory would be under some form of control. That control, however, would cover four out of every five dollars of the total value of inventory.

Remember that inventories are typically an extremely large asset. Many times, they are second in size only to plant and equipment. This justifies significant management attention. Also remember that the EOQ model is not terribly sensitive to misestimates. If exact figures aren't available (and they won't usually be, since you are dealing with the future) get the best estimate affordable and proceed. It is better to estimate too high than too low. For example, holding cost may be based on the following estimate: The cost of money plus warehouse cost may end up about 25 percent of the value of inventory on an annual basis. If inflation in prices is expected, subtract that percentage. Further, ask questions if ordering costs are estimated at less then $50.00. Frequently people tend to overlook or underestimate the cost associated with placing an order. Significant paperwork and handling are required to ensure that orders are timely and properly placed. These costs are significant.

MATERIALS REQUIREMENTS PLANNING (MRP)

Materials Requirements Planning is a sophisticated method of controlling work-in-progress inventories. In order to qualify for the use of MRP as a planning and control device, you must have an in-place, sophisticated system of bill of materials and complete inventory records.

The first step in setting up an MRP plan is to take the exploded bill of materials for a unit and multiply it by the planned units of production. In this matter the total number of each subassembly, part, and material can be determined. The inventories are then examined to determine which parts, materials, or subassemblies have to be ordered. Orders are placed so that parts, materials, and subassemblies will be in the work centers when needed. Lead times and EOQs must be considered. When successfully applied, MRP has resulted in sizable savings in reduced inventory levels, increased validity of schedules, and increased labor utilization. When unsuccessful, confusion and production shut-downs may result. The keys to success are a computer and an accurate record-keeping system. Some quick tests to determine whether the firm will have a likelihood of success in using an MRP system include:

1. Disassemble a completed product and compare the parts with the bill of materials. If 100 percent accurate, go on to the next step.

2. Select one high-value part and one low-value part in inventory. Count each part in inventory and compare that number to the inventory records. Do the same for one item in the work-in-process inventory. If the count is within 5 percent of the amount indicated on the inventory records, go on.

3. Obtain the current status report for current month's targets and next month's plan from:
   A. A production control supervisor;
   B. An assembly supervisor; and
   C. An inventory supervisor.
   If all three agree, you are ready to consider MRP.

If you have failed any of these screening questions, you are probably not ready to attempt implementation of MRP. However, you may be able to effect some considerable savings by improvements in record keeping, even if MRP is not subsequently adopted.

MRP is an expanded version of the EOQ model, applied at successive stages in a production line. Remember that at each stage in the MRP model, where EOQ is applied, the "make or buy" decision is equally applicable. Often, some of the work on subassemblies can be carried out as easily or at lower cost by subcontractors. However, when using subcontractors, you may be building into the system additional delays in receipt of completed subassemblies or components. These can be adjusted if management is aware of the magnitude of the delays. The simple EOQ model is not equipped to take into consideration the lag time in receipt of completed components.

Many successful companies have used subcontractors for the provision of subassemblies and components. This has the advantage of allowing the company a margin in which to call back work in periods where demand falls off.

By "farming out" work, you have the flexibility to call it back when demand drops off and in this way avoid lay-offs and improve direct cost allocations. When you call this extra-work back into the plant, you spread your overhead and reduce labor uncertainty.

The EOQ model can set up some of the parameters necessary for the calculation of the level of subcontractor work. It was discussed in the CVP model that there are cases where you seek to have your production exceed the optimum point of maximum profitability. One of the ways that this can be accomplished is through the use of subcontractors.

JUST-IN-TIME PRODUCTION SYSTEM

This system's objective, as with MRP, is to reduce the costs involved in the production process. Both systems are more than simple inventory management systems. The difference between them and the EOQ is primarily one of degree. The Just-In-Time (JIT) system goes beyond the MRP in that it requires:

- Balancing production lines.
- Multi-function workers.
- Minimizing set-up times and special paper work systems (including those of the suppliers).
- Automation of quality control.

Toyota has developed and successfully used the JIT system. Toyota has assisted suppliers in their implementation of the system and has reduced inventory below that required for other production systems. While Toyota has shown excellent results, and wishes to export the methodology, it should be remembered that the system is basically a special case of MRP requiring management dedication and employee attitudes seldom found outside Japan. A full discussion of the JIT model can be found in current publications related to production.

SUMMARY

One of your larger assets may be your investment in inventories. In thinking of inventories, most individuals think of finished goods sitting in a warehouse awaiting shipment. In fact, those finished goods only represent a part of the inventories you have on hand at any time. Another large segment of your production may be tied up in work-in-process inventories and raw materials. These partially complete products act as a buffer to keep production going in the event that a process or machine critical to the operation fails.

When ordering materials or in determining set-up costs versus run durations (and other inventory control problems) Economic Order Quantity analysis can be used to minimize the cost implications of these decisions. One of the often overlooked components of ordering stock is simply the cost of placing an order. Ordering costs are significant and assignable.

In doing so their hidden impact can be considered and minimized. These ordering costs should be balanced against holding costs to determine that level of ordering where total cost is minimized. This same analysis can be used to determine manufacturing lot sizes where set-up cost is the same as ordering cost and run expenses equate to holding cost.

Another powerful application of the model is to the problem of evaluating quantity discounts. That problem has, in addition to ordering and holding costs, an element of discounting the price for purchasing various quantities of the product. The problem calls for treating a step function.

For many, the 80/20 rule applies—that is, 80 percent of the inventory amounts to about 20 percent of the value of the inventory. Emphasis should be placed on controlling the most costly or valuable inventory items first.

Sophisticated models have been developed to control inventories such as MRP and Just-In-Time production. These models work well where the firm has accurate records and good material control processes; the exercise of evaluating the probable ability to implement the system may have beneficial results for such a firm. It is, simply, a useful form of self-analysis.

8

Pricing

Pricing the product or service of the company can be quite simple. Someone simply establishes a price—cost-based, volume-based, market-based, or without a basis. The trick for success is to price so that the product or service will be purchased *and* the company can make a profit.

An acceptable price usually falls within the bounds of a "price ceiling" and a "price floor." The market generally determines the price under which products will sell and thus establishes a price ceiling. Costs and desired profits establish a price floor below which one cannot sell and make the desired profit. Pricing practices often get out of date as a result of rising costs, material shortages, wide swings in economy, difficult access to funds for expansion and operation, and tougher competition at home and from abroad. Good pricing practices require an understanding of the influences of market factors: the economy, technology, competition, and the competing pressures on limited resources. In addition to these factors, you must constantly consider those related to internally generated costs.

BASIC RULES OF PRICING

Good pricing practices generally recognize that there is more to pricing than consideration of only internal costs. Two important factors in developing prices for small companies are:

1. Recognition that the market, not your costs, determines the price at which the product will sell.

2. An awareness that your costs and desired profits only establish a price floor below which you cannot sell and still make a profit.

The area between the price ceiling, established by the market, and the price floor, determined by cost and desired profit, is one view of the "relevant price range" often discussed but seldom defined in textbooks. It is only when a business can produce at a cost that will permit recovery of those costs plus a desired profit margin that the price determined by the market will sustain the business in a profitable mode.

COST AS A FACTOR

Without good cost information any pricing policy is inadequate at best. Good cost data are as important for pricing as they are for operational management of the business. If you do not have adequate cost figures, you should require the accounting department to develop them for use both in operations control and for the necessary pricing decisions.

Methods of Pricing Using Cost as a Basis

There are several methods of establishing price floors using your costs. Each has advantages and disadvantages.

1. *Mark-up on cost method.* Among non-manufacturers the simplest, and a frequently used, method for developing price floors is mark-up on cost of goods. This generally involves adding a percentage to the cost of goods. This mark-up is intended to cover all other costs and the necessary profit levels for the business. Keystoning (doubling the invoice cost) is an example of this method.

2. *Full cost basis.* This method has been designed to recover all costs plus a margin. It is calculated by developing the total cost for manufacturing the product and then adding a mark-up, or fraction, to those costs. The formula is:

$$P = TC + [M\% \times TC]$$

or, price = the total cost per unit plus a mark-up as a percentage times the total cost. The advantage of this method is clearly its simplicity of application. The major disadvantage is that the methodology used for the allocation of overhead expenses (as a part of total cost) may create an artificial number.

3. *Incremental cost basis*. Using this method, total cost is abandoned in favor of the use of direct labor and direct material costs as the basis for setting price. It emphasizes the incremental cost of producing additional units. In using this method, normally, a larger mark-up is required on a smaller base than in the full cost system mentioned above. The emphasis is shifted toward production that can absorb more overhead. The formula is:

$$P = (DL + DM) + [M\% \times (DL + DM)]$$

$$= [(1 + M\%) \times (DL + DM)]$$

or, price = direct labor plus direct material plus a mark-up, as a percentage, times the sum of direct labor plus direct materials. This method is often used to price special orders. In the longer term, one must be sure the mark-up is sufficient to cover both overhead and profit.

4. *Conversion cost basis*. Conversion cost–based pricing emphasizes the value added, or the direct labor plus overhead (costs needed to convert materials into product), in developing a price floor. The formula for this method is:

$$P = (DL + OH) + [M\% \times (DL + OH)]$$

$$= [(1 + M\%) \times (DL + OH)]$$

or, price = direct labor plus overhead plus a mark-up as a percentage times the sum of direct labor and overhead. A necessary condition of this system is that overhead allocation must be based upon some clear rationale. For this reason, it offers the higher potential for errors in pricing.

Other Cost-Based Approaches

There are methods that have been designed to determine prices required to accomplish the firm's objectives, such as:

- A specified or target margin.
- A return on investment objective.

Target Margin. If the objective is to establish a price that will return a specific margin on sales, the method is simply: price = total cost / (100%

– PM%), where PM is the expected profit margin. This method clearly identifies a price at which we must sell in order to achieve a desired margin on sales.

Target return on investment. As in the profit margin example, this method determines a price that must be charged in order to achieve a desired rate of return on investment. The formula is:

$$P = \frac{\left[(ROI) \times \left(\frac{I}{2}\right)\right] + \left(\frac{I}{Y}\right) + FC + [(VC) \times Q]}{Q}$$

or, price = the targeted before tax return times the average investment, plus the amortized return of the investment plus, fixed costs, plus the variable costs per unit times the quantity sold, all divided by the quantity sold. The critical variable in the formula is an estimation of the quantity that will be sold. Often sales volumes are very sensitive to price. Marketing experts may have to vary their projections and estimates after recalculating the price. One gets caught in a chicken-and-egg problem here in that in determining the price, the quantity may vary and making adjustments for the quantity may alter the price.

Take as an example Newtown Mfg. Co, which has a new product and wishes to set the price. The accounting department has established the following costs:

Direct labor (DL)	$.20/unit
Direct materials (DM)	.25/unit
Overhead (OH)	.11/unit
Total Cost	$.56/unit

It calculates the price using three of the pricing methods:

1. Full cost pricing with a 50 percent margin:

$$\text{Price} = TC + (M\%)(TC)$$

$$= \$.56 + (50\%)(.56)$$

$$= .56 + .28$$

$$= \$.84$$

2. Incremental cost pricing with a 100 percent margin:

$$Price = (DL + DM) + (M\%)(DL + DM)$$

$$= (.20 + .25) + (1.00)(.20 + .25)$$

$$= .45 + .45$$

$$= .90$$

3. Conversion cost pricing with a 200 percent margin:

$$Price = (DL + OH) + (M\%)(DL + OH)$$

$$= (.20 + .11) + (2.00)(.20 + .11)$$

$$= (.31) + 2.0(.31)$$

$$= .31 + 62$$

$$= .93$$

Target Margin on Sales. The Newtown Mfg. Co. believes it can get a 25 percent sales (gross profit) margin. The firm wants to calculate a price using a target margin on sales method. The formula is:

$$Price = \frac{Total\ Cost\ per\ Unit}{100\% - (PM\%)}$$

$$Price = \frac{.56}{1.00 - .25}$$

$$Price = \frac{.56}{.75} = \$.75$$

Target Return on Investment Pricing. The Newtown Mfg. Co. has developed a new product that requires a substantial investment. The company wants to be sure that it gets a satisfactory return. It requires a 30 percent (before taxes) return. It is in the 46 percent tax bracket. This will give the firm about a 16 percent after-tax return. The accountant estimates the following costs:

Investment required	$2,000,000.00
Fixed costs	$40,000.00
Variable cost/unit	$2.50

The investment is targeted for repayment in five years and the firm estimates sales at 100,000 units per year. Using the equation for target return on investment pricing, the following price is calculated:

$$\text{Price} = \frac{[(ROI) \times (I/2)] + (I/Y) + FC + [(VC) \times Q]}{Q}$$

$$\text{Price} = \frac{[.3 \times (2,000,000/2)] + [2,000,000/5] + 40,000 + [2.50 \times 100,000]}{100,000}$$

$$\text{Price} = \frac{[.3 \times 1,000,000] + [400,000] + 40,000 + 250,000}{100,000}$$

$$\text{Price} = \frac{300,000 + 400,000 + 40,000 + 250,000}{100,000}$$

$$\text{Price} = \frac{990,000}{100,000}$$

$$\text{Price} = \$9.90$$

The "proof" of this price follows:

Annual Sales	$990,000
Less: Fixed Costs	(40,000)
Variable Costs	(250,000)
Straight Line Depreciation	(400,000)
Before Tax Profit	300,000
Taxes at 46%	(138,000)
After Tax Profit	$162,000

Average Investment = ($2,000,000/2) = $1,000,000
Before Tax Return = $300,000/1,000,000 = 30%
After Tax Return = $162,000/$1,000,000 = 16.2%

THE PRICE CEILING

The other half of the pricing concern is the price ceiling. The price ceiling is generally determined by the market and is often more difficult to estimate than the price floors. Many factors such as the economy, the nature of the market, the number of competitors, the aggressiveness of the competitors, consumer influences, and advertising may affect the price ceiling. Generally there are two approaches to determining a price ceiling—hit or miss, and market research.

The hit or miss approach requires an estimate of a selling price based upon the simple principle that it is often easier to lower prices than it is to raise prices. Therefore, for a new product, it may be better to put the product on the market with a little higher margin than the firm would normally sustain. If the market accepts the product at that price, the extra margin can be considered windfall or the price could be lowered to stimulate further market acceptance and buying. In the event that the market rejects the product at that price, it is simpler to remove the excess margin and lower the price. In this manner, risk has been lessened. One danger in reducing the price of a new product is giving the consumer the signal that the product may be a "failure" in the market. However, this risk is often less than the risk of turning the consumer off by raising the initial price for the product. When the firm raises the initial price, it gives a signal to the customer that, in effect, a form of bait-and-switch has gone on. In other words, the consumer will feel that the lower price was a come-on, and now that an inroad has been established in the market, the price is raised. This may turn off the consumer, especially if price was the motivating factor to buy to begin with.

The market research approach offers the benefit of minimizing the risk associated with the introduction price of a new product. However, it does not avoid the cost of doing the necessary research to determine the appropriate price. One point to be considered in establishing the price is to ask the question: What did the consumer do before this product was available? In this manner, the marketing department is trying to make a "value of benefits" determination to establish the appropriate price for the product. It steers the mind away from a strictly cost-based approach.

WHAT IF THE MARKET BALKS?

If the market will not accept the product at the established market price (that covers the cost and a desired margin), four alternatives are generally available:

- Discontinue the product.
- Accept a lower margin.

- Reduce costs.
- Differentiate the product from that of the competitors' in the minds of the buyers.

The first two solutions generally should be used as fall-back positions. Reducing costs is always an acceptable alternative and should be reviewed continuously regardless of the market's reaction to the price. However, reducing costs may often be difficult especially at the introduction date of a new product. Simply put, learning takes time, and achieving cost reduction often comes later in the process. The fourth alternative, product differentiation, though sometimes overlooked, is often the best.

PRODUCT DIFFERENTIATION

Frequently, a product can be distinguished from competing products not on the basis of price but of other factors that may influence buying habits. Such factors may include:

1. Superior quality, or an emphasis on extra features or reliability. Rolls-Royce has often been used as the prime example.

2. Better service. At one time Caterpillar tractor built a tremendous market presence by stressing the fact that its equipment could be serviced within 24 hours at any location in the world.

3. Product performance. A good example is the claim by BMW that it is the "ultimate driving machine."

4. Delivery time. Federal Express's overnight delivery created a market niche.

5. Financing arrangements. This method is frequently used with great success by the automotive industry. Low APR financing has put a number of people into showrooms who might not otherwise have gone at that time.

6. Engineering and design help. Many construction firms offer "pre-bid" assistance.

7. Packaging. One professor at a major university wanted to sell a used Corvette, so he offered a package of two tickets to the premier football game and a car to get to the game in for several thousand dollars.

Product differentiation will work best under the conditions where price sensitivity is low. Several factors influence buyer sensitivity to price and are therefore considerations in product differentiation:

- The availability of comparable substitutes.
- The frequency of the purchase of your product by an individual buyer.
- The impact of the purchase on the buyer's budget.

If competing products are not readily available, sensitivity to price diminishes. Price sensitivity increases as the frequency of purchase increases. And, if the product does not have a significant impact on the individual's budget, it will be less price sensitive.

PRICING AS PART OF STRATEGIC PLANNING

A pricing philosophy is not a separate document to be placed alongside a strategic plan or an operating plan. Pricing is a management tool in every sense. It is a means of attaining your objectives rather than an objective itself. A pricing strategy, therefore, should become an integral part of planning for your product, market, and profit. In order to establish a written strategy for pricing, you may consider the following:

Operating Environment.

- Establish whether the industry in which you operate is stable or fluctuates. If it fluctuates you should try to determine what drives the fluctuations.
- Establish what the trend is in the industry for growth and the introduction of new products into the market.
- Where do you stand in the industry? Is yours the oldest company? Is it the leader? Is it the smallest?
- How innovative are you and the industry with new products?

Marketing Strategy.

- How is the industry structured? How many companies together command 80 percent of the market? How many smaller firms are there? Where do you intend to emphasize your products and position?

- Is brand loyalty a key factor in the business? Is it your intention to concentrate on the wholesale market or do you intend to deal directly with the retail customers?

Product Strategy.

- What market do you intend to target your products for? How extensive a product line do you intend to manufacture or carry?

Profit Strategy.

- What economic factors will affect your products? Is the market for raw materials unstable or is it showing the pressures of an expanding industry by increasing prices?
- Can you substitute less expensive raw materials, such as plastics, for steel to lower the cost to produce?
- Are incremental profit opportunities available for a budget segment of your product line? Is the market in which you operate very stable for revenue profit projections?

Once these considerations have been made, the process of developing a pricing philosophy should begin with describing and defining the market price patterns and overall price environment (retail, wholesale, etc.). Next, take your own internal corporate, market, product, or other plans and consider each of them for potential pricing actions. This will be discussed later.

To improve internal strategies, for instance, you must give full recognition to how price works in the market and then decide how and when to follow these established practices and when to strike out on your own using new pricing ideas, which vary from tradition. Only then does pricing become a tool that is part of your strategies rather than a stand-alone plan.

THE MASTER CHECKLIST OF KEY FACTORS THAT AFFECT PRICING

The foundation for analyzing key factors lies in these questions:

- What information do I need?
- Where do I look for it?

- How do I get it?
- Who will have the information?
- How reliable is the source?

Once you have answers to these questions, you can proceed to analyze and use the information to make pricing decisions and devise strategies accordingly.

Internal Factors

Internal data and feedback are usually the most reliable pricing information. In order to accumulate sufficient data internally, feedback of information should be encouraged at all levels of management.

Customers and Users. Customers and users can be a good source of pricing information if the appropriate questions are asked and data are gathered. Ask such questions as:

- What do customers feel about the worth of the product?
- How much do they value the product? (It is important to remember that price is ultimately determined by the final consumer, based upon the concept of value received.)
- Understand how the buyers feel and what motivates them to buy. This calls for insight and perception. The most likely individual to possess that insight is the one who has to make that sale for a living.

Intermediate Customers. If you sell to wholesalers, do not lose sight of the fact that resellers are really customers. These "middlemen" exert a profound influence on pricing decisions. You should continuously assess the following:

- What is going on with the business of the broker, agent, distributor, or dealer?
- Where are actual prevailing prices compared with list or suggested retail prices? An important matter to consider here is why there is a deviation between the manufacturer's suggested retail price and the prevailing market price.
- What unique pricing structures are prevalent? Are they becoming more complex? Areas to explore are the nature and basis for discounts, advertising, and promotional allowances, special terms, rebates, and occasionally indirect concessions relating to inventories, receivables and payables.

- Are there any needed changes in the distribution channels?
- Are the middlemen doing the job for which they are being compensated and are they bringing added value to the end user?

It is indeed important for you to work toward building a loyal, competent reseller network that keeps management supplied with necessary and well-founded information about the salability of products and the adequacy of pricing arrangements.

Company Developments. Some of the keys to company developments include:

- New and replacement products
- Shifts in your objectives and financial targets.
- Regular sales reports and average actual selling price reports for the entire selling pipeline.

External factors

Competition. Perhaps the most important information you need concerns the activities and pricing policies of competitors. No one should be more sensitive to the efforts of competitors than the sales force and regional sales managers. Focus on the following:

- Pricing. What are competitive price ranges for equivalent products and how are the prices constructed in terms of discounts, allowances, etc.? Analysis should be made between prevailing and list prices for competitive products.
- Innovation. Are new products entering the market from competitors? In addition, are new uses being made of the existing products? Will minor modifications to our products better meet the needs of the current market? What changes are there in packaging, product features, delivery schedules, servicing, warranties, and a host of other areas?
- Programs. Are your competitors offering new sales promotion devices or sales force incentives to motivate sales of their products?
- Markets. Are competitors shifting into new markets or market segments and expanding their existing sales? What are the competitors' market-share philosophies?
- New competition. Are there any new firms entering your industry or your market?

Overall Economic Trend. Market trends are the primary data needed to signal whether customers are willing and able to buy your products.

Comparisons of past historic trends between the overall market indicators and your sales will give some correlation between these two factors. With the use of this correlation, marketing can evaluate ongoing economic trends so as to project sales forecasts for the future. Price effectiveness is a direct result of gathering and analyzing meaningful data on future economic trends.

Trends in Substitute Products. Home buying and apartment rentals, at least in the short run, offer an example of trends in substitute products. It is important to look to the trend that may necessitate price shifts in order to maintain market shares. Remember, however, that these price shifts may be only temporary substitutes for the necessary innovation needed to maintain current market.

Effective Strategies to Combat Profit Erosion. Often, negative market reaction to a price increase can be offset by stressing the addition of more value to the product. Very frequently someone will advertise that her product is "new and improved" to give the impression that additional quality has been added to justify the price increase. This approach emphasizes the concept that the price is more reflective of the market value than of the cost. With this approach, you attempt to show that you are reacting to the market's need for a higher quality product and consequently the price is reflective of that additional value.

Profits may erode due to market reaction to prices or price changes.

1. You may wish to announce new prices, but delay their effective date for 30 days. Any orders placed in that 30-day period will be honored at the current, lower prices. This strategy, commonly referred to as "grand-fathering," serves the useful purpose of accelerating sales for the next month from price-conscious customers. Therefore, even at a lower price you will be receiving the benefit of accelerated cash flows. If price increase is based upon anticipated increases in cost, there will be little erosion in profits in the short term since a decrease in buying at a higher price will be offset by the older, lower embedded cost.

2. Another strategy often used to offset the effects of an increased price is to unbundle services or options. You do not raise the price for the existing base product or service. However, the services or options that once were included as part of the price are now spun off as differentially priced items. Thus the seller is offering the service or option at an additional cost.

As an example, assume you have traditionally sold a product with a one-year warranty included. You may "unbundle" nine months of the warranty and offer the product with a three-month warranty at the old price and an extended nine-month warranty at an additional cost.

3. Another strategy is to maintain the price but to decrease the quantity in the package. For example, a 15-ounce package of Soapies has sold for $1.50, or $.10 per ounce. If the price per box ($1.50) is maintained but the box content is reduced to 12 ounces, the price per ounce has increased by 25 percent to $.125 per ounce.

4. A combination strategy is to increase prices per unit slightly and to decrease unit content simultaneously. This appears to have been the approach of candy bar manufacturers several years ago.

5. On some large ticket items consumers are more concerned with the payment amount than with total price. Therefore, making financing arrangements for extended terms, which hold payments, rather than price, at a constant level, may mask a price increase.

6. An interesting strategy can be effected when the product is sold primarily through vending machines. Because of the operation of the machine, prices can go up only in pre-set increments. For example, the minimum increase to the price of a bag of chips now priced at $0.50 is $.05, or 10 percent.

Municipalities have employed a variation of this strategy with parking meters. In addition to raising the price per minute, some meters accept only certain coins. Therefore, the consumer can't buy just the quantity desired and the effective price per unit to the consumer is increased by time left on the meter.

SUMMARY

The cost of producing a product has a great deal to do with pricing, for if you cannot price above cost, you cannot stay in business. Factors outside the business influence the price at which you may sell your products or services. The price floors—that price below which you cannot sell and still make a profit—can be set using several pricing formulas set out in this chapter. Other pricing methods have been developed to attempt a target rate of return on investment or a target margin.

The other half of the pricing problem is the price ceiling—the price set by the market above which the product generally will not sell. Many factors affect price ceilings and usually a marketing research approach can estimate this market or ceilings price.

Techniques have been developed to minimize the adverse affect of consumer rejection of price increases. You can discontinue the product, accept a lower margin, reduce costs, or attempt to differentiate the product. Discontinuing a product is rather radical (but sometimes necessary); accepting a lower margin may not compensate for the risk and an effort toward lower costs should always be encouraged. The emphasis on product differentiation can exploit whole submarkets for existing products or product lines. Sometimes carving out a previously indistinguishable part of a bigger market may give you a product advantage that may comfortably justify higher prices. One clear example is emphasis on product quality—priced a bit more but well worth it.

Pricing, an integral part of market strategy, should occupy a position in your strategic plan. You must consider the effects of many external factors, such as competition, the overall economy, and trends in the introduction of and change in competitive and substitute products.

You should constantly monitor the market's reaction to the product and the price. Where profits start to erode you can effect a change in strategy to combat this erosion and neutralize the consumer's resentment or reaction to a change in price. You can explore such methods as packaging changes, like the reduction in coffee cans from 16 ounces to 13 ounces, to unbundling "extras," and grandfathering existing prices for a certain time before new prices become effective. The emphasis, again, is on planning for change—not crisis management.

9

Marketing Analysis

This chapter will discuss the use of the well-known product matrix analysis. We will show how this may be used to assist in planning both the marketing and manufacturing strategies. We will also examine how to analyze marketing costs and will provide an outline for a marketing-oriented cost accounting system. We will cover the nature, behavior, and assignment of marketing costs and their relationship to contribution margin accounting. A section will be devoted to correcting product weaknesses in the market and another to segmenting markets. We will examine the channels used for the distribution of products, how to handle changes, and how to improve distribution either through existing channels or by seeking new channels. Finally, we will give a checklist of questions to be asked in order to establish how well your marketing plan is meeting your business objectives.

PRODUCT MATRIX ANALYSIS

Very often a company carries lines of similar and even competing products. For a retail business this may cause inventory control problems and additional costs associated with storage, ordering, and handling. Questions arise as to which products to continue or discontinue, and where you may need to add new lines or products.

One method of using the product matrix analysis is a two variable matrix analysis. Each product the firm sells may be evaluated in this method. It is a simple analytical tool for determining the constituent parts of each product's market. On a square matrix, quality or any variable of interest is plotted across the bottom from low quality on the left to high quality on the right. Going down the side, a price scale is made, from high on the top to low on the bottom. Fair value would be along the diagonal. Figure 9.1 is an example of this tool.

Then, using a separate graph for each of the firm's products, the marketing department can establish where each product is on the graph. If the product is priced fairly, for the quality it represents, it should be somewhere on the diagonal.

As an example, assume that Shirts, Inc., manufacturer of casual shirts for men, is a solid brand carried by several large chain department stores. Also within the market are three old, established brands (O1, O2, O3) and two designer brands (D1, D2). The company first plots where it believes its product fits in the quality/price matrix and then plots where the other businesses appear to be. Figure 9.2 depicts what the market for men's casual shirts looks like for the business.

An Analysis. Shirts, Inc., and firms O1 and O2 have priced their products competitively, based on the value analysis. They are giving fair value to

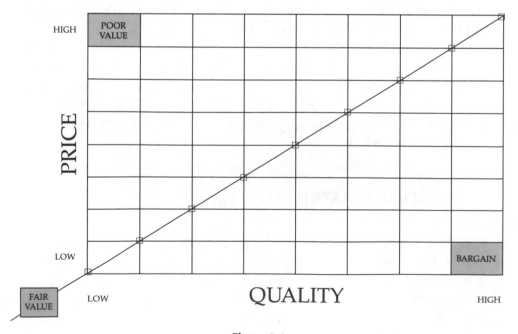

Figure 9.1

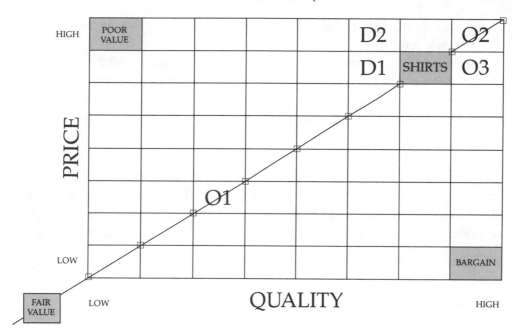

Figure 9.2

the consumer, pricing their goods in accordance with quality. Firms D1
and D2 are selling shirts at prices higher than the quality dictates, meaning
that something other than quality (label, prestige, advertising, etc.) is
driving the market.

Firm O3, on the other hand, is selling high quality goods at a price
less than fair value. This should be a warning sign. Firm O3 may be
trying to cut into the other firms' existing market share, they may have
a bad pricing policy, or they may be trying to increase sales because of
financial problems. For whatever reason, Firm O3 should be monitored
as a potentially dangerous competitor in this situation.

This analysis does have some limitations:

- It assumes knowledgeable matrix users who analyze the price/quality
  relationship.
- It does not consider other extrinsic motivating factors: name recognition, fashion, styles, fads, etc.
- It assumes comparable products.

Another interesting outcome of this analysis is that it points out that
the firm selling a low-price, low-quality product is still selling a fair value
product for which there may be a market. If gaps in the market are

evident, you could produce a different "value" product to meet these market opportunities.

For example, for a particular product line you could produce and price a shirt for each level of quality along the diagonal. In this manner, it would blanket the market. Competition might then be forced to focus upon those other extrinsic factors that differentiate their products.

Each of your products can be evaluated in this manner. Also, other variables could be placed on the bottom axis (prestige, sex appeal, image, etc.), with various conclusions to be drawn. Additionally, complementary products can be placed on the same grid to analyze any linkage between the sales of each. Conceptually, this analysis can be extended to three dimensions (price, quality, and image), but that is very difficult to visualize and to depict.

UNIT PRODUCT CONTRIBUTION ANALYSIS

In looking at the aggregate product line versus the price-quality relationship, more information may be needed to evaluate the effectiveness of product mix. Cost and contribution provides the necessary data. Consider the Unit Product Contribution Analysis sheet shown as Figure 9.3.

UNIT PRODUCT CONTRIBUTION ANALYSIS
(BY UNIT)

| PRODUCTS | NET SELLING PRICE | COSTS | | | | | CONTRIBUTION PER UNIT | PERCENT CONTRIBUTION |
		MATERIAL	LABOR	VARIABLE OVERHEAD	OTHER	TOTAL		
LINE A								
A1								
A2								
A3								
LINE B								
B1								
B2								
B3								

Figure 9.3

UNIT PRODUCT CONTRIBUTION ANALYSIS
(BY UNIT)

| PRODUCTS | NET SELLING PRICE | COSTS | | | | | CONTRIBUTION PER UNIT | PERCENT CONTRIBUTION |
		MATERIAL	LABOR	VARIABLE OVERHEAD	OTHER	TOTAL		
LINE A								
A1	$5.47	$1.35	$2.01	$0.17	$0.00	$3.53	$1.94	35.47%
A2	$6.15	$1.39	$2.10	$0.19	$0.00	$3.68	$2.47	40.16%
A3	$6.27	$1.20	$2.15	$0.20	$0.05	$3.60	$2.67	42.58%
LINE B								
B1	$7.99	$2.10	$1.75	$0.16	$0.07	$4.08	$3.91	48.94%
B2	$8.99	$3.27	$4.97	$0.30	$0.50	$9.04	($0.05)	−0.56%
B3	$9.99	$3.15	$3.10	$0.27	$0.00	$6.52	$3.47	34.73%
B4	$10.50	$4.00	$2.97	$0.39	$0.00	$7.36	$3.14	29.90%

Figure 9.4

When you compile the necessary data to prepare this spreadsheet, it becomes apparent which products make a contribution to overall fixed costs and which do not.

The performance of Product B2 should be of concern to the firm, as it does not sustain its directly attributable costs (or make any contribution to the corporate fixed expenses).

Carrying the analysis further to demonstrate contribution as a percentage of price can also be a helpful exercise. The matrix can quickly point out where your attention should be concentrated. Other types of comparisons can be generated by grouping product lines together and evaluating the comparative contributions between lines.

One other factor may be introduced into the analysis: the existing and projected sales levels. You may not produce enough of certain products in your line to have a significant cost or profit effect. However, in order to be competitive, you may need these products to have a "complete line" and to service your customers.

You should consider sales forecasting with an eye on the percentage contribution each line and each type within each line gives to the bottom line. The next logical step in the process is to project sales by product line and type.

There are two sources of sales forecasting: internally generated numbers and customer-generated projections. Sometimes internally generated numbers are produced by people who don't know the market. It is better to have the customer-contact people, the salesmen, generate these data.

PRODUCT AND PRODUCT LINE CONTRIBUTION ANALYSIS

| UNIT CONTRIBUTION | | PRODUCT LINE A | | | | PRODUCT LINE B | | | | | GRAND |
		1	2	3	TOTAL	1	2	3	4	TOTAL	TOTAL
BY %		36.00%	40.00%	43.00%		49.00%	0.00%	35.00%	30.00%		
BY $		$1.94	$2.47	$2.67		$3.91	($0.05)	$3.47	$3.14		
BY VOLUME		10,000	25,000	27,000		8,000	2,000	21,000	37,000		
TOTAL CONTRIBUTION		$19,400	$61,750	$72,090	$153,240	$31,280	($100)	$72,870	$116,180	$220,230	$373,470

Figure 9.5

CUSTOMER SALES ANTICIPATION

CUSTOMER _____   SALESMAN _____

	1 QUARTER	2 QUARTER	3 QUARTER	4 QUARTER	YEAR
PRODUCT LINE A					
PRODUCT A1					
PRODUCT A2					
PRODUCT A3					
PRODUCT A4					
PRODUCT LINE B					
PRODUCT B1					
PRODUCT B2					
PRODUCT B3					
PRODUCT B4					

Figure 9.6

A format such as that in Figure 9.6 can be very helpful in getting the salesmen to think at the level of the specific customer, specific product, specific time frame. This detailed information is very beneficial for planning purposes.

In order to compile projected sales information from customers in a uniform and consistent manner, the following survey form can be used to solicit estimates from customers as salesmen visit with them.

CUSTOMER SALES AND CALL PLAN

CUSTOMER NAME	CUSTOMER CATEGORY	EXISTING (E) NEW (N)	PRIOR YEAR'S SALES	PROJECTED SALES	CALL PLAN
		EXISTING			
		NEW			

Figure 9.7

As the salesmen call on customers they can be polled concerning their expectations for sales of your products. Obviously, the more details addressed (specific products, colors, time, etc.) the better. From this information the salesmen can produce their call plan for getting back to the customer on a timely basis.

By using the above outline approach to product matrix analysis you can generate useful information displayed in an easily recognizable manner. The process is another tool available to you for the quantification and comparison of your marketing program.

ANALYZING THE IMPACT OF MARKETING DOLLARS

In order to maximize the utility of marketing dollars, it is important to establish quantified objectives for each marketing program and carefully monitor the results of those programs. The programs should embody significant feedback loops to allow for the modification of the marketing plan in the event it fails to be effective.

ANALYZING MARKETING COSTS

The foundation essential to success in monitoring marketing plans is a good system for identifying and assigning costs. Such foundation permits you to pinpoint wasted effort and ineffective programs. The real problem lies in the fact that many owner-managers do not have the necessary information to begin to make an analysis. Is that information not available?

Accounting systems. Typical accounting systems, following generally accepted accounting procedures, may be oriented toward external reporting and not toward sales or marketing decision-making. Such systems frequently lump all marketing costs into one or a handful of "selling expenses." The categories often used by accountants may be too broad for useful analysis of sales and marketing considerations.

Accountants' appreciation of marketing costs. Often accountants have not been adequately educated to appreciate the nature of all the various marketing elements, components, and costs. Accountants, therefore, may concern themselves chiefly with getting all marketing costs assigned somewhere—often with little regard for the appropriateness of those assignments or the behavior of the costs.

Lack of objectives. Many owners of small businesses fail to establish marketing programs with the care used to establish other objectives.

Often marketing programs are established on the basis of tradition, industry practices, or rules of thumb. Frequently, small companies try to match a competitor's sales force on a one-to-one basis, instead of setting clear, measurable objectives for marketing endeavors.

What you need, then, is to establish a marketing-oriented, cost accounting system, with the proper assignment and allocation of marketing costs, as well as a working understanding of the behavior of these costs. Finally, you should establish a formal program of marketing objectives with the obvious "results management" follow-up. This would also require the necessary feedback loop to ensure that marketing programs do not operate without close supervision and control.

Checklist for a Marketing-Oriented Cost Accounting System

Here is what a reasonable chart of accounts for sales and marketing should address.

1. *Salaries and commissions*
   a. Sales representatives
   b. Marketing management and administration
   c. Sales management
   d. Marketing communications
   e. Shipping
   f. Credit and collections
   g. Market research
   h. Order processing

2. *Marketing communications*
   a. Advertising
   b. Sales promotion
   c. Merchandising
   d. Publicity
   e. Trade shows and exhibits
   f. Direct mail
   g. Samples
   h. Literature
   i. Telephone expenses
   j. Package design

3. *Shipping*
   a. Materials
   b. Freight
   c. Depreciation

4. *Customer Service*
   a. Entry of orders
   b. Order processing
   c. Billing
   d. Telephone expenses
5. *Other marketing costs*
   a. Finished goods inventory, inventory carrying discounts
      and mark-downs
   b. Marketing research
   c. Sales office
   d. Returns
   e. Travel and entertainment
   f. Credit and collections
   g. Refunds
   h. Warranties

The above checklist is not intended to be an exclusive marketing-oriented cost accounting system. Such a system must be tailored to your specific needs. There may be other elements not on this list that should be considered in setting up the system. The objective should be to establish a marketing-oriented accounting system that permits an analysis of marketing costs and results in some detail. The marketing accounting system should also be capable of providing cost analysis on the basis of the following categories:

1. Market or market segment
2. Channel of distribution
3. Product and product line
4. Geographic region, distribution center, or sales territory
5. Account type and individual accounts

You may not feel the need for this level of sophistication. However, if you generate this information the analysis can show you what costs, other than sales and advertising, are being incurred and the results of these costs.

Nature, Behavior, or Assignment of Costs

Marketing costs do not fundamentally differ from other types of business costs; they can be broadly classified as either fixed or variable.

Variable costs. Those which vary in relation to the amount or frequency of an activity or function. Some marketing costs that may typically be classified as variable: trade discounts, cash discounts, freight charges, and sales commission.

Fixed costs. Those which do not vary in the amount of product manufactured or sold. Typically such costs include: district sales managers' salaries, base salaries for sales representatives, and cost of operating regional sales offices.

In addition, there are other fixed, general expenses that usually are treated as overhead. Such costs may include: salaries of chief operating officers and administrative staff; the cost of operating electronic data processing systems and the cost of maintaining the company's headquarters; insurance; property taxes; etc.

Contribution Accounting

In essence, contribution accounting answers the question of how much money a particular unit contributes in excess of certain agreed costs to meet the continuing demands of carrying general overhead. As shown in Chapter 3, to measure contribution to fixed expenses of a particular product, a four-step procedure is undertaken:

1. Calculate the income generated for that product.
2. Subtract the variable portion of direct labor, direct material, and any variable overhead associated with that product, at that production level.
3. Subtract other variable costs, such as commissions, freight, etc.
4. Finally, subtract the total program cost incurred solely for that product (this is a little more difficult to identify but such costs as product advertising will fall into this category).

When you have concluded this four-step evaluation, you are left with the amount available for contribution to the company's general expenses, which may also be calculated as a percentage, by dividing the contribution by the income generated in step one. Such a number is quite useful in determining a product or product line's overall effectiveness.

Continuing Programs

Even marketing programs that appear to be working effectively should be assessed periodically to guard against a decline in effectiveness. Continuous measuring of programs usually results in better program control. Complacency is one of the biggest dangers to marketing effectiveness.

Keeping products and services aimed at customers and prospective customers is a delicate combination of looking forward for trends and looking back at an analysis of accomplishments and failures. You should examine present and past records to determine weaknesses and strengths in the market. You should also look ahead and plan for the necessary changes to correct weaknesses and exploit strengths.

CORRECTING WEAKNESSES

1. One method of correcting weaknesses is to look at your product matrix and determine which items are slow movers, versus those which may be up-and-comers.

2. A second correction may come from looking to the margin available to retailers and wholesalers. A different, more liberal policy here may encourage pushing the firm's products over those of its competitors.

3. In a highly competitive market, smaller segments of that market may be targeted and efforts concentrated in those areas to improve marketing potentials. An example would be support hose for ladies, an attractive submarket of the overall hosiery market. Looking for an opportunity to target a specialized product in a segment of a general market is often rewarding. It is noteworthy that both the opportunity and associated costs in segmenting a market have to be considered. There are identifiable expenses associated with product differentiation. Advertising must be specialized and directed at the target market. Manufacturing may incur additional costs to handle the special materials used in a specialized product. Different packaging may be required.

4. Established products can drift off target when a substitute product, with more appeal to the consumer, appears in that market. You may need to look to those elements which make the competing product more attractive to customers: price, convenience, novelty, etc. If the adverse trend cannot be reversed, rather than abandon the product a viable alternative may be to find a substitute use for the product. Look at the growth in use of shock-absorber type products. They are now used for automobile rear hatch openers, rowing machines, and other weight-lifting and exercise equipment.

EXAMINING CHANNELS

Marketing channels may also be potential areas of weakness for small manufacturers. Distribution channels can lose their effectiveness for many reasons. Consumer buying habits may change, competition may develop, different cost incentives cause the channels to shift emphasis, or the company may simply develop alternative objectives. Therefore, channels should be reviewed periodically to see that they are in fact performing effectively and consistently with your objectives.

Checklist for Channel Review. Determine whether the channels are a means to an end by asking such questions as:

1. Who buys my product?
2. Where do they buy it?
3. How do they buy it, by single lots or by the dozen?
4. How frequently do they buy it?
5. Are my ultimate users satisfied in buying through present channels?

Sources of Market Information. Examine the following:

1. Warranty return cards
2. Information provided by distributors
3. Trade associations
4. Trade journals
5. Government publications

Improving Channels. Some helpful hints in improving marketing channels include:

1. You should actively seek cooperation with your resellers who have active feedback opportunities. It is through such cooperation that resellers can increase their effectiveness in moving your product.
2. Provide resellers with selling tools such as counter cards, displays, and other helpful promotional information.
3. Better cooperation may be obtained by providing distributors with technical aid and help in inventory control.
4. Monitor resellers' margins available from competitors and, if necessary, take corrective action to keep your products competitive in the eyes of the seller.
5. Finally, it may be necessary to seek new channels when present channels become ineffective.

Creative planning may offer alternatives and new methods of channeling your product to the ultimate consumer. Some examples:

1. Paperback book manufacturers found that magazine wholesalers could provide mass distribution to newsstands, drug stores, and supermarkets.

2. Producers of inexpensive throwaway pens found that distribution through tobacco wholesalers got the pens into many small stores.

3. Sometimes, as a manufacturer, you may have to set up your own organization to overcome such problems. It should be noted, however, that such action can be exceptionally costly.

Normally, changing distribution channels is not without additional costs. Old established relationships may have to be broken, and moving into new channels may interfere with relationships already existing in those channels.

In some cases, it may be necessary to change your entire business image to compensate for changing marketing strategies. For example: A drug company refused to sell its drugs through discount houses. Ultimately it had to modify its business decision and compromise to the extent that it would sell through discount houses where there were licensed pharmacists. In this way the firm increased the exposure for its product but maintained a more exclusive image.

Seven Points to Assist in the Definition of Your Business

In order to market products effectively, there are many things management should know. Some information is easily obtained, other information is difficult and expensive. The following questions may be of value in determining what you know.

1. List your five major classes of customers.
   a. What are the common characteristics of those customers?
   b. Why do they buy your product? Be *very* specific.
2. Analyze each product or product line in terms of:
   a. Revenue
   b. Percent of total revenue
   c. Profit and percent of total profit
3. List three potential customers who do not currently do business with you. *Why* don't they do business with you.

4. List five adjectives your customers use to describe the business or product. What do these words mean to you?

5. Is there any obvious ethnic, age, religious, gender, or other majority in the firm's customer base?

6. What is the most effective sales outlet?

7. If customers could not buy what you sell (even from a competitor) what would they do? This last question has some profound significance in determining how your product is perceived in the market—as luxury, necessity, etc. A well-reasoned answer will reveal the need the product meets and might also indicate alternate ways to meet that need.

Fourteen Questions to Assist in the Definition of the Market

Knowing what need you meet (or could meet) leads to the question of who has that need and what prompts them to buy. The following questions can assist you in focusing in on your market.

Demographics

1. Are products purchased primarily by any particular age group?

2. Are products purchased by any specific ethnic group?

3. Are products purchased by any one gender?

4. Are products purchased primarily within any one geographical area?

5. Are products purchased by any income level group?

6. Are sales of products tied to sales or use of other products?

7. Are sales of products tied largely to any occupational category?

8. What is the education level of the primary purchasers?

9. Who, according to the above categories, is the heaviest user of the product?

Psychographics

10. List the benefits each class of customer derives from using the product. Be *very* specific.

11. List the adjectives customers use to describe your product.

12. Which advertising has been most effective?

13. Whose endorsements might cause a person to buy the product?

14. Where are the products primarily purchased (type of store, channels of distribution, etc.)?

Demographics and psychographics are two useful approaches to gathering data to determine the characteristics and attitudes of buyers. Demographics specify groups by age, sex, income, marital status, education, and geography. It then correlates buying responses with those characteristics. Psychographics deals with buying patterns motivated by attitudes rather than external characteristics. Psychographics chart personality, values and interests.

ASSESSING THE COMPETITION

As important as it is to assess your own products and marketing processes, it is at least equally important to do a thorough analysis of the competition. Sometimes this is relatively easy and does not need to be sophisticated; sometimes it requires a great deal of research and expertise. Much of what needs to be done was referenced in Chapter 1. We will refer to a number of forms and concepts already dealt with in that material.

The Strategic Factors Analysis (Figure 1.5) and the related Suggestions for Use (Figure 1.6) can be very effectively used in the competitive assessment. Finding out who the competitors are, what their strengths and weaknesses are, and what you believe their most immediate moves might be will be very revealing. Then, a Strategic Plan of Action (Figure 1.7) will provide specific steps to be taken relative to those competitors.

Information developed in the formulation of the Saleman's Sales Forecast (by Customer) (Figure 1.9) and the Sales Forecast Summary (Figure 1.10) can produce interesting field-based perceptions of what the competition is doing and what responses are appropriate.

Another interesting and revealing approach is to apply the Thirty Questions to Assist with Strategic Planning (Appendix C of Chapter 1) to your competitors. You may find it even more difficult to answer these questions about your competitors than it is to answer them about yourself. However, the process of asking the questions and trying to determine the answers, particularly as you involve more people from your organization, will be an excellent competitive analysis.

You may also want to try to apply the Internal Data Monitoring (Appendix D of Chapter 1) to various competitors. The more information you are able to develop about how they conduct business, where they make their money, and why, the better able you will be to devise plans to improve your ability to compete. In fact, almost any of the planning tools presented in Chapter 1 can be used as competitor assessment tools as well.

Reverse engineering of products and services is a valuable tool. The process is more obvious with tangible products than with intangible services, so we will discuss products. However, it is applicable to services as well and is very helpful when so applied.

Reverse engineering of products requires you to acquire the product and to take it apart, noting every detail of its design and composition. It is an attempt to determine exactly how the product is made, what all of the components are, and why the competitor chooses to do it that way. From this you may determine a number of changes to your process that will be cost saving and/or improvements to quality.

SUMMARY

One of the initial concerns for the firm is the nature of the market, the competitors present in the market, and the availability of competitive products. This can be quickly visualized using a product matrix analysis. On the market grid, your products are located according to an analysis of the quality and price or other appropriate relationships. These relationships are based upon the assumption, for example, that demand reacts to the perception that a product's price accurately reflects the value of that product. If it does not, that too indicates an important market fact about the product or the firm. For example, if the product is selling at a price above that warranted by the quality, other factors are causing this market acceptance. This is typical for designer clothes. They are generally priced—and do, in fact, sell—above the price normally dictated for their quality. The factor driving this "price premium" is fashion or prestige. Extrinsic variables often affect the pricing policies of the firm.

Analysis of your product lines using a contribution margin analysis will indicate the financial strengths and weaknesses of your product distribution. To this you can add an analysis of the impact of your marketing dollars on sales. In doing these analyses, it may become apparent that your accounting and control systems do not account well for the marketing function. Accountants are generally concerned with fitting costs into appropriate categories and often lump all marketing costs into one or two accounts. This is probably inadequate to serve as a basis for proper marketing analysis. As part of the existing accounting system, an accounting subsystem can be developed to provide the necessary cost information for marketing decision making.

In any marketing analysis you should consider the demographics and psychographics of the markets in which you operate or intend to operate. By doing this, you identify how you are perceived, who the target of your marketing effort is, and even what business you are truly in.

Marketing analysis is, however, never complete with only an internal look. You must also look at your competitors. Virtually any information you might be interested in about yourself is also information that would help you if you knew it about your competition.

10

Financing

When considering business financing it is important to distinguish between businesses just beginning their life cycle and those that have an established business record upon which to build.

NEW BUSINESSES

Many new businesses begin operations using "stolen funds," by which we mean funds diverted from other normal financial activities unrelated to the project. Often with the inception of a new business the capital for start-up will come from personal resources. Even in larger businesses, start-up funds may come from stolen funds. As such, they may appear in another budget, not directly earmarked for the project to which they are applied.

Another source of stolen funds may be personal loans advanced by individuals using homes and items of personal property as collateral. Finally, an ultimate source of venture capital for a small business may be funds invested by, or loaned from, friends or family.

In all events, these funds represent a source not to be counted on for long-term or continued financing. As businesses start to grow, additional funds from these sources probably will not be available for continuing operations and growth. Additional resources and capital will be needed for inventory, equipment, operations, and to support accounts receivable.

Many people with new businesses are surprised to learn the amount of money needed to support accounts receivable. As the business grows, accounts receivable may seem to eat money.

Later in the chapter we will discuss sources of equity capital. At this point, however, it is important to mention that, in many circumstances, it is better to borrow money than to seek money from outside equity sources. Equity sources often dilute entrepreneurial control—a significant potential problem for smaller businesses.

Debt may be the best form of financing for at least two reasons:

- It is sometimes cheap. Interest payments on debt are made in before-tax dollars. Dividends paid on equity are in after-tax dollars. However, interest payments are mandatory and dividends can be discretionary.

- Debt has an amplifying effect on earnings. Provided the business is profitable "after debt service," as the percentage of debt to equity increases, the earnings available to stockholders increase for a given amount of earnings. That is, once debt is serviced, the additional earnings on that capital go to the stockholders, not the creditors.

TYPES OF FINANCING

Typically, businesses are financed using either or both of two forms of capital investment: debt and equity. Within these two general classifications there is an array of alternatives as diverse and creative as human imagination. Probably the only thing more complex than the means of financing available is the tax code that is intended to finance the country. The first and most common form of financing is debt.

DEBT

Debt—borrowing—can be structured with repayment in the short term, intermediate, or long term. It can be unsecured or (as is more commonly the case) secured by the assets of the business and/or owners. It typically has conditions or covenants that define the terms of the commitment and repayment of the loan.

Short-term debt is generally intended to be self-liquidating in that the asset purchased with that loan will generate sufficient cash flows to pay off that loan within one year. It is often used to finance inventory build-ups and seasonal increases in accounts receivable. Trade credit, lines of credit and commercial paper (for the large firm) are sources of short-term, unsecured financing. With some forms of short-term, unsecured financing, some extra compensation is required. For example, for a line of credit, a bank may require a compensating balance to be deposited. If you wish to establish a line of credit for $200,000, many banks require you to maintain a balance of, say, 15 percent, or $30,000, in a demand-deposit account during the year. If the compensating balance is above the amount you would ordinarily have on deposit, the cost of the incremental amount represents an additional cost of borrowing. In the above example, if you wish to borrow $200,000 and the bank rate is 12 percent, with the compensating balance of $30,000 *more* than you ordinarily have on deposit, you would net only $170,000 to use. The nominal annual dollar cost is 12 percent of $200,000, or $24,000. The actual cost of the loan as a percentage is:

$$\frac{\$24,000}{170,000} = 14.11 \text{ percent}$$

The use of compensating balances is falling with the advent of variable interest rates. Some banks are charging higher interest rates more in line with their incremental cost of money and de-emphasizing compensating balances.

Another method used by banks to improve their return is discounting. For example, under a "regular" loan a bank lends $20,000 for one year at 14 percent simple interest. At the end of the year, the borrower repays the $20,000 plus $2,800 in interest. If the loan is discounted, the bank collects its interest at the time of lending. You receive a net loan of $17,200. At the end of the year, when you repay the loan of $20,000 the actual effective interest rate is higher. It computes to:

$$\frac{\$2,800}{17,200} = 16.28 \text{ percent}$$

Secured Loans and Intermediate Financing

Many new firms cannot obtain credit on an unsecured agreement because they have no proven track record. First, banks look to your cash flow ability. Failing that, the security of the collateral pledged to insure payment must be considered. The lender will seek collateral in excess of the loan value to guarantee a margin of safety. The greater the margin of safety the more liquid the collateral, because the asset can be discounted further (and still realize full repayment) and sold more quickly to meet the call on the debt.

One method you may employ to secure your debt is borrowing against accounts receivable. The collateral to the lender is the debt owed the borrower on goods or services provided to customers. From the lender's standpoint, there is a cost to process the collateral and there is a risk of fraud and default. Therefore, this may be an expensive method of borrowing.

A loan against accounts receivable is generally made through a commercial bank because the interest rate is lower than that offered by finance companies. The lender discounts the face value of the receivables and may even reject from consideration some that have low credit ratings, are unrated, or are slow to pay.

Another factor of concern to the lender is the size or amount of each receivable. There is a trade-off: the larger the amount of the receivable, the larger the amount of potential default. But, with fewer accounts to keep track of, the cost of administration is less. A large number of small accounts have higher administrative costs, but any single default has less overall impact.

Accounts receivable financing is a continuous financing arrangement because as new accounts are added and assigned, additional security is added to the base. New receivables replace old and the amount of the loan may fluctuate with each change in the base. This form of financing is advantageous to growing companies that have growing receivables.

Selling or factoring receivables is another form of financing. When receivables are sold (with notification), the purchaser steps into the place of the seller and the customers pay the purchaser of the receivables. The sale of receivables may be with or without recourse against the seller. When the sale of receivables is without recourse, the discounting will be much higher than when the buyer of the receivable still may see recovery from the seller. Sometimes receivables are sold "without notification." In this case, customers continue to pay the goods or service provider who acts as agent for the purchaser.

The problem with selling accounts receivable is that it is often done by companies that are in financial trouble. If you are not in financial trouble and you attempt to sell accounts receivable, you may send a signal that will be incorrectly interpreted by both the customers and your lending institutions. This may have a detrimental effect despite the offsetting benefits received from the sale. You may lose customers as a result of selling their accounts. Sometimes firms that purchase accounts receivable do not have the same equitable treatment of customers in mind when they undertake collection policies. Their rigidity in collection is based upon one and only one premise—collecting their money. Your interest in collecting from your customer includes maintaining the good customers for a long time. The goals of the collection department of the receivables purchasers are not congruent with your goals.

As was stated earlier, accounts receivable financing is expensive. And selling, or factoring receivables, is quite expensive. This is because:

1. The firm purchasing receivables incurs substantial costs in collecting.

2. It also incurs front-end costs in analyzing the worth of the receivables. This analysis cost has to be recovered somewhere, and that somewhere is in the discount rate for the receivables.

3. The collection firm stands the risk of non-collections. Since there is a risk associated with non-collections, the purchasing firm will additionally discount the receivables to compensate for the percentage of potential bad debt.

4. The purchasing firm might not purchase high risk-of-default accounts, leaving the selling firm with the "worst" receivables still on its books.

Inventory Loans

Inventories, as discussed in Chapter 6 dealing with working capital and in Chapter 7 on inventories, represent a significant investment. The lender making a loan secured by inventory generally discounts the market value of the inventory based on a perception of the ease of liquidation. The advance on an inventory secured loan may be as high as 90 percent. However, lenders do not want to be in the sales business and prefer to have the loan repaid rather than have to seek foreclosure on the stock. These loans can be ongoing and variable in amount depending on the size of the inventory.

Long-Term Financing

Long-term financing is generally considered as equity-based investments. Acquiring such investment often requires the services of investment bankers who act as middlemen between a firm issuing securities and sources of funds wishing to invest those funds. Investment bankers take some of the risks associated with the selling of a company's offering. Investment banking firms are used because of their expertise.

Investment banks use two methods of obtaining offerings: bidding and negotiation. In either case, the investment banker makes a margin in the issue between the selling price and the price at which the banker purchases the offering. This margin may be small—often less than 1 percent of the offering price. This function is called underwriting and relieves the offering company of the risk of selling the issue.

Convertible Debt

The firm may issue bonds that are convertible to common stock at a given ratio. One of the arguments against convertible debt is that it may lead to further stock dilution. Other conversion options are available to corporations besides conversion of long-term debt to common stock. For example, you may convert short-term debt to long-term debt or vice versa. This later conversion can have dangerous consequences but is really no different from a creditor accelerating payments as a result of failure to meet a loan convenant.

COMMON STOCK

Common stock represents an ownership right in the firm issued to investors in return for the input of capital. Common stock has two statements of value: that which the stock certificate says and that which the market says. The stock certificate may indicate a par value, a stated value, or that the stock is issued without par or stated value. Ideally, the par or stated value should approximate the market value at date of issuance. That need not be the case. In any event, these values have legal ramifications as to the required legal capital in the company. And because various state laws govern in these cases, we recommend you see a competent corporate attorney concerning your state requirements.

The truly important value is the market value. Simply, that is what someone will pay to acquire a share of the stock. This is the perception of worth that governs how much ownership percentage you may have to surrender to acquire sufficient money to make the business go.

Investors buy common stock for cash dividends and/or appreciation in stock prices. The reason you sell common stock is to raise money. The advantage of common stock is that there is no obligation for the corporation to pay dividends in any given year. Dividends are declared at the discretion of your board of directors, assuming the company is profitable and there are sufficient additional dollars to pay the dividend.

   Unlike debt, there is no maturity date on a stock. Therefore, common stock is a financial cushion for the firm (and the creditors). The common stockholders are the ones who absorb the bad times and enjoy the profit in the good times. Common stock ownership is considered residual ownership and should be considered a risky investment.

   Companies can have approximately the same yields but different dividends and growths. A formula for yield or cost of stock equity (depending on whether you are a buyer or seller) is:

$$\text{Yield, or cost of stock equity} = \frac{\text{Annual dividend}}{\text{Stock price}} + \text{Growth}$$

Thus the real cost of common stock cannot be measured by the dividend alone; consideration should be given to the growth rate in the stock's value as well.

   When you issue more stock you are in effect selling ownership interests in the business. The problem with the sale of new stock is that it dilutes the percentage ownership of existing stockholders. For example, take a company that has three stockholders who own respective interests:

Shareholder	Percentage	Dollars	Shares (@ $100/share)
A	23%	$23,000	230
B	41%	41,000	410
C	36%	36,000	360
Total	100%	$100,000	1,000

If you sell 300 additional shares at $100 per share to D, the resulting ownership looks like:

Shareholder	Percentage	Shares
A	17.7%	230
B	31.5%	410
C	27.7%	360
D	23.1%	300
	100%	1,300

   By selling 300 new shares of common stock to D, the percentages of ownership for A, B, and C have been reduced. Sometimes, the price of the stock will also drop to reflect the additional stock selling on the market. This reaction is caused by the perception (or mis-perception) that the total value of the business hasn't changed, but is just being spread over more shares. This dilution in value may give existing stockholders certain legal rights. In the above example, if the market believes the business is worth $100,000, by selling 300 additional shares the price might drop from $100 per share to, say, $77.00. This happens because the business is perceived to be worth $100,000/1,300 shares. The value of each shareholder's interest would then be:

Shareholder	Shares	Value	Change in Value
A	230	$17,692	(5,308)
B	410	31,537	(9,463)
C	360	27,692	(8,309)

The initial stockholders may file a lawsuit against the company for these losses through a proceeding called a "derivative suit." They can claim a real loss in value as a result of a sale of additional stock by the company. For example, stockholder A claims a loss of $5,308 because the firm sold 300 shares of new issue. To protect against such a suit, you could offer the option to purchase a pro-rata share (usually this preemptive right is granted to shareholders by covenant) of the new issue to existing stockholders. In this example, the following would be offered:

A: 23% of 300 shares or   69 shares

B: 41% of 300 shares or 123 shares

C: 36% of 300 shares or 108 shares

In this way, their ownership percentages could be maintained, but the value per share may still decline. One of the governing criteria of the market price (or price per share) will be the use to which the additional funds are put and whether the value of the business appears to increase in the eyes of the market. It comes down to what the potential buyers *believe* the value of the business is. The decision to sell additional stock should be carefully considered and planned for in advance of issue. You should consider an information release indicating what plans you have for the funds. The intent is to let the market know that the value will increase with the new issue.

Common stockholders are the last to receive a return when times get difficult. There being no legal obligation to pay dividends, the business may choose not to pay them. Also, when the business is forced to liquidate assets to capital contributors, common stock owners are the last in line to share in the asset distribution.

The question, then, might be "Why not always use debt financing?"

- The stockholder may lose the expectation of future returns if you add new debt capitalization. Additional debt increases the debt service against gross profits and decreases earnings, which translates directly into a risk of reduced dividends.

- There may be a decrease in the amount of managerial freedom. Debt reduces the amount of unaccounted-for profits by increasing debt service and the fixed obligations of interest payments. This may also reduce the operating latitude of management because of the covenants to which management agrees when accepting the debt.

- As a company issues more debt, it approaches its debt capacity. As it nears this limit, it reduces the margin of safety available to issue more debt if it needs additional capital, particularly if it needs capital quickly. The company has reduced its financial flexibility.

PREFERRED STOCK

Often called a compromise investment, preferred stock has some of the attributes of common stock and some of the features of debt. Usually, a company's interest in selling preferred stock increases under the following conditions:

- The company cannot issue further debt but wants to use further leverage.
- The company does not want to dilute the interests of current common stockholders but wants more stock equity.

In either case, the company may wish to sell preferred stock. These are some of the distinguishing characteristics of preferred stock:

- While it may have a fixed rate of return (like debt) the dividend is optional and paid only when declared by the directors (but the dividend may be "cumulative" and therefore payable before any common stock dividends are paid).
- Preferred stock may have sinking funds provisions for the repurchase of the stock.
- Debt holders have a superior claim to assets in case of liquidation and have first claim to earnings. However, preferred stockholders' claims are superior to common stockholders'.

Taxes affect the amount of earnings needed to meet debt service and preferred stock dividends. However, because they receive different tax treatment, they affect earnings differently.

Suppose that both debt and preferred stock command a return of 12 percent and the applicable corporate tax rate is 46 percent. To pay the 12 percent interest rate on debt, the firm has to earn 12 percent before taxes. Interest on debt is paid in before-tax dollars. To pay the 12 percent dividend for preferred stock, the firm has to earn 12 percent in after-tax dollars.

For a 12 percent earnings after taxes, 22.2 percent—12 percent/(1 − .46)—is required in before-tax dollars. Because dividends are paid in after-tax dollars, the firm has to earn more to pay a dividend of comparable worth to an investor than it has to earn for interest.

You can see that the tax rate you pay will have a great deal to do with the amount of dividend paid for two reasons:

- The lower your real tax rate the more disposable cash you will have to reinvest and pay dividends.

- The lower your tax rate the more flexibility you can have in designing dividend policies to be attractive to investors and enhance the goodwill and value of the firm.

HOW TO OBTAIN A BANK LOAN

A businessman making a first-time loan application has greater reporting responsibilities and requirements than does a borrower who has been dealing on a continuing basis with a bank for short-term financing. Once a bank has had good experience with a borrower, a loan request is much simpler. Usually the borrower need only provide updated information for an application that is on file.

Bankers are also interested in information that is not always reflected in the financial statements. For example, they like to be informed about the borrower's management capability, organizational strength, experience, and reputation. However, in addition to this reputation information, the bank will generally require completion of certain standardized reporting forms in order to evaluate the creditworthiness of the borrower. Some of these filing requirements will be discussed below.

Projected Cash Flow Statements

One of the most effective tools to determine the amount of the loan needed and its repayment date is the projected cash flow statement. The projections should disclose the significant assumptions used by management in preparing the cash forecast. Generally, past performances will serve as the basis for preparation, but it should be adjusted to reflect current trends. Two ways of making these adjustments are 1) pro forma and 2) an attrition allowance. Pro forma adjustments reflect changes in a company's projected cash flow that are nonrecurring; an attrition adjustment can be used to reflect recurring changes and expenses. For example, if you have an agreement with labor for an annual increase of 7 percent, this would be treated as an additional allowance and grouped together with other recurring costs as an overall percentage adjustment to expenses. Nonrecurring expenses can be treated as one-item adjustments to individual expenses. An example of a typical nonrecurring item may be the payment of damages due to a loss in a personal injury lawsuit. It is not anticipated that in any succeeding period the company will lose a similar lawsuit. If it does, it should be treated as an attrition allowance.

The cash flow statement should show a monthly estimate of receipts from all sources, such as: cash sales, accounts receivable, miscellaneous income, and loans. The estimated expenditures should include capital improvement, accounts payable, taxes, payroll, other operating expenses, and repayment of loans. Many bankers request projected income statements and balance sheets as well as cash flow statements.

Financial Trends

When a banker looks at a company's figures or ratios, he is concerned not only with cash flow but also with other financial trends. The question may not be what the ratios are for the year, but rather how they compare with those of the previous years. The question that will be asked is: How does your financial picture (past, present, and projected) relate to the general economy and to the borrower's industry? Banks generally keep a record of clients' financial trends by periodically transcribing all of the vital balance sheet and operating statistics to a worksheet.

The following is a list of some of the key financial factors that banks may calculate:

1. Profitability
2. Net working capital
3. Working capital or current ratio
4. Net quick ratio
5. Ratio of debt to net worth
6. Number of days of sales in accounts receivable

7. Numbers of days of purchases in accounts payable

8. Number of days of supply of inventory (related to cost of sales)

These are discussed in Chapter 12 on ratios, but the relevant ones will be defined and briefly discussed here.

Profitability. Profitability is a measure of how well the business has been doing. At least three ratios generate meaningful potential measures of a firm's profitability:

- Net profit to net sales
- Gross profit to sales
- Net profit to net worth

It is important that your company be able to earn profits in a manner consistent with the capital invested and the expected growth. When your company shows that it has a high net profit, it not only shows that it has debt paying dollars but also that it has fresh capital to reinvest and support its own growth. These are indications of good management. A bank will be interested in looking at your year-to-year profitability and noting any trends in your ratios.

The banker will also want to see if your company's flow of net profits into its working capital is growing. He will be interested in whether profits must constantly be reinvested in fixed assets. Also, a company that pays out all of its profits in dividends and salaries will be unable to show growth in net worth from this source.

A banker will usually add back non-cash items, such as depreciation to the net profit of the company to arrive at the cash flow or debt servicing dollars available from profit. Caution must be emphasized here, for what the bank might be doing is looking to funds you have earmarked as a "reserve" for equipment replacement. While the bank may be interested in the potential use of those funds for debt servicing in the worst case, enlightened bankers will also care about replacement of worn-out assets. The best bankers are concerned with the long-term needs of the business as well as protecting their own interests.

Net Working Capital. The net working capital of the company is defined as the excess of the current assets over the current liabilities and is a significant factor to be considered for credit purposes. A bank expects a company to provide enough of its own normal working capital to carry its inventory, accounts receivable, and other current assets at prudent levels. You should be able to meet these obligations during non-peak sales periods of the year. Thus, even during slow times, the bank expects you to cover your current liabilities within the customary terms of trade.

Working Capital or Current Ratio. This is the ratio of current assets to current liabilities. It is even more significant in the bank's appraisal than in the working capital budget. Example:

Company A has current assets of $200,000
            current liabilities of 100,000
            net working capital of 100,000

The working capital ratio is 200,000 to 100,000, or 2 to 1.

Company B has current assets of 500,000
            current liabilities of 400,000
            net working capital of 100,000

The working capital ratio is 500,000 to 400,000, or 1.25 to 1.

Both firms show the same net working capital of $100,000, yet the first company is in a more favorable position in that it has $2.00 in current assets from which to pay for each $1.00 in current liabilities in the event that it must liquidate assets. The second company, on the other hand, has only a $1.25 to meet its current liabilities of $1.00. Therefore, based upon this ratio, Company A would be considered to be in a much stronger financial position.

Net Quick Ratio. Another indicator used by bankers to determine the ability of a company to pay its bills is the net quick ratio. This ratio is generally determined by taking the total of cash, short-term marketable securities, and net receivables, and dividing it by the total of current liabilities. This is a simple measure of the firm's liquidity or the ability of the company to pay its debts. Again, a bank will be more concerned with the trend established by several years of net quick ratios. This will show the bank whether you are increasing or decreasing your liquidity and hence your ability to meet your debt. Since cash and accounts receivables are far more current than inventory, this ratio is a good indicator of the relative short-term liquidity risk of the company.

Ratio of Debt to Net Worth. Another test of the adequacy of the company's net worth is the ratio of total debt, including current liabilities, to net worth. Banks will, again, generally rely more upon the trend in the ratio than in the specific number itself.

Other debt ratios are discussed in Chapter 12.

Number of Days of Sales in Accounts Receivable. In calculating this number, the following assumptions are made:

- An even flow of sales.
- A uniformity in collecting accounts receivable.

The question here is the average number of days it takes you to collect your accounts as compared with other firms within the same industry. The banks will factor in the number of days normal for the terms of the sale and those of the industry. For example: Assume a firm has average daily credit sales of $20,000 and accounts receivable are $1,800,000. The terms of the sale are 30 days. The first step is to divide the accounts receivable of $1,800,000 by 20,000, the average daily credit sales. This indicates that 90 days of sales are still in accounts receivable and that the accounts receivable are taking longer to collect than the normal 30-day terms. In fact, on average, this company is collecting its accounts receivables 60 days after the expiration of the due date.

This is 60 days more than the pricing policy allows; it is probably having considerable financial effects on cash flow.

This also indicates that management may not be doing a good job of managing its accounts receivable. However, this may also be typical for the industry. If this is your situation, you should take some steps to try to improve your accounts receivables collection policy. You are loaning money to your customers for *an average* of 60 days *more* than you intended when you set your terms of sale. This has significant cost consequences.

Number of Days of Purchases in Accounts Payable. This figure is computed by dividing the average daily purchases into the accounts payable. If, for example, the average daily purchases are $5,000 and the accounts payable are $150,000, the number of days purchases in accounts payable is 30 days. This number tells a banker quickly if you are paying your bills promptly. Significant variations from normal trade terms must be explained. If you are on a net 30-day cycle, then you are meeting your obligations and perhaps obtaining all of the discounts you are entitled to under the terms of your purchase agreements. That question requires further examination. The ratio is helpful but you should also be concerned with those accounts payable for which discounts were lost and not only the average payments.

You should be examining your aging of payables and monitoring discounts lost.

Number of Days of Supply of Inventory. This number is computed by dividing the *cost* of the inventory by the average daily cost of sales, assuming an even flow of sales. The answer gives the banker the average number of days it takes the company to turn over inventory. The abuse that the bank is looking for here is excess inventory. This ratio will vary substantially from business to business. Supermarkets generally have very short inventory cycles, whereas automobile dealers have longer cycles.

Other Supplemental Data. Other information that should be considered for submission in the loan request presentation includes:

1. A summary of insurance coverage.
2. An analysis of profitability by product line, if available and applicable.
3. Unusual events, historical or prospective, affecting the company.
4. Concentration, if any, of sales within a small number of customers. This shows the bank the reliance upon a few select customers. If sales are concentrated in very few buyers, as in the aerospace industry, the risk associated with that industry may be considered to be somewhat higher.
5. Analysis of the effect of special situations on the company, such as a LIFO method of inventory evaluation.

Letters of Credit

You may not want to borrow any money from a bank; however, a prospective subcontractor or provider of raw materials may be unsure as to your creditworthiness. A method for improving your assumed creditworthiness that may be available at low cost is the purchasing of a letter of credit.

If your company is new or is experimenting with a new product or product line, some vendors will refuse to sell you materials on a trade accounts payable basis. They would instead prefer to have you establish creditworthiness by showing good payment records. A possible way around this problem is to obtain a letter of credit and, in effect, to use the good credit standing of a bank. By obtaining a letter of credit you are is saying: "If we fail to pay you, the bank will pay you." The bank then has recourse to you for its money.

In this way you are advancing the bank's creditworthiness. Typically, letters of credit cost 1 percent of the amount you wish to advance and the letter of credit is normally good for one year. The real cost of a letter of credit depends on how frequently you wish to purchase using the letter of credit as a guarantee of payment.

For example: Suppose a supplier of raw materials wants his money net 30 days, but is willing to extend credit for 90 days if you provide a letter of credit. Also, suppose that the letter of credit costs 1 percent. Since you are having money advanced for two additional months for the cost of 1 percent, this is the same as borrowing money at 6 percent per annum, assuming the letter of credit and the materials purchased are the same amount. However, each time you use the guarantee of the letter of credit during the year it is still taking advantage of that one-time payment of 1 percent. The more the firm uses the letter of credit, the cheaper (on a cost-per-transaction basis) the cost of the guarantee.

You may consider joint ventures. Joint ventures are, essentially, a technique whereby you change your organizational structure. However, this is still a form of financing whereby you use the financial creditworthiness of a collective entity to improve the market appearance to lenders and investors. The financial strength of two or more entities is put behind the joint venture entity.

THE SOURCES OF DEBT FINANCING

A business may consider a number of financial institutions as possible lenders. The large and popular ones include:

1. *Banks.* Both commercial banks and savings and loan associations grant a significant portion of all the available credit they have on hand to businesses.

2. *Commercial finance companies.* Most commercial finance companies have a specialty, such as discounting accounts receivable. Interest rates are generally higher with finance companies because as a financing source they seem to be institutions of last resort. Companies that are unable to find other means of financing may resort to commercial finance companies.

3. *Insurance companies.* Many large insurance companies participate in investment banking both directly and indirectly. Typically, insurance companies loan substantial blocks of money. Because of this, the typical

insurance company borrower is a large company. They do not as often or as readily extend credit to smaller companies. Insurance companies prefer transactions of $1,000,000 or more. Some insurance companies are interested only in transactions greater than $5,000,000.

4. *Brokerage houses.* Many stock brokerage houses offer or arrange financing that ranges from bonds and commercial paper to private loans from individual investors. Brokerage houses do just as their name suggests: they broker money from sources to ultimate users.

5. *Investment bankers.* Investment banking may be a function of any of the previously named lenders. They generally facilitate the sale of security issues, through either a bidding process or a contractual arrangement. For a fee, they use their expertise and market contacts to sell securities.

In some financing agreements, the lender takes an equity position in connection with a loan or takes an option or warrant to buy stock in the event that the company grows. This is known as a "kicker" or "sweetener" and is generally viewed by borrowers as giving up some possible future control over the business in exchange for controlling current costs. Many investors wish to have some financial or managerial say over the direction and nature of the business. Typically, when substantial funds are loaned to your business, you have to give up some measure of control.

6. *Venture capitalists.* Venture capitalists may be investment bankers when they invest capital, make loans, and give management advice intended to assist the company to achieve significant growth. Many companies financed by venture capitalists convert from closely held corporations to public corporations during the course of their growth.

7. *Government loans and grants.* A wide variety of loan programs are offered by the federal government. Some are direct loans, others are government sponsored or guaranteed loans channeled through banks. Small Business Administration loans are available to smaller businesses. Additionally, the federal government has a program for small business innovation research grants. These grants are intended to assist small businesses in obtaining financing for the development of specific ideas.

8. *Federal tax laws.* The federal tax code provides some options for deferring taxes. This is essentially an interest-free loan. Many large corporations, by taking advantage of deferred taxes, have in effect put off the payment of taxes for many years.

TYPES OF LOAN ARRANGEMENTS

1. *Commercial loan.* The terms of a commercial loan are designed to repay the loan on the basis of specific assets or business cycle activities.

These loans may take the form of either short-term or long-term commitments.

2. *Leases.* Many lending institutions offer a choice between debt and a lease. Leases are obligations for the specific assets, and are generally fixed as to rate and payment. In addition, most offer a purchase option. Some caution must be exercised in selecting between leasing and outright purchase with a mortgage. Very often, under the terms of the lease, significantly higher costs are incurred over the costs of the outright purchase of the item.

3. *Mortgage.* A mortgage secures a loan by pledging an asset as collateral, with an associated repayment schedule. Amortization schedules of repayment show the principal and interest payments over the life of the mortgage.

4. *Balloon loan.* Balloon loans are very similar to mortgages except that the maturity date occurs before the end of amortized schedule. The repayment terms are based on a long-term commitment. However, an unpaid balance or balloon payment is due and payable after a specified time. A typical example of a balloon payment would be a 20-year mortgage with a requirement that after five years of payment on the mortgage the unpaid balance of the principal is due. The advantage to a lender of a balloon mortgage is that he obtains significant interest payments during the early years of the mortgage. It is during this period that the interest constitutes the bulk of the payment. The benefit to the borrower is that he expects to pay off the principal without incurring further interest liabilities after a few years of operation. In addition, these interest payments represent significant deductions for tax purposes. Remember that if the firm is paying taxes at the rate of 46 percent on profits, the federal government is returning $.46 on *each* dollar of interest paid. Very often these loans provide for refinancing in the event that the balloon payment cannot be met.

5. *Leverage-financed loans.* These loans are used to acquire businesses. The largest percentage of funds used to acquire a business is supplied by a lender, who secures all assets. These loans ostensibly are attractive to borrowers because if a firm is heavily leveraged a smaller increment of profit yields a much higher percentage return on equity. For example, compare:

Firm A: Makes $100,000 profit (after taxes) and is capitalized for $1,000,000. It has 50% debt, 50% equity.

The firm realizes a return on equity of:

$$\frac{100,000}{50\% \times 1,000,000} \text{ or } \frac{100,000}{500,000} \text{ or } 20\%$$

Firm B: Makes $100,000 profits (after taxes) and is capitalized for $1,000,000. It has 80% debt, 20% equity.

The firm realizes a return on equity of:

$$\frac{100,000}{20\% \times 1,000,000} \text{ or } \frac{100,000}{200,000} \text{ or } 50\%$$

For the same level of after-tax profits, for the same size firms, the higher the leverage the greater the percentage return on equity. The fallacy in the cited example is that Firm B would have to pay interest on the additional $300,000 of debt.

The greater the debt to equity ratio the greater the risk, because the fixed obligation to pay debt service increases. However, this relationship to risk may be incorrect if you can show substantial cash flow ability to service the debt. Therefore, the debt to equity ratio can be misleading without additional information.

6. *Bonds.* Bonds represent debt sold to lenders either privately or through public underwriting. Usually, a business needs to be fairly substantial in size to float a bond issue. Bonds typically are not available to small businesses except in some special cases, where they are backed by local governmental units.

7. *Commercial paper.* Commercial paper is offered by large, stable companies intent on raising working capital for short periods of time. Commercial paper generally is sold in a public market and is in the form of short-term, unsecured promissory notes. The usual denominations are $25,000 and over.

Small Business Administration loans. The SBA generally guarantees a bank loan, thereby lowering the risk and interest cost for the borrower. These loans are intended for business people who can qualify based on certain profiles. Usually these loans are offered only after a firm has been turned down by two banks but otherwise qualifies for an SBA loan. These loans may be based on needs such as a business in a hardship area or areas where unemployment is high. Occasionally, these loans are extended for areas in which a natural disaster has occurred.

9. *Economic Development Authority loans.* EDA loans generally relate to social goals promoted by the authority, such as increasing minority employment or employment in depressed areas. These loans are made and administered through state agencies. The nature of these loans is to obtain working capital allowances and not generally to purchase specific assets.

10. *Industrial revenue bonds.* Industrial revenue bonds are issued through governmental agencies and are intended for use in the acquisition of real estate and equipment. The governmental agency issues the bonds, which

are then purchased by investors, often banks. Because they are governmental bonds, they are tax exempt. As such, the prevailing interest rate on IRB's is lower than the prevailing market rate. A great deal of criticism has been leveled against IRB's because some businesses, which compete with others that get IRB's, complain they are unable to acquire similar low-interest money and thus are less able to compete.

11. *Research and development financing arrangements.* Often companies and private investors have entered into creative financing arrangements in order to raise necessary funds to pay for research and development. These have taken the shape of limited partnerships in recent years. Typically, the sponsoring company contributes the right to a product in a limited partnership, in exchange for an interest in the partnership, often as the general partner. Capital contributions by limited partners usually provide funds for R & D that may be subcontracted to the sponsoring company or even to other entities. The limited partners expect to receive income in the form of royalties from the sale and development of the product. They may also receive income tax breaks in the form of capital gains rates. The major advantage to the sponsor is that in the event that the project fails, no repayment of the loan is required and there is no liability for interest cost.

RESTRICTIONS ON LOANS

Very often when an institution is considering making substantial loans to a company, it requires, as part of the loan, agreements to control the business activities and obtain reports about the current status of the firm. Typically these arrangements will include:

1. *Limitations on the purchase of new assets.* Some lenders have a policy to keep additional expenditures low after a loan has been made. This has the effect of slowing or stopping growth. You should negotiate with the lender to ensure that this is not an absolute limitation on acquisition of new assets. Be sure that additional new assets can be purchased on a regular basis if there is provable growth associated with the need for those purchases. Show the lender that through planned growth, the risk of default is lessened. Planned growth can be accomplished only by the acquisition of additional assets based upon a schedule and a good business plan.

2. *Limitations on additional debt.* Once again, a lender may try to restrict the incurring of additional debt. This too has the detrimental effect of limiting growth. When you negotiate with the lender, make it clear that

additional debt may have to be incurred in order to sustain regular growth. An adequate business plan will certainly help as bargaining leverage for the execution of the appropriate terms in the lending agreement. The selling point to the lender is that additional debt supports additional income through growth. As you grow, so does the lender's security of repayment.

3. *Salary restrictions*. Because salaries of chief executives and other executives are a direct expense, lenders will typically want some restriction on these salaries so they do not skyrocket. Large increases in these salaries will dig into the profits of the firms, sometimes radically increasing expenses. You should counter with a reasonable alternative, which may include tying the increases to profitability, earnings, or the general growth in the gross income of the firm. This also has the beneficial effect of motivating management.

4. *Dividend restrictions*. If the company pays dividends, you should attempt to negotiate a reasonable formula for payment. You are confronted with the competing interests of debt holders and holders of equity. The lender may try to put an absolute prohibition on the payment of any dividends. This allows for the additional retained earnings to be used for debt servicing. But it may have a chilling effect on the raising of additional equity capital. Your attraction as an equity investment opportunity is based on two factors: your absolute growth in net worth and the income stream of dividends. A "no dividends" policy reduces your attractiveness of an equity investment possibility.

Typically, firms will be required to provide lenders with regular financial reports. Lenders will generally require financial statements accompanied by a certified public accountant's report. Audited reports certified by CPA's are costly and time consuming documents to prepare. Look to reduce the requirement to a cheaper alternative such as a review or even a compilation.

If You Are a Small Firm

Some people think that when they incorporate they absolve themselves of any personal liability for the debt incurred by the business in its operation. Legally that might be true. However, lenders too have learned that people try to limit their personal liability by incorporating and often require certain personal guarantees by the business owner. Some banks may want you to sign a general guarantee of the business loan as a sign of "good faith" or as a "personal commitment" to the business. That kind of guarantee can be dangerous because it typically has no limits.

1. *Specific personal assets.* As a rule it is not wise to risk everything you own. If a pledge of "good faith" is required by the lender, pick one particular asset to risk. Do not risk more than you are willing to lose in any situation.

2. *The value of business collateral already offered.* Typically, lenders will require as much collateral as they can reasonably get. They may even seek collateral that is unreasonable. In such cases, it may be a benefit to you to prepare reports showing the extent and valuation of those assets pledged to secure the loan. Often appraisals by independent groups as to the value of real estate and other assets tend to dissuade the bank from seeking further collateral.

3. *Stock in the business as collateral.* If the business has some attractiveness and a reasonably high probability of success, the lender may take back some stock as collateral. You should be wary that you are not giving up so much stock that you lose control of your business.

CONDITIONS THAT A BORROWER SHOULD SEEK

The success of the business depends on you. Too much reliance upon the lending institution to help run the business may prove disastrous. There should, therefore, be flexibility in the agreement to let the business grow and be successful. Advice and help from the lender should not be overlooked. It may be a lifesaver. Lenders may have had experience with other similar businesses and you can profit from that experience. As a borrower, you should request the following considerations in the lending agreement:

1. *There should be an option available to you to refinance at any time.* Often the lender will qualify this provision to permit refinancing only after a certain period of time or with a prepayment penalty. You may need this provision in order to take advantage of lower prevailing interest rates should they occur.

2. *A conversion agreement should allow for more favorable loan conditions once certain "growth forecasts" have been met.* You should require that this provision take into consideration the fact that as your business grows its risks may decrease. Because interest rates should be tied to perceived risk, as you prove your viability and success you are entitled to pay less of a loan premium; arguably your riskiness has been reduced.

3. *Agree on no prepayment penalty.* Changing financial conditions may provide you with sufficient cash to prepay the loan. This may be done to realize significant tax benefits, as a requirement for the obtaining of

additional financing, or to put you in a better business posture. Prepayment generally will work no hardship on the lender other than to take away the guarantee of expected future earnings. There would be nothing to stop the lender from reloaning this money to other individuals and thus recovering the future earnings from someone else. The lender's risk is that the money cannot be reloaned at equal or better rates.

4. *Request limitation on interest rates.* Currently the vogue is variable interest rate. The federal government has placed certain requirements on capping the variability of some interest rates. You should be aware of limitations or caps on rates and make this a major consideration in determining whether to enter into the financing agreement.

5. *Agree on the possibility of increased loan based upon meeting certain tests.* Very often if you are successful and the business is growing within certain predictable ranges, additional debt financing may be necessary to continue the growth pattern. As such, you may want the loan agreement to provide for additional advances of debt to aid in sustaining that growth. A lender should consider himself an ongoing business partner in these agreements. As you grow, so does the income of the lender. Some loans have an absolute upper credit limit and you may borrow up to that limit without further formal application.

6. *The agreement should specify identifiable assets that are pledged as collateral.*

7. *Seek a loan "grace" period of 30 to 60 days for noncompliance with debt arrangements.* Very often this provision will require a notification by you to the lender in advance that you will use the provision. There will probably be a limit on how frequently this can be done. Lenders may be more willing to permit minimum defaults when there is a plan submitted showing how you will make it up after appropriate notice to the lender. The worst thing you can do is surprise your lender. In most cases, they would rather work out a mutually agreeable accommodation than seek legal redress.

SUMMARY

Financing is in some respects similar to the operational side of the business. They each have associated risks and returns. Each has strategic consequences for your firm.

There are two fundamental sources of financing: debt and equity. Each has certain consequences. Debt, either secured by property or unsecured, is the most common form of financing. It has fixed repayment requirements for both principal and interest. Failure to make interest payments, unless otherwise provided for, generally results in default. Additionally, interest payments are made with before-tax dollars. As such, depending upon the tax rate, interest payments are in effect discounted by your federal tax liability. The relative amount of debt financing has a multiplying effect on your earnings. The greater the percentage of debt to equity for a fixed amount of profits, the greater the percentage return on equity.

You may seek to raise capital through the sale of ownership. This is done through the issuance and sale of stock. There are two forms of certificates that businesses generally sell: common and preferred stock. Common stock carries with it no obligation to pay a dividend. Preferred stock, on the other hand, may have a fixed rate, as does debt, but payment is optional if no dividends are declared. Dividends on preferred stock (sometimes cumulative over a period of years) have to be met *before* payment can be made to common stock holders.

Obtaining financing is a matter of convincing conservative lenders or investors to part with their money. As in all selling, it is a process of convincing these people that risks are low and that reasonable returns will compensate them for taking the risk. Your best method of selling is through the use of a good business plan showing good ratios and a sound financial picture. One of the chief objectives should be to build a lasting, sound financial relationship with these sources.

Remember that many of the terms of a financial agreement are negotiable. Therefore, when approaching any such situation, try to be prepared to negotiate from strength. The more preliminary work you do in getting ready to deal with lenders and investors, the greater the likelihood of a more favorable financial agreement.

III

EVALUATING THE OPERATIONS OF THE BUSINESS

The first two sections addressed the tasks to be accomplished before the business, or operating period, begins, and those that are ongoing during the operating period. Naturally, there is a close connection between what you determine to do—your plan—and what you actually do.

In this section we discuss what happens when the operating period is completed. This may be an intermediate time—not necessarily the end of a complete fiscal year. For example, some of what we discuss in these final five chapters is equally appropriate to monthly or quarterly considerations.

As Section I and II were closely related, so Section III is closely linked to both of them. The topics to be covered here—

Reporting

Ratios

Taxes and Insurance

Business Valuation

Professional Advisors

—flow directly out of your intended accomplishments as well as actual ones during the fiscal period.

__11__

Reporting

Every business organization has numerous reporting responsibilities. In this chapter we will discuss some of the reporting requirements of the federal, state, and local governments; creditors; and equity owners. In view of the variety of responsibilities that governmental units place on various types of businesses, you are advised to use the services of a competent accountant and/or attorney to assure compliance with all reporting requirements. Because they change so frequently, specific rates, caps, and eligibility rules have been avoided.

FEDERAL GOVERNMENT REQUIREMENTS

Federal Employer Identification Number

Every new business must file for and obtain a proper Federal Employer Identification (FEI) number from the federal government. This number identifies the business and is the key for filing and reporting taxes. All federal taxes paid or filed by a business use the FEI as a reference. It is obtained upon request by filling out Federal Form SS–4. Some states also use an employer identification number of their own. Information concerning this requirement may be obtained by contacting your state's department of revenue or taxation.

The FEI number is used to identify the business entity for more than tax purposes. Other federal agencies reference the number for compilation of other information relative to business activities such as employment statistics. It is comparable to an individual's social security number.

Employment Reports

When your business employs and pays wages to even one employee it becomes subject to the provisions dealing with payroll taxes. As an employer you are responsible for the state and federal income taxes and social security taxes withheld from your employees' paychecks and for the taxes assessed directly against you, such as social security and unemployment. Payroll taxes must be deposited by specific dates, which vary according to the amounts payable. You should contact the Internal Revenue Service for booklets that provide this information.

- *New employees.* You are required to have each new employee fill out a W–4 form. This form requires the employee to produce a social security number. On the W–4 form, the employee specifies the number of withholding allowances claimed. With that number, and the marital status and salary of the individual, you can compute withholding tax amounts.

- *Social Security Taxes.* Social security taxes are calculated at rates which vary almost annually. The important thing to remember is that this tax is paid by both the employer and the employee. You not only have to withhold appropriate amounts, you also contribute to this fund.

The income tax and the social security tax must be withheld, deposited, reported, and paid by employers to the government. The social security tax withheld from the employee is matched by the employer when deposited.

- *FUTA (Federal Unemployment Tax).* This tax is deposited, reported, and paid by you, the employer, only. The employee does not pay this tax. The tax applies to wages paid to each employee during the calendar year up to a maximum. Once an employee reaches this cap, no additional tax is due.

What Are Wages Subject to Taxes? The IRS makes available publications on what constitutes wages for the purpose of tax liabilities. It is difficult to do the subject justice; however, wages subject to taxes include all compensation given to an employee for services performed. The pay may be in cash, vacation allowances, bonuses, and commissions. Other special considerations to be checked in current IRS publications include:

- Partially exempt employment
- Moving expenses
- Fringe benefits
- Taxable tips

Depositing Taxes. Federal Deposit Coupon Books (Form 8109) are used to deposit paid and withheld taxes. The preprinted coupons are basically a form with boxes for the amount of each tax paid, the FEI number and the tax period against which the payment is being made. The coupon is mailed or delivered along with a single payment covering the taxes to a Federal Reserve Bank (serving your area) or, more likely, to an authorized financial institution. The frequency of payment depends upon the amount due at the end of the month; you should determine your required deposit periods in consultation with your accountant or attorney.

Filing Returns and Reporting Taxes. FUTA taxes are reported quarterly, using Form 940. The deposit is due by the last day of the first month after the quarter. If the amount due for any quarter is less than $100, it may be carried over and paid in the next quarter's report.

For income taxes withheld and for social security (FICA) taxes, the employer files a quarterly report on Federal Form 941. There are some exceptions to this rule related to agricultural employers, household employers, state and local governments, and some others.

Willful failure to file returns and pay taxes when due will result in criminal and civil penalties. The same is true for willful filing of false or fraudulent returns. In some cases, where income and social security taxes are not withheld and not paid to the IRS, individuals of the corporation or partnership may be held individually liable for the payment of these taxes along with a penalty of up to 100 percent of the taxes wrongfully uncollected.

Some hints on filing:

- Do not report more than one quarter of taxes on a return.
- If your business is seasonal and you temporarily stop paying wages, file returns even though you have no taxes to report.
- Use the IRS's preprinted forms and envelopes for filing returns and reports.

Wages and Tax Statement. By January 31 of each year an employer must provide each employee a statement of wages and taxes. This report, form W–2, includes all wages, tips, other compensations, and withheld income and social security taxes. Other payments may be included when applicable: bonuses, vacation allowances, severance pay, moving expenses, taxable fringe benefits, some kinds of travel expenses, and others.

Income Tax Return

Tax rules vary according to whether the operation of the business is as a sole proprietorship, a partnership, a regular C-corporation, or an S-corporation. These tax rules may affect how the firm carries out its business activities.

Sole Proprietorships. In order to qualify as a sole proprietorship, you must be self-employed and the sole owner of an unincorporated business. Schedule C is filed with a Federal Form 1040 (personal tax return) by April 15 of the year following the fiscal year reported.

In a sole proprietorship there is no tax effect for taking money out of the business for personal use or transferring personal money to the business. However, you should set up and keep separate accounts to keep track of identifiable business expenses and personal withdrawals. Failure to keep adequate business records has been the downfall of many sole proprietorships.

Partnerships. A partnership is the relationship between two or more persons for the purpose of carrying out a trade or business for a profit. Each person contributes money, property, labor, or skill, expecting to share in the profits or losses of the enterprise.

If a husband and wife carry on a business together and expect to share in the profits and losses, they may come under the definition of a partnership for the purposes of taxes. This may occur even by operation of law, where the husband and wife have not executed a form of partnership agreement.

Income from a partnership is reported on Form 1065, U.S. Partnership Return of Income. Also included will be a separate schedule SE Computation of Social Security Self Employment Tax. These are "information only" returns. Taxes will be paid in quarterly estimates as a part of the partners' personal (1040) tax reporting.

But for a few exceptions, a partnership determines its income in much the same way that an individual determines his income. In determining their income tax liability for the year on their own income tax returns, partners must take into account, separately, each partner's *distributive share*. This consideration must be made whether or not the following items are distributed:

- Gains or losses associated with the sale of capital assets.
- Gains or losses from sale or exchange of certain property used by the business.
- Charitable contributions.
- Dividends or interest for which there is an exclusion or deduction.
- Other items of income, gains or losses, as explained in Schedule K, Form 1065.

Corporations. Many areas of corporation taxation are quite complex and cannot adequately be dealt with here. For a more complete discussion of corporate tax consequences, the IRS publication 542, *Tax Information on Corporations*, may be helpful to you.

Every corporation must file a tax return, even if it had no taxable income for the year and regardless of the amount of its gross income for the year. The income tax return for the regular corporation is Form 1120. As in the case of individual taxpayers, the federal government has a short-form application for taxes of small U.S. corporations; Form 1120-A, U.S. Short-form Corporation Income Tax Return. In order to qualify to use the short form, the business must meet certain requirements which have usually been:

- Gross receipts do not exceed $25,000
- Total income does not exceed $25,000
- Total assets do not exceed $250,000
- No foreign owners, direct or indirect, of 50% or more of its stock.
- It is not a member of a controlled group or a personal holding company.
- It is not a consolidated corporation return filer.
- It is not undergoing liquidation or dissolution.
- It is not an S-corporation, life or mutual insurance company, or other company filing a specialized form. For more information, use the instructions for Form 1120 and 1120–A.

If the corporation files a return on a calendar year basis, then the return is to be filed by March 15 following the calendar year. If the corporation uses a fiscal year other than a calendar year, then the report must be filed by the 15th day of the third month after the fiscal year. The return is filed with the Internal Revenue Office serving the area where the corporation maintains its principal office—that is, where it maintains its principal books and records.

A corporation will receive an automatic six-month extension for filing a return by submitting an application for an extension on a Form 7004. The IRS can terminate this extension at any time prior to the expiration of the six-month period. Interest is charged on the difference between the tentative tax reported on the Form 7004 and the actual tax the corporation must pay when it files its Form 1120.

Failure to file on the date required without good cause shown may result in the imposition of a delinquency penalty of 5 percent of the tax due. This penalty will apply to the first month due and may be increased by 5 percent per month for each subsequent month, up to a cap of 25 percent. To avoid penalties you will have to give an explanation of good cause; that statement will be made under penalty of perjury.

If after filing a Form 1120 or Form 1120–A you wish to correct an error on the return, you may do so by filing a Form 1120X, Amended U.S. Corporation Income Tax Return. You can use this method when you discover that you may have misstated income, or failed to claim a deduction or credit.

Estimated Income Tax. Many, if not most, corporations are required to file and to pay an estimated tax. A corporation's estimated tax is the amount of its expected tax liability less its allowable tax credits. You must deposit this estimated tax with an authorized financial institution or with the Federal Reserve Bank. Each tax payment must be accompanied by a federal tax deposit coupon, according to the instructions in the coupon book.

S-Corporations. Some business owners prefer not to be subject to federal corporate income tax liability. If the corporation qualifies, its income will be taxed to the shareholders individually, like a partnership, rather than the corporation. For a complete discussion of the tax liabilities and calculations, the Internal Revenue Service provides *Publication 589, Tax Information on S-Corporations*.

To qualify as an S-corporation the following requirements have normally been applicable:

- All shareholders must elect to be an S-corporation.
- You must have a permitted tax year.

- You must file *Form 2553—Election by a Small Business Corporation,* indicating your choice to be treated as an S-corporation.
- You must be a domestic corporation.
- You must have only one class of stock.
- You must not have more than 35 stockholders.
- You must have only individuals or their estates as stockholders.
- You must not have a nonresident alien as a shareholder.
- You must not be a member of an affiliated group of corporations.
- You must not be:
  1. A domestic international sales corporation.
  2. A company that serves as a financial institution, taking deposits and making loans.
  3. An insurance company taxed under Subchapter L.

The permitted tax year is generally a calendar year ending December 31. Other years may be requested but require approval from the IRS.

Other Specialized Reporting Areas

Specialized business. Certain businesses have specialized reporting for reasons of the exercise of the federal police powers clause. Businesses such as those dealing in firearms sales and transportation, tobacco sales, liquors and spirits, ethanol production, travel agencies, and others have special reports. Most have some relation to the health, safety, morals, and welfare of citizens. These reporting requirements vary for different businesses. For example, dealers in firearms require federal licenses depending on whether the dealer sells rifles and shotguns, handguns, or transports weapons in interstate commerce. In addition, sales have to be reported on various forms prepared and submitted by the dealer.

Special agencies. Many federal agencies require periodic and regular reporting of various business functions. For example, EPA—air and water quality, OSHA—workplace safety and employee health, FERC—utility fuel costs, ICC—motor and rail carrier rates and charges, FCC—depreciation rates, service charges, and terms and conditions of service. This is not meant to be an exhaustive list. Such a list would comprise a book in itself.

The discussion of federal reporting requirements has been, by necessity, brief and general. You should contact an accountant and/or attorney to assure compliance with all reporting requirements. Also, it is a good idea to make use of the publications provided by the various agencies.

STATE GOVERNMENT REQUIREMENTS

Unemployment Insurance

Unemployment insurance provides a temporary source of income to make up a part of the wages lost by workers who lose their jobs through no fault of their own and who are willing and able to work. Although the programs may vary from state to state, the following description is representative.

You, the employer, generally pay for unemployment insurance as one of your businesses expenses. Typically, workers pay no part of the premium. The premiums go into a reserve fund to pay claims as they arise. Many states consider the stability of an employer's employment history when establishing your tax rate.

As a new employer, you are required to report your initial employment in the month following the calendar quarter in which employment begins. The regulating agency then determines whether you are liable for taxes. Typical state eligibility requirements include:

- That in a calendar year a business has:
  1. A $1,500 quarterly payroll, or
  2. One or more employees.
- Liability for Federal Unemployment Tax.
- Purchase of a liable business.

Reporting. If you are liable for the payment of unemployment insurance, you will be required to make periodic reports and payments of taxes. You may be required to report:

- Total wages paid to covered workers, excess wages, taxable wages, and taxes due.
- Individual wage listings with each employee's social security number, name, weeks worked, and total wages paid.

This report is usually required to be filed along with the proper amount of taxes one month after the quarter in which the qualifying employment occurred.

Timely filing is necessary in order to:

- Receive the maximum amount of credit against the Federal Unemployment Tax for the State Unemployment Taxes paid.
- Get proper credit for calculating the experience rating.
- Avoid penalty and interest charges established by law for late payment and late reports.

Sales and Use Taxes

Sales and use taxes vary greatly from state to state. Their applicability, rates, and exemptions from taxation are dissimilar across state boundaries. In addition, many counties and cities have local option sales and special use taxes. Information relative to your state and local government should be obtained from the offices of the state department of revenue or taxation *and* from the county or city government. The following discussion will serve as an example but may not be typical of your state.

Registration. Every person, partnership, corporation or S-corporation desiring to engage in business in the state will generally be required to secure a certificate of registration for each place of business within the state. You may not have to comply with this requirement if your business is engaging in an enterprise not subject to sales and use tax. There is usually a nominal fee ($5–$25) associated with the filing for a certificate. Sales tax of about 4–8 percent is levied on qualifying sales made within a state. A use tax is generally the same rate but the tax is paid on qualifying items brought into the state to be used, consumed, distributed, rented, or stored for use or consumption.

Exemptions in Some States Include:

- Groceries and produce, except those prepared within a premise for consumption
- Medical—prescription and household medicines
- Telephone and utility service (other taxes, however, may apply to these transactions
- Sale of livestock, poultry, and produce if the sales are made by the producers
- Professional services
- Subscriptions
- Rentals

Payments. Sales taxes are usually payable to the state by a certain date, for example, the 20th day of the month following the collection of the tax. Some states offer quarterly filing of the tax. Some offer quarterly filing for small businesses and even monthly estimated filings for business that collect large sums of tax in any one month. Some states allow the business or person collecting the tax to retain a portion of the collection as a fee for the collection process itself. Finally, items purchased for resale may be exempt from the tax. This is usually the case, to avoid double and sometimes triple taxation of an item.

State Corporate Income Taxes

Many states have a form of corporate income taxes. These taxes are imposed upon all domestic and foreign corporations for the privilege of doing business, or earning or receiving income within the state. Generally, individuals, partnerships, and estates or trusts are not liable for this tax.

Reporting. A return is generally required by a state if 1) a federal income tax return is filed or 2) the taxpayer is liable for payment of taxes. The return is usually filed on the first day of the fourth month after the close of the taxable year or the 15th day after the due date for the filing of the related federal returns for the taxable year. Some states allow for automatic extensions. However, they usually require payment of estimated taxes. Any underpayment of estimated taxes will usually be assessed both penalty and interest. These can be as much as 12–15 percent on the amount of underpayment. Remittance of the tax is due at the same time the return is filed. Some states have provisions related to the federal penalty provisions for nonfiling without just cause. Interest is generally applicable at a fixed rate and the state may even penalize a company for fraudulent returns. Some states assess a penalty for failure to file a return even when no taxes are due.

Tax Basis and Rates. The tax is generally applicable to all forms of income, including capital gains at (usually) a uniform rate. States typically model their code provisions so as to be consistent with applicable federal code provisions.

Individual Income Tax

If the business operates as a sole proprietorship, a partnership, or an S-corporation, the profits of those entities may be subject to individual state income taxes. One of the initial considerations that should be made in setting up the form of business is the tax considerations of the entity and the individuals involved. Therefore, the state's individual personal income tax (if it has one) may be a valid consideration in the operation of the business and the policy for the distribution of profits.

Other Possible Tax Returns

Intangible tax. This is a tax levied on the ownership, control, or custody of taxable intangibles such as notes, bonds, and other obligations to pay money that are secured by a mortgage, deed of trust, or other lien on real property within the state. In addition, the state generally levies this tax on shares of stock in incorporated businesses, bonds, notes, accounts receivable, and other obligations for payment.

Ad valorem tax. This is a tax on the value of real estate as assessed by a duly authorized appraiser appointed or elected to serve in that capacity. The rate of taxation—the millage—is usually expressed in one-thousandths of a dollar. For example, 23 mils means $.0023. Various states and even counties within a state will apply various rates (and even various values) for tax purposes. This tax applies to land, buildings, fixtures, and all other improvements to real estate physically located within a jurisdiction.

Some states may have special taxing districts, which will assess an ad valorem tax on the property for special services (water management, flood control, fire, school, and many others.)

Documentary stamp taxes. Documentary stamp taxes are taxes assessed against the execution of certain documents. Although varying in rates across states, this tax is generally applicable on promissory notes, mortgages, trust deeds, security agreements, and other written promises to pay money. Typically not a significant tax (usually being about $.15–$.20 per $100 face value), it is an obligation that must be met in the consummation of certain financial transactions.

Tangible personal property tax. Tangible personal property taxes, like ad valorem (real property) taxes are generally assessed by counties at a rate sometimes equal to the ad valorem tax. This tax is based on the assessed value or the value declared by the owner, for business supplies, fixtures, furnishings, etc. Some states extend this tax to motor vehicles, rail cars, trucks, busses, aircraft, and even ships and boats. Often states which exempt these items from this tax collect a like amount through licenses. Some states include inventories and work-in-process in this class of taxable property.

Others. States may have enacted various other miscellaneous taxes and fees that may impose both a reporting and filing requirement. For example:

- Charter Tax: A fee or tax associated with the filing of articles of incorporation, amendment to the articles, merger, consolidation, or dissolution.
- Excise Tax: Tax usually collected directly from the ultimate consumer on the sale of utility services.

LOCAL GOVERNMENT REQUIREMENTS

Local governments—cities and counties—have varying amounts of licensing and taxing authority. These powers arise as a result of constitutional provisions, state statutes, county ordinances, special acts of state legislatures, and charters and municipal code provisions. Some of these requirements may include:

Occupational licenses. Counties and incorporated municipalities may be authorized to levy a tax for the privilege of engaging in or managing a business, profession, or occupation within the jurisdiction. The basis and rates for license payments vary considerably. Inquiries concerning these restrictions can usually be handled by individual county or city clerks.

Zoning restrictions. Land use restrictions and limitations may be governed by a local zoning board. This may be under the authority of city or county governments. Zoning restrictions are usually established for an area or a parcel. Variances to restrictions may be petitioned for on an exceptional basis. Often, the nature, character, and use of parcels will change over time, bringing about updating and change to land use plans. For example, with the growth of suburbs, land previously zoned agricultural may be changed to residential; some may change to commercial to accommodate malls, shopping area, and business activities.

Sales taxes. Sometimes counties or cities impose local option sales taxes. These may be ongoing taxes or may have limited durations designed to meet specific needs (e.g., construction of a jail or courthouse; road improvement; modernizing a hospital or school; etc.). These taxes may be collected by the state and remitted back to the city or county.

Gasoline and special fuels tax. Generally all gasoline and diesel fuel used for on-road vehicles is taxed by the state and federal governments. However, counties may have an additional local option tax. Sometimes, special fuels sold for residential, agricultural, or commercial marine purposes are exempt from this tax.

Local income tax. Some large cities (notably New York City) have local income taxes. These are levied in addition to federal and state income taxes. There is often a credit or deduction applicable for state and local income taxes against federal income tax.

CREDITORS

Companies that have advanced credit to your business or who have invested money in the enterprise want to know how their investment is faring. They will generally insist upon some form of status report on a timely basis—weekly, monthly, quarterly, or other regular period. The frequency of the necessary reporting will depend upon various factors: risk, volatility of the market, past performances, solvency, and others.

Often, you will have to prepare several documents to inform creditors of the business status and financial conditions:

- Balance sheet
- Income statement
- Cash flow

Together these reports afford a comprehensive model of the operations, liquidity, and the past and current operations of the business. Creditors may also request pro forma or forward-looking financial statements to create an educated future forecast of the business operations of the enterprise.

When loaning money to you, creditors may require notes and mortgages to carry conditions or covenants. In the chapter dealing with financing the business, we explained how the investors of debt capital will probably condition the loans on a showing of certain ratios. We also discussed how you can and should, to the extent practicable, negotiate these covenants. Covenants are conditions or assurances. They may include:

- Maintenance of specified current ratios or quick ratios.
- Limitations on payments or salaries to officers or directors.
- Ratios of debt to equity.

- Restrictions on dividend payments.
- Restrictions on additional debt obligations.

Again, these conditions are negotiable and the reporting of changes of status are subject to the assessment of risk.

EQUITY HOLDERS

Equity holders are not dissimilar to creditors in their interest in the business results. Secured debt holders have a lien against the property superior in claim to equity holders in the case of default. Debt holders have a superior claim to the equity holder's claim. Equity holders have claims, if any, to dividends in after-tax dollars (if any). Therefore, the risk to equity holders is higher and, with luck, so is the expected return.

MANAGEMENT

In Chapter 5 we discussed how a business will generate a budget for operations including targets for materials, labor and overhead by product and/or by operation. These operating budgets are monthly projections and targets against which actual performance can and should be measured. An overall report against the business plan should be prepared to assure that the objectives set are being approached.

These reports can be generated based on standards showing variances from plan. Variance reporting permits you to address variances with reports of performance and exception reports, which identify reasons for the various and curative steps taken. Finally, these reports can be economically generated—by centers, by departments, or in any other way you desire.

SUMMARY

You will have varying reporting responsibilities to federal, state, and local jurisdictions. You will have other external reporting requirements to creditors and investors. Finally, you will have internal reporting functions used for planning and control.

The federal reporting requirements include employment reports on wage-earning employees, tax reports, and social security taxes. You will pay unemployment taxes for your employees. The federal government has arranged for banks and federal depositories to receive taxes collected from employees and those paid by the employer. The employer will withhold federal income tax and social security taxes and pay those into the federal depository pursuant to IRS guidelines. Annually, the IRS requires you to report to your employees the wages and taxes paid and withheld.

Depending upon the form of the business organization, you will have various reporting requirements for federal tax liabilities. Sole proprietorships, S-corporations, and partnerships pay income taxes for the business entity. However, S-corporations and partnerships file information returns. Corporations, on the other hand, are taxed as a separate legal entity.

Other reporting requirements arise out of the nature of the business. For example, dealers in firearms are strictly licensed and regulated by the United States Treasury Department. Other businesses are regulated as to rates, charges, and services offered. Utilities, transportation companies, banks, and other such industries are closely regulated. Some, because of the dangers associated with working conditions, are closely scrutinized. Coal mining, toxic chemical companies, and airlines are just a few such activities.

State governments also regulate and tax many businesses and activities. States generally tax the real property of businesses and the structures attached to the property through their ad valorem taxing authority. Your equipment, fixtures, appliances, and even inventories might be taxed using tangible personal property taxes. Intangible items of ownership, such as stocks, bonds, and notes are taxed through intangible personal property taxes. In some cases, sales and even purchases made in other states are taxed. Some products, such as groceries, medicines, and telephone services, are exempt in some states.

Local governments may impose taxes, licensing requirements, and zoning restrictions on the operations of some businesses. Some county or city governments may have franchise requirements for the provision of services; these may be exclusive rights to provide services, such as cable television.

Creditors have or seek certain information to assure the likelihood of payment. You may prepare and distribute balance sheets, income statements, and statements of cash flow. Investors, likewise, are concerned with these reports.

Finally, you will have internal reporting requirements for planning and control. These needs vary with the size and type of business and with the style of management used.

12

Ratios

Ratios, like many of the tools discussed earlier, can be used to make rational decisions in keeping with your objectives. Ratios are analytical tools used by outside suppliers of capital, creditors and investors, and by you to evaluate how well you are doing. You may also use ratios to evaluate how the business appears to the investor. The type of analysis undertaken varies according to the specific interest that the party seeks to satisfy.

- A trade creditor who has supplied goods, services, or raw materials would generally be interested in liquidity—your ability to pay bills.
- A bond holder is more interested in long-term financial stability. As such, he would be interested in cash flow and your ability to service your debt.
- The present and expected future earnings and the stability of these earnings may be primary concerns to an investor in common stock.

Depending upon the planning horizon of each person interested in the ratios, the value of trend analysis may be greater than any point-in-time or present ratios. How well you have done over time and are expected to do in the future are pieces of information necessary to make reasoned decisions.

Finally, you too should be concerned with the trend depicted through ratios. In order to bargain more effectively for outside funds, you should be aware of all of the aspects of financial analysis that outsiders use in evaluating the business. Financial and operating ratios can also be effective tools for managing and controlling the business.

There are two broad categories of ratios that will be of concern in this chapter. The first set is financial ratios. We have briefly discussed financial ratios in Chapter 10. Therefore, we will not endeavor to repeat that material, but rather only supplement it here. The second set of ratios, which you should consider in setting up controls, are the operating ratios. Operating ratios can be designed to meet specific needs of the user. These ratios are intended as a tool for analysis and control of business operations.

FINANCIAL RATIOS

Some unit of measure is necessary to evaluate the financial condition or the performance of the business. A system frequently used is a ratio, or index, which connects two pieces of financial or operational information. Interpreting a ratio correctly gives the analyst an understanding of the financial condition and performance of the firm, which may not be readily apparent from the traditional forms of reporting. It is important to remember that a single ratio in itself may not be a particularly meaningful piece of information. Often a trend showing past historical ratios will indicate more than will the current individual ratio alone. When financial ratios are listed on a spread sheet for a period of years, a study of the composite change will quickly indicate whether there has been an improvement or deterioration in the financial condition over time. In addition, the productivity, profitability, or performance of the firm relative to past performances is easily demonstrated. For example, by arraying the last five years of current ratios—that is, the ratio of current assets to current liabilities—you can compare the ability of the business to pay its bills and determine if that is improving or deteriorating.

The second comparison method involves evaluating the ratio of one company against others similarly situated for the same period. Such a comparison, if properly done, will give some insight into the relative financial condition of the company. If improperly done, the information derived from this study may be worse than meaningless—it may be harmful. The primary problem is comparability.

Avoid using "rules of thumb" indiscriminately. The comparison of your financial ratios with the ratios published by major sources may be inaccurate. For example, you may have multiple product lines and may not have the same product mix as other companies in the industry. You may be differently diversified, crossing industry boundaries. It is preferable to build comparable numbers over time for your own business rather than seek comparisons with others. However, sometimes outside comparisons, properly used, can be helpful. A rule of thumb, if it is to be used, should be from your industry. Trade associations can be a source of good financial ratio information.

For example, the standard rule of thumb for the current ratio—that is, the ratio of current assets to current liabilities—is 2:1. It is considered advisable for a small business to maintain a current ratio of at least 2:1 for the sake of sound cash flow and healthy financial condition. Remember, however, that rules of thumb are averages. As such, there may be as many companies above the average as below it. To show how this rule of thumb may be misapplied, take the example of a fast food outlet. It may have a current ratio of 1:2 or even 1:3. Comparing this current ratio with the rule of thumb, one quickly concludes that the business has a liquidity problem and may not have sufficient liquid assets available to meet all of the debts falling due. However, this is probably not the case. A typical fast food outlet has:

- *Receivables*. There are generally no credit sales and no delayed payments at a fast food store.
- *Inventory levels*. Fast food stores generally carry very small inventories and deliveries are small, frequent, and fresh.
- *Normal or extended trade payables*. Some profitable franchises can delay payments to local suppliers for longer than is normal because of their volume of business.

Fast food outlets, therefore, turn over inventory at a tremendous rate and generate continuous streams of cash. At any one point the company may not have large amounts of cash on hand if it is using cash to retire longer-term debt or to acquire additional fixed assets. By comparing the company's own historic trend in the current ratio, and examining those ratios with other fast food outlets, you can perhaps see that a 1:4 ratio may be even better than a 1:2 ratio. The traditional rule of thumb may not be applicable or representative of the fast food industry. The point of this example is that you should consider:

- Those ratios which make sense for you.
- Those ratios which give usable management information.
- Those ratios which can be obtained on a timely basis.

It is often important to have the financial information generated by ratios on a more timely basis than can be generated from full blown financial statements. In some cases, by the time the financial statements are prepared it may be too late to take corrective action. In determining how timely the information should be, the trade-off between timeliness and accuracy must be considered. Full-blown financial statements may produce extremely accurate, audited information. However, it will likely be too late for many important decisions.

"Per book" ratios may be generated monthly by your bookkeeper or accountant. While this information may not be as accurate as a fully audited financial statement, by generating the data on a monthly basis, you get periodic, consistent reports that may point out problems long before the audit is even undertaken.

The following balance sheet and statement of earnings will be used to demonstrate the financial ratios.

FRUIT CRATE MFG. CO., INC.
ASSETS

	1983	1982
CURRENT ASSETS		
Cash and marketable securities	$ 21,285	$ 20,860
Accounts receivables	83,473	91,155
Inventories	164,482	157,698
Prepaid expenses	2,554	2,049
Accumulated prepaid tax	4,261	3,475
Current assets	$276,055	$275,237
FIXED ASSETS		
Fixed assets	$198,760	$192,666
Less: Accumulated depreciation	107,330	99,030
Net fixed assets	$ 91,430	$ 93,636
Long-term investment	$ 8,229	$ -0-
OTHER ASSETS		
Goodwill	$ 23,839	$ 23,839
Debenture discount	751	833
Other assets	$ 24,590	$ 24,672
TOTAL ASSETS	$400,304	$393,545

LIABILITIES AND NET WORTH

	1983	1982
CURRENT LIABILITIES		
Bank loans and notes payables	$ 53,638	$ 42,544
Accounts payable	17,560	16,271

Accrued taxes	4,321	15,186
Other accured liabilities	22,775	19,608
Current liabilities	$ 98,294	$ 93,609
Long-term debt	$ 75,562	$ 74,262
Stockholders' equity		
Common stock @ $1.00 par value	$ 50,420	$ 50,420
Capital surplus	43,179	43,016
Retained earnings	132,849	132,238
Total stockholders' equity	$226,448	$225,674
TOTAL LIABILITIES AND NET WORTH	$400,304	$393,545

FRUIT CRATE MFG. CO., INC.
STATEMENT OF EARNINGS

	1983	1982
Net Sales	$492,374	$464,383
Cost of goods sold	$330,383	$311,601
Selling, general, and administration expense	98,475	90,555
Depreciation	13,786	14,396
Interest expense	10,340	8,823
EXPENSES	$452,984	$425,375
Earnings before taxes	$ 39,390	$ 39,008
Less: Income taxes	18,907	19,114
Earnings after taxes	$ 20,483	$ 19,894
Less: Cash dividend	12,495	12,732
Retained earnings	$ 7,988	$ 7,162

TYPES OF FINANCIAL RATIOS

Liquidity Ratios

Liquidity ratios give an indication of your ability to meet short-term obligations. These ratios give some insight into the present cash solvency and are a measure of your ability to meet adversity. Generally, liquidity ratios look at the short-term assets or resources and the short-term debts and obligations.

Current Ratio. As discussed in Chapter 10, the current ratio is the ratio of:

$$\frac{\text{Current Assets}}{\text{Current Liabilities}}$$

For Fruit Crate Mfg. Co., Inc., the current ratio for 1983 is:

$$\frac{\$276,055}{\$98,294} = 2.81{:}1$$

Supposedly, the higher the ratio the better your ability to pay bills. However, the ratio does not take into account how liquid the "current" assets really are. For example, if your current assets are mostly cash and current receivables, these are more liquid than if most of the current assets are in inventories. To refine the ratio as a measure, we eliminate the effect of inventories, prepaid expenses, and prepaid tax.

Acid Test Ratio

$$\frac{\text{Current Assets} - (\text{Inventories} + \text{Prepaids})}{\text{Current Liabilities}}$$

For Fruit Crate Mfg. Co., Inc.:

$$\frac{\$276,055 - 171,297}{\$98,294} = 1.066{:}1$$

The acid test ratio eliminates the least liquid components of the current assets and therefore focuses on the assets most easily converted to debt payment.

Liquidity of Receivables. Analyzing the current assets by components enables you to detect problems in your liquidity. One thing you can examine is how current are your receivables. Receivables are a liquid asset only if they can be collected in a reasonable time. The first of two ratios that examine receivables is *average collection period ratio:*

$$\frac{\text{Receivables} \times \text{Days in Year}}{\text{Annual Credit Sales}}$$

For Fruit Crate Mfg. Co., Inc., the average collection period rate for 1983 is (assuming all sales are credit sales):

$$\frac{83,473 \times 365}{492,374} = 62 \text{ days}$$

This tells you the average collection period receivables are outstanding, in other words, how long, on average, you wait to convert receivables to cash.

The second basic receivable ratio is the *receivable turnover ratio:*

$$\frac{\text{Annual Credit Sales}}{\text{Average Receivables}}$$

For Fruit Crate Mfg., Co., Inc., the receivables turnover ratio is:

$$\frac{\$492,374}{\$83,473} = 5.90 \text{ times}$$

If you do not have a figure for the amount of credit sales, you must resort to the total sales figure. Care should be taken to analyze all ratios, especially receivables ratios. Often the numbers available are year-end numbers, which may not recognize seasonal fluctuations or significant, steady growth. If you have significant seasonal sales, the average of the monthly closing balances may be a more appropriate figure to use. If you are experiencing a steady growth in sales, the year-end receivables will not match accurately with the annual sales figure. If this is the case, the number may be calculated based on the annualized sales from the last six months and the end-of-year level of receivables.

Some questions to ask when analyzing these ratios are:

- How does the average collection period compare with the sales terms? For Fruit Crate Mfg. Co., Inc., the credit terms are 2/10; n/60. The bulk of the collections are made around the due date.
- How does the collection period compare with others in the industry? This can give you some insight into your investment in receivables.
- Is the average collection period so low that it may be inhibiting sales? The firm may have an excessively restrictive credit policy.
- How old are your receivables? Here you must ask "What does the average tell us?" Fruit Crate Mfg. Co., Inc., had 433 accounts and

found the average collection period ratio was 62 days. But when it grouped the accounts by age it discovered the following statistics:

Number of Accounts	Paid in How Many Days?
110 (25%)	10
80 (18%)	30
170 (39%)	60
73 (18%)	180 days

You have 82 percent of your receivables collected before or by the due date and only 18 percent extending beyond the due date. But the late receivables are *really* late: averaging six months after shipment of goods and four months after payment was due.

By adding an aging of receivables, you gain more usable information than the average collection period ratio alone. This tells you:

• Where collection efforts need to be concentrated.

• How much investment you have in receivables.

• Accounts that may require discontinuation of service.

• Whether your terms are speeding up the recovery of receivables.

Another question the aging would raise: "Are the good accounts paying in the 10–30 period taking the cash discounts even though they have no right to it?" If the answer is yes, the cash discount terms are really 2/30; n/60.

Debt Ratios

Up to now we have been concerned with short-term liquidity measures. Depending upon the use, certain long-term solvency ratios may be of interest to you and your investors. These ratios give an indication of your ability to meet long-term obligations.

Debt to Net Worth. This ratio is computed by dividing the total debt, including current liabilities, by the net worth (total stockholders' equity):

For the Fruit Crate Mfg. Co., Inc.:

$$\frac{\text{Total Debt}}{\text{Net Worth}} = \frac{\$98,294 + 75,562}{\$226,448} = \frac{\$173,856}{\$226,448} = .77{:}1$$

Frequently, intangible assets, if relatively large, are deducted from net worth to obtain the tangible net worth. Note that for the liquidity ratios discussed earlier, we used assets divided by liabilities. Here we are creating debt ratios—putting liabilities over other measures. For liquidity, the higher the number the "better" the ratio. For debt ratios the reverse is true: the lower the number the "better" the ratio. Sometimes in computing this ratio, preferred stock is included with debt instead of net worth. This acknowledges that preferred stock represents a claim superior to the claim of common stockholders. It also points out that when using "comparable ratios" one must be certain that the calculations are truly comparable; you must compare the definitions of the ratios.

The debt to net worth ratio varies from industry to industry. One factor often contributing to this variation is the volatility of cash flows. The more stable and predictable your cash flow, the greater the debt you may be able to service consistently. Because this ratio is a good measure of ability to pay debts over time, it is sometimes used as a measure for approximating financial risk.

Debt to Total Capital. Another useful debt ratio is the ratio of total debt to total capital. In this ratio, only the long-term capitalization of the firm is considered.

$$\frac{\text{Long Term Debt}}{\text{Total Capitalization}}$$

The total capitalization is composed of long-term debt and net worth.

For Fruit Crate Mfg. Co., Inc.:

$$\frac{\$75,562}{\$75,562 + 226,448} = \frac{\$75,562}{\$302,010} = .25{:}1$$

This ratio shows the importance of long-term debt financing relative to other financing in the capital structure. When computing this ratio, it may be more informative to use market values instead of book values for the stock components. (Book values have been used in the calculation above.) If market values of stock are available, this computation may indicate a very different leverage factor.

Coverage Ratios

Coverage ratios are used to examine the relationship between finance charges and your ability to service them. One of the traditional coverage ratios is the interest coverage ratio. To compute this ratio for a given period, divide the annual earnings before interest and taxes by the interest charges for the period.

Different coverage ratios use different interest charges in the denominator. For example: the overall coverage method considers all fixed interest regardless of the seniority of the claim. By ignoring the seniority of some debt, the implication is that senior debt obligations are only as secure as your ability to meet all debt servicing. A method that gives some consideration to the seniority of debt is the cumulative deduction method.

For cumulative deduction methods, assume the following hypothetical data: The Fruit Crate Mfg. Co., Inc., has

$49,730 = earnings before interest and taxes. ($39,390 + 10,340)

$4,210 = interest on 7% senior notes.

6,130 = interest on 9% junior notes.

The coverage on the senior notes would be

$$\frac{\$49,730}{\$4,210} = 11.81 \text{ times}$$

The coverage on the junior notes, after the senior debt has been covered, is:

$$\frac{\$49,730 - 4,210}{\$10,340} = 4.40 \text{ times}$$

Using this method, the coverage ratio on the junior notes takes into consideration the fact that there are outstanding senior obligations.

Both of these methods ignore the fact that the payment of interest is only part of the obligation covered by debt service. Debt service includes both payment of interest and principal. And because these payments are made from cash, a more appropriate ratio may be the cash-flow coverage ratio. One adjustment should be made in computing this ratio. Interest payments are accounted for before taxes, whereas principal payments are treated as after-tax dollars. To adjust for the tax effect you must adjust the principal by the factor $[1/(1 - t)]$ where t is the effective tax rate. So:

$$\frac{\text{Cash flow}}{\text{coverage ratio}} = \frac{\text{Annual cash flow before interest and taxes}}{\text{Interest \& Principal } [1/(1 - t)]}$$

If you had a $10,000/year principal payment and a 46 percent tax rate, it would require:

$$\$10,000 \times [1/(1 - .46)] \text{ or}$$

$$\$10,000 \times (1.85), \text{ or } \$18,500 \text{ in before-tax dollars}$$
$$\text{to meet that principal obligation.}$$

This type of analysis can, in some cases, be expanded to consider other fixed obligations like dividends on preferred stock, lease payments, and long-term essential capital expenditures.

Debt ratios or coverage ratios may not give you an accurate picture of your ability to meet obligations. Because of the timing of the payment of debt obligations, the average interest rates, and other factors, you may wish to calculate other ratios showing the relationship of profitability to sales or to investment.

Profitability Ratios

When the profitability on sales ratio and the profitability on investment ratios are considered, they can given an indication of your efficiency of operation. The first such ratio is the *gross profit margin*:

Gross Margin on Sales. For the Fruit Crate Mfg. Co., Inc., the gross profit margin is:

$$\frac{\$492,374 - 330,383}{\$492,374} = \frac{\$161,991}{\$492,374} = 33\%$$

This ratio gives the percentage of profit relative to the sales after deducting the cost of goods sold. A more reflective ratio of profitability is the *net profit margin*:

$$\frac{\text{Net Profit (after taxes)}}{\text{Sales}}$$

For Fruit Crate Mfg. Co., Inc., the net profit margin is:

$$\frac{\$20,483}{\$492,374} = 4.2\%$$

This ratio gives a measure of your overall efficiency after taking into consideration expenses and taxes but not extraordinary charges. With these two ratios you can, over time, evaluate operational changes. For example, if the gross profit margin remained relatively constant over time, but the net profit margin declined, it shows that either the tax rate has changed or your selling and administrative expenses have increased. The relative change between these ratios can identify areas where management attention may be necessary.

As another example, if the gross profit margin declines, the cost of goods sold has increased. This could signal several things:

- The firm may have had to lower price to be competitive.
- Cost of labor, materials, or purchased components may have increased.
- Overall efficiency may have declined.

Another group of profitability ratios relate profits to investment. For example, *rate of return on common stock equity*:

$$\frac{\text{Net profit after taxes} - \text{preferred stock dividend}}{\text{Net worth} - \text{par value of preferred stock}}$$

For the Fruit Crate Mfg. Co., Inc. (no preferred stock involved):

$$\frac{\$\,20{,}483}{\$226{,}448} = .090 \text{ or } 9\%$$

This ratio gives an indication of the earning power on the book investment of the shareholders' interest. A more general ratio used to analyze profitability is the *return on assets ratio*. To calculate this ratio:

$$\frac{\text{Net profits (after taxes)}}{\text{Total assets (tangible)}}$$

For the Fruit Crate Mfg. Co., Inc.:

$$\frac{\$\,20{,}483}{\$375{,}714} = 5.5\%$$

Profits are considered after interest is paid to creditors; to some extent this ratio may be inappropriate because some of these same creditors provide the means by which part of the assets are supported. When the finance charges are large, it may be better for comparative purposes to calculate a different ratio. An arguably more appropriate ratio may be the *net-operating profit rate-of-return*. It is calculated from:

$$\frac{\text{Earnings before interest and taxes}}{\text{Total assets (tangible)}}$$

For Fruit Crate Mfg. Co., Inc.:

$$\frac{\$ \ 49,730}{\$375,714} = 13.24\%$$

Turnover and Earning Power Ratios

The asset turnover ratio relates total sales to total tangible assets. Like many of the ratios discussed before, the meaningfulness of this ratio lies in the trend you establish and how you compare with similarly situated, comparable businesses in the same industry. The ratio is used as a measure or indicator of how well you use your resources to generate output.

The *asset turnover ratio* is calculated as:

$$\frac{\text{Sales}}{\text{Total Tangible Assets}}$$

For the Fruit Crate Mfg. Co., Inc., the asset turnover ratio is:

$$\frac{\$492,374}{\$375,714} = 1.31$$

A shortcoming of this ratio is that it puts a premium on businesses that have more fully depreciated equipment than on more new investment. This ratio may distort efficiency. New equipment should be producing goods at lower per unit costs than older, out-of-date equipment. As a consequence, this ratio should be used in conjunction with other ratios.

The earning power ratio on total assets is obtained when the asset turnover is multiplied by the net profit margin, generating the *earning power percentage*:

$$\text{Earning Power} = \frac{\text{Sales}}{\text{Total assets (tangible)}} \times \frac{\text{Net profit (after taxes)}}{\text{Sales}}$$

$$= \frac{\text{Net profits (after taxes)}}{\text{Total assets (tangible)}}$$

Because the net profit margin ignores the asset utilization and the turnover ratio does not consider profitability, each by itself is an inadequate measure of operating efficiency. The earning power ratio resolves these shortcomings. From this ratio it is clear that earning power will increase if there is an increase in turnover or an increase in net profit margin or both.

USING RATIOS FOR PREDICTIONS

Belief in the predictive power of ratios is based upon the idea that a knowledge of historical trends decreases future risk for investors and businessmen. The best use of ratios is made where they are used in connection with one another, compared collectively over time, and compared with other businesses. Any one snapshot of ratios may indicate misleading conclusions. You may look to trade associations if you desire a comparison of ratios with other businesses similarly situated. Trade association information will, in all likelihood, be more representative of comparability than the use of ratios from other sources. Reliance upon trends may be more useful if the same trends are found to be industry consistent.

One final warning: Financial ratios are a simple tool that has the potential for good, timely information—but it can also be a source of incorrect information if improperly compiled and used.

OPERATING RATIOS

Operating ratios may be even more useful to you than financial ratios because of the timely nature of their calculation and the decision-specific nature of their use. While these ratios are in keeping with the thinking of most engineers and managers of sales, service *and* manufacturing can also use the principles of operating ratios effectively.

Comparison of Financial and Operating Ratios

Similarities

- Both financial and operating ratios are most useful when the information generated by the ratio is timely. Ratios are like other tools; they are beneficial only if you have them when you need them.

- As with financial ratios, operating ratios can be generated for any two numbers, for example: the number of salespersons and the dollars of sales per month. These two numbers will generate an average sales per salesperson, against which you may have a relative performance index. Also like financial ratios, unless there is a relationship the resulting ratio is meaningless.

- Like financial ratios, operating ratios should not be accepted at face value. For the sales per person ratio, assume we find the average to be 17 sales per salesperson per day in an automobile dealership. Two of the salespersons make 43 and 53 sales per day, respectively, and the remaining 5 salespersons make 3 sales, 6 sales, 5 sales, 5 sales, and 4 sales, respectively. It would appear that you could replace the 5 salespersons with one aggressive person and be better off. However, additional information may reveal that the low volume employees are automobile showroom salespersons, and the other two are in the parts department. The parts room accounts for only 17 percent of the revenues but has 28.6 percent of the sales force. Several more ratios can be generated that would help in determining whether the sales force is well managed, efficient, and economical. Standing alone, no one ratio is as useful as a series of related ratios.

- Ratios for operations, like financial ratios, can be more effective if they are "trended." Taking the salesroom salespersons' past 12 months average ratio of sales per day we observe the following data:

Jan.	3.6	July	4.9
Feb.	4.2	Aug.	2.1
Mar.	5.4	Sept.	4.7
Apr.	6.1	Oct.	7.0
May	7.7	Nov.	6.3
June	6.3	Dec.	4.1

From this we see a two-peak cycle of automobile sales. The dealership can plan when it should order more cars to increase the inventory in anticipation of seasonal sales. It also may help plan for sales incentives, promotional advertising, vacation schedules, and other operational elements.

- The cost of generating the data necessary for any ratio should not exceed the benefit derived from the information produced from the data. As with any tool, a ratio should itself have a favorable cost/

benefit relationship. In other words, the benefits should outweigh the costs.

- Ratios are useless if they do not meet a need. Looking back, the ratio of average sales per salesperson per period was designed to measure the relative performance of sales personnel. It did not adequately do that. It failed to inform management what the meaningful performance was for automobiles versus parts sales personnel.

- Properly structured, an operating ratio or series of ratios can be used for planning and control. As an example, some of the financial ratios mentioned can be used to evaluate credit policy. The same is true for operating ratios. If we monitor how well auto sales personnel are doing individually, compared to the monthly historical figures, we have a quantitative measure of individual performance. If we look at the aggregate sales figures of average sales per person per day against the historical average, we have a measure of how well the business is doing compared with past performance.

Dissimilarities

- Financial ratios relate to numbers from the balance sheet and income statement, whereas operational ratios are oriented more toward production, service, and sales—figures which may not be accumulated in the accounting system. Because of this, standard financial ratios are more likely to be routinely prepared, whereas operating ratios are more often tailored to meet particular needs. There is a greater tendency to compare financial ratios among businesses almost indiscriminately—resulting in bad comparisons among dissimilar businesses. Since operating ratios may be tailored, there is less of a tendency for misapplication and greater reliance upon historical trends.

- Operating ratios can often be calculated very quickly from obvious data. For the example of average sales per salesperson, management can have an accurate number for the previous day's sales for each member of the sales force at the start of each work day. It is often more difficult to compile and verify the financial data.

Use of Operating Ratios

Operating ratios can be used to evaluate any function. There may be a very large number of data-gathering efforts necessary to compile the needed input for ratio generation. Data gathering is costly and time consuming. It represents an investment that should have an expectation of a return to justify the expenditure. Therefore, you should first implement the use of ratios that have the greatest return or control. The ability to improve control through ratio generation and evaluation should be directed at critical steps in the process.

Breakdowns at critical steps may halt all production. For example, in a law firm specializing in appeals, time constraints are externally generated by rules of court with limited opportunities for extensions of time or deviations. Operationally, research is accomplished using sophisticated terminals connected to national data banks. Writing and editing is done on electronic word processing equipment. All work flows through personnel highly skilled in the use of word processors. A breakdown in the word processor/printer could be very serious for the meeting of critical deadlines. Typing a draft into the machine may be a critical function or a potential bottleneck. Often the speed of input into the word processor is slower than dictation. Therefore, the ratio of skilled typists to writers may be critical. Ratio analysis can play a key role in determining a proper relationship.

There is a general five-step process for designing and implementing a control system based upon ratio analysis. These five steps may not all be necessary if the system is not complex. More steps may have to be added if the process or system is very complicated. This five step system is a good outline of an analysis control system.

The five steps are:

1. Analyze the process or system: Write out a step-by-step description of the process.
2. Look for and identify critical steps: Is there any one step through which most or all work flows?
3. Analyze the critical step: Is it a potential bottleneck or constriction? Why is it a bottleneck?
4. Set a target performance ratio: Determine from past historical data how well you have done and ask, "How much better can we do?"
5. Evaluate performance and feedback: How well are you now doing? How do you improve the system? What is the justification?

Applications

Operating ratios can be applied to any business. The following case study applies a ratio analysis to a service company (a law firm). Other suggestions will be given for a retail store and a manufacturing firm.

Case I: The firm of Simmer, Braize, and Broyle, P.A., is a Midwest law firm composed of six partners and 11 associate attorneys. They represent three large automobile insurance companies in defense litigation. The firm's business is basically steady with two small seasonal variations. The firm has a sophisticated word processing system with satellite terminals, one draft, high-speed printer, one letter-quality printer, and a new laser printer. The firm has two senior secretaries, two junior secretaries, and one clerk-typist/receptionist. As the case load has grown, one senior secretary spends almost all her time setting up new case files.

The firm noticed that the secretaries were putting in more overtime and the senior partner was concerned that things were getting done only just in time. Ratio analysis was undertaken by an associate who had an undergraduate degree in business.

1. She analyzed the flow of paper from the receipt of a complaint through the final order of the trial court. She prepared a flow chart of what work was done, when, and by whom.

2. She discovered two critical steps:
   a) All work product passed through the two junior and one senior secretary as they input, edited, and printed out lawyers' work products.
   b) The reproduction and mailing of letters, pleadings, and briefs.

3. a) The technical word processing function was on the verge of becoming a bottleneck. The work just seemed to take too long to process.
   b) The reproduction facility was a disaster. The equipment was always breaking down; when it worked, people were constantly seen walking back to work without copies because "the line was too long" or "a long critical job was on the machine."

4. a) After studying the number of words processed by each of the three secretaries she found an average of 52 words per minute. Not to be fooled by averages, she looked at the distribution. The two junior secretaries typed at 38 and 42 words per minute each and the senior secretary typed at 75. The other senior secretary, who only set up files, could type at 81 words per minute. The associate, told that this secretary had been hired because of her typing speed, calculated that if the senior secretary switched roles with the junior secretary, the firm could target word input at 67 words per minute, average, without changing personnel (a 29 percent increase). The junior secretary and the receptionist would be able to prepare all the files as they came in. The associate

found that the senior secretary had started or updated 61 files per day. She set a target of 45 files for the junior secretary and 20 for the receptionist (because of her other duties).

b) The copier: She ran a study of the copier by asking each user to log in the number of copies made of each original and the number of originals. From this she learned several things. There were only two basic types of copying requirements: 1) long runs (many copies of large jobs with many originals) and, 2) short runs (few originals, few copies). The long runs, on average consumed 6 hours a day total time, and the short runs 1.5 hours. The average short run took less than 30 seconds, but the average long run took 17 minutes. Twenty-one long runs and about 200 short runs were run each day. With the machine breakdowns considered, the copier (owned by the firm), worked properly on average 8.2 hours each 9-hour day. Often copies were run through lunch hour on a staggered secretarial shift.

5. From these ratios the associate made the following recommendations: Buy a highly reliable, small copier and dedicate it to short runs. Hire a clerk to do the copying. As justification, she made the following findings based upon ratio analysis:

a) On average, each secretary saved up five small runs or one long run before going to the machine.

b) On average, the machine was tied up doing long runs or broken down 6.8 hours out of every 9 hours, roughly 75 percent of the time. On three out of every four trips to the machine a secretary found it occupied by a long run. Because the secretaries made 40 successful trips to the copier per day (200 short runs/5 runs per trip) they were making appropriately 120 unsuccessful trips to the machine. If they waited for a long run to finish rather then returning to their desk, they waited 8½ minutes (17/2).

c) By assigning a clerk to copying, all unsuccessful trips were eliminated. Even though an unsuccessful trip to the copier took only 45 seconds, 1.5 hours of secretarial time was saved (120 trips × 45 seconds).

d) By reducing the demand on the copier, the breakdown rate was expected to improve.

e) The biggest bonus to the firm was the actual freeing up of 7.5 hours of secretarial time. Simply to do the copying, a secretary stood at the machine for 6 hours a day for long runs and 1.5 hours per day for short runs. This, coupled with the 1.5 hours of time saved on unsuccessful trips, amounted to enough savings in dollars of overtime to pay for the small run copier in nine months and still pay the salary and benefits of the clerk.

Ratio analysis improved the operation of the firm, gave it quantifiable measures of performance and got some control over the operation.

OTHER RATIOS

The following is a list of other operating ratios a firm might generate; it is not meant to be complete.

1. For the law firm other ratios were considered:
   a. Total hours worked to hours spent on task for which hired.
   b. Clerical hours to professional hours.
   c. Billable hours to hours worked.
   d. Billable hours brought to firm (new clients, new or repeat work) to hours billed.
2. For a retail store:
   a. Number of customers making purchases to the number of customers coming through door.
   b. Number of sales to number of customers waited on (by each salesperson).
   c. Number of sales per hour of the day.
   d. Dollars of sales per dollars of inventory (by product or product type).
   e. Number of sales to number of salespersons.
3. For a manufacturing firm.
   Lower management
   a. Hours of set-up time to hours of run time.
   b. Hours of downtime to available hours.
   c. Hours of downtime to run time.
   d. Hours of sick time to hours worked.
   e. Labor hours per product produced.
   f. Hours of rework to hours of production.
   g. Number of quality control steps or inspections to hours to product or steps to produce.
   h. Work area per employee.
   Middle management
   a. Number of supervisors to direct laborers.
   b. Number of indirect laborers to direct laborers.

   c. Scrapped product to good finished goods.

   d. Number of returns to goods sold.

Upper management

   a. Dollars of profit to cost to produce.

   b. Number of products back-ordered to number delivered.

   c. Dollars of sales to number of employees.

   d. Lost time accidents to hours worked.

   e. Number of service employees to manufacturing employees.

   f. Number of units shipped per day.

Each manager or supervisor concerned with the operations of the firm or store should monitor at least two or three critical ratios on a continuous basis. This information may be plotted on a daily basis to accumulate historical information that could be used for planning, control, and budgeting. Often, this information will point up areas of critical concern before it has a fatal effect. Therefore, ratios, if properly structured and monitored, can be powerful management tools.

SUMMARY

Ratios are an analytical tool used for reporting and control. They have external and internal applications. Externally, trade creditors, bond holders, and banks are interested in the ratios and the trends depicted by a historical progression of those ratios. Internally, financial and operating ratios depict how well the firm is doing and serve as an instrument of feedback for control.

In trying to determine what a ratio "means," analysts sometimes resort to "rules of thumb." Rules of thumb are nothing more than averages. As such, they may be inapplicable, thus generating faulty comparisons and conclusions. Financial ratios generated internally over time may be the most useful for your purposes. Next, you might compare other similar firms' ratios generated by trade associations.

For financial ratios, you might possibly generate liquidity ratios, debt ratios, long-term liquidity measures, coverage ratios, and profitability ratios.

After financial concerns, you may generate operating ratios as a measure of how well you are doing, where bottlenecks occur, and where objective measures of performance can be established. Creating operating ratios is an individual endeavor for each business. Although some of the ratios established—for example, acceptable parts to parts produced—may be common, what is acceptable will vary from business to business. Also, where you want to emphasize control will vary according to your individual costs.

A five-step analysis of a process or system helps point out areas where you may have critical steps or potential bottlenecks. These may be areas where you should expend some effort in generating ratios for control and reporting.

The generation of *useful* ratios is the guiding star for this analysis. If you undertake to generate the information necessary for implementation of a ratio control or feedback system, the ratio should be meaningful and the information useful.

Ratios are guides and that implies movement over time. Taking a snapshot look at ratios may tell management something, but that something may be misleading. Trends in ratios indicate what is going on with the business and they may even indicate what may go on in the future.

Properly applied, analyzed, and interpreted, ratios are a powerful tool for internal and external reporting, control, and evaluations.

13

Taxes and Insurance

Many of the tax consequences to a firm are covered in Chapter 11 (Reporting). This chapter will point out how to manage taxes on a continuous basis in order to take advantage of the benefits associated with various liability-limiting provisions in the tax code. Without consideration on an ongoing basis, taxes can become a significant drain on the business's cash flow.

If you consider that under the federal corporate tax rates one of the largest percentage deductions from your profits may come as payment of taxes on an annual basis, you quickly realize that significant gains can be made if taxes can be deferred or, better still, eliminated. There are many tax choices available to businesspeople that may eliminate or defer payment of taxes on the profits. Although very few situations permit the permanent deferral of taxes, the law will permit deferral of tax payments in certain situations. The deferral of taxes has many benefits:

1. By deferring taxes, you lower your cash flow commitment to the government. This means more cash will be available for withdrawal and use for profit-making opportunities.

2. If taxes can be deferred long enough, there is a chance that the federal government will change the tax code so as to make the payment of taxes more favorable or eliminate some tax liability entirely. In effect, the deferred taxes may be less when paid after the law changes instead of before. The rate, or the method of calculation of liability, could change. Of course, the reverse may also be true.

3. A tax deferral is, in effect, an interest-free loan from the federal government. It can be recognized as a valid financing source because there can be no more favorable rate than a zero interest rate for a loan.

4. Many tax options are under your control. When one option fails to be favorable, you can change to another.

Tax planning can have significant advantages. It can help conserve cash flow by deferring the payment of taxes. It can make available interest-free capital for the financing and purchase of new fixed assets or expansion. It can free up additional cash and make more disposable cash available for payout.

CONTROLLING TAX LIABILITIES

When planning for your treatment of tax expenses, you should consider the following accounting methods and choices of accounting periods for controlling the amount of tax liabilities that may be incurred. Of course, you should discuss these issues with a competent advisor familiar with your circumstances.

Deferred Installment Sales

You may be able to defer income if you make sales of personal property on an installment sales basis. This deferral is permitted even if the overall method of accounting used is an accrual method. You realize a cash flow improvement by not having to prepay the tax on profits until they have been realized in cash payments. If you sell on installment sales contracts do not fail to utilize this deferral method.

An installment sale is defined for tax purposes as requiring two or more payments. Therefore, a company that sells personal property on a credit basis requiring only one payment in a certain period would not qualify for use of this deferral method.

Another consideration is your credit policy. In establishing a credit policy, one thing that the firm may wish to consider is the tax advantages of certain installment sales. This deferral gets particularly beneficial if you are experiencing an increase in accounts receivable. Typically, big ticket item retail stores, such as furniture and appliance dealers, can take significant advantage of installment sales deferment. By looking to the installment sales method of tax deferments, you may not only have the benefit of deferring income taxes, but it may also provide an opportunity to charge slow paying customers interest in consideration for extended payment terms. In this manner you may be able to take advantage of a tax code benefit to improve the percentage return on your accounts receivable.

Bad Debt Method

One company may choose to recognize its bad debts for tax purposes at the point where these debts actually become known to be worthless. Another company may set up a reserve and obtain a tax deduction based upon an estimate of the debts that will be bad. The reserve method simply accelerates your tax deduction for bad debts. This is true because the deduction is allowed in the year the reserve is established, based upon the probability of some accounts going bad, rather than when the specific debt is determined to be bad.

Accounting for Inventory

Sometimes, by changing accounting methods, you can eliminate short-term profits associated with inflation and the cost of inventory. In other words, if you have significant inventory levels that were produced at lower costs and you are currently producing inventory at much higher expenses, by selling off the most recently made or purchased inventory items you will then realize a profit only between the current selling price and the current higher costs. In doing so, you retain, as a matter of bookkeeping only, old inventory at lower costs. This is a change from a "first-in-first-out" (FIFO) accounting system to a "last-in-first-out" (LIFO) system.

State Tax Considerations

When locating offices and plants, a company with multistate operations should take into consideration the states in which legislation has been passed giving lower taxes for business. Lower state taxes can substantially reduce tax liability and will not inhibit the business from engaging in interstate commerce.

Another important consideration is whether the state has a tangible personal property tax. In some states, on particular days of the year tangible personal property located within the state will be subject to taxation. Many large companies (particularly airlines and railroads) ensure that the majority of their movable assets are not in states that levy tangible personal property taxes on the day of levy (and can prove it).

Consideration of the Taxable Entity

In planning the creation of a business, the principals should consider discussing tax liabilities associated with the various forms of business entities available. Consideration of whether to incorporate, enter partnerships, subchapter S-corporations, or domestic/international sales corporations should be reviewed. Each of these has particular tax liabilities. Some of them are associated with particular types of businesses and may not be applicable to the business in which you engage.

Partnerships and subchapter S-corporations can be useful to avoid double taxation, which arises because the corporation is taxed on its profits and again when the profits are distributed in the form of dividends. Again, there is an income tax liability associated with a receipt of the dividends by the owners.

Partnerships and subchapter S-entities, on the other hand, shift income from the entity to the shareholders' or partners' tax return. Tax losses, as well, flow directly through to the owners or partners.

One of the criteria that should be considered when setting up the business entity is the relative tax rate for the individuals as compared to the corporate rate. The corporate rate may be higher than the rate at which the principals are taxed.

The qualifications for subchapter S status change periodically. The IRS can provide up-to-date information on revisions.

Financing Considerations for Fixed Assets

Rapid Depreciation Methods. When a fixed asset is purchased, new accelerated cost recovery systems can be used, which at the same time increase cash flow. The law in this area changes frequently and consultation with a good tax advisor will help you to understand how the depreciation deductions work and what is currently available.

Investment Tax Credits. The laws regarding Investment Tax Credits also change frequently. Congress permits and withdraws such credits as a means of altering tax revenue and/or stimulating the economy. The following describes the normal situation when an ITC is available.

An ITC affords the taxpayer an opportunity to reduce income tax liability by buying or constructing equipment or other qualifying properties. Property that qualifies for ITC normally includes tangible depreciable property. This property typically must have a useful life of at least three years. Due regard must be given to the fact that usually no ITC is permitted for buildings or permanent structural components.

In the case of leased property, a lessor for a qualifying piece of property may be able to pass the credit on to the lessee. ITC or any portion may be carried back for three years or carried forward for 15 years. Unused credit for the current year is generally carried back for the earliest carry-back year and any other remaining unused credit is applied to each succeeding year in chronological order.

Again, serious consideration should be given to consulting with a tax advisor in this area. The tax laws are changing on a fairly regular basis, and before you make any capital decision ITC should be considered.

Leasing

There are certain tax benefits to leasing, although the controversy surrounding these benefits still exists. Leasing may have the following advantages:

1. The cash needed to purchase the property is available for other uses.
2. The lessor may pass through the ITC, if any, to the lessee for his use. This benefit probably will not be passed on without a corresponding payment to the lessor.
3. The lessor bears the risk of obsolescence or loss.
4. Lease payments may exceed depreciation and interest. In this respect it may give the lessee a higher deduction in the form of immediate expense dollars.

Cash Management through Tax Planning

Compensation Plans. There are three types of compensation plans: basic, deferred, and pension- and profit-sharing funds. Funded and unfunded deferred compensation plans offer numerous advantages. For example, in the funded pension plan, the employer's contribution to the fund is currently deductible as an expense. Any earnings generated internally by the trust fund are tax exempt. Finally, the employees are not taxed on an individual basis until after retirement. After retirement, the employee's income should be less than he is receiving as an active employee. The employee gets the benefit of a lower tax rate at a later date. This is an income-deferred plan available to employees through the cooperation of their employer. There are firms and businesses that plan compensation packages. These groups can be very helpful in demonstrating different ways in which you may save cash flow through the design of compensation plans.

Employees' Stock Ownership. Like compensation plans, many firms offer their employees participatory ownership plans. These plans offer two advantages:

1. By giving the employees some participatory ownership in the firm, there is greater loyalty and greater concern for the firm's well being. Each employee has a vested interest in the success of the firm. As the firm grows and succeeds so does the personal worth of the individual.

2. The second benefit of an employee stock ownership plan is that it offers an employer a deduction without the payment of cash. You should be careful that the contribution of stock should not significantly change ownership. When significant dilution of the ownership is caused by a stock purchase plan you may become subject to a suit called a derivative lawsuit by those owners who have had their percentage ownership decreased by sale of additional stock. This is generally associated with the issuance of new stock and is discussed more fully in Chapter 10.

An employee stock ownership plan may use a profit-sharing or stock bonus format. In a profit-sharing format, there are two basic limitations:

1. The employees' contributions to the stock ownership plan trust may come only from current or accumulated profits; and,

2. The plan may not borrow funds on the basis of corporate majority stockholder guarantees to purchase employee stock. There is a major advantage to a profit-sharing format: It allows distribution of benefits to employees in the form of cash or securities as well as employer stock. This may be an important consideration if the employer's stock is not publicly traded or does not otherwise have a ready market.

INSURANCE

You should periodically review insurance coverage to ensure that your coverage on buildings, equipment, and inventory is adequate. The liability insurance should cover bodily injuries. You should familiarize yourself with the obligations to employees under both the common law and workers compensation. This will require some time with an attorney in order to evaluate the rights and liabilities occurring under both. There are some areas that workers compensation may not cover. However, in those cases, the English common law, as adopted by the United States Constitution, may apply.

Another major area or concern is whether your insurance coverage is spread among various agents. In some cases there will be overlapping coverage and care must be taken to try to ensure that there are no gaps in the insurance coverage. This may raise the question as to which insurance company is responsible for payment of claims arising from a particular occurrence. Consultation with an insurance agency may show you how to cut premiums in areas such as fleet automobile coverage, proper classification of employees under workers compensation, and the cutting back on seasonal inventory insurance.

Another consideration should be whether to take out insurance coverage on business interruptions. Finally, you may consider whether fringe benefits insurance for employees (group life, group health, or retirement insurance) is a competitive benefits package. You may wish to give to your employees these benefits in order to retain good employees.

Split-Dollar Life Insurance

A split-dollar life insurance plan is a way in which you can create significant cash reserves through the payment of employee life insurance while at the same time offering the employee a benefit in the form of a term life insurance policy. The insurance policy is not actually a term insurance policy except as it appears to the employee. The employee is sold life insurance protection at low cost, but the company owns the cash surrender value of the policy. Under such an agreement, the employee has the benefit of the insurance and the company has a significant portion of the cash surrender value. The cash surrender value can be borrowed against under most policy provisions. This offers a low-cost source of additional capital.

SUMMARY

Detailed coverage of tax liabilities, exemptions, and deductions can be readily obtained at no cost from the IRS. Two good federal publications are *Publication 334, Tax Guide for Small Businesses*, and *Circular E, Employer's Tax Guide*.

You should plan for the tax effect of your decisions on a daily basis. Certainly each financial decision and most operational decisions have direct, if not immediate, tax consequences. Knowing what the tax effects are may enable you to defer the payment of taxes. Many large firms use tax deferral methods to postpone the payment of some taxes indefinitely.

The form of the business—whether a corporation, an S-corporation, a partnership, or a sole proprietorship—changes the form of reporting and the nature of the tax liability. You should look at the tax rates applicable to the entities at various income levels.

Liabilities should be calculated using various scenarios dealing with both the level of income and the payment of that income under various business formats. As incomes grow and the business prospers, changing the business form may be an integral part of the business plan. Methods of financing capital assets have tax consquences that should be part of the acquisition plan.

Overall, the business should integrate tax planning as part of the operating budget and capital budgeting functions of the business. When taxes cannot be reduced, they sometimes can be deferred, which in some cases can be almost as good as nonpayment.

Finally, you should on a regular basis review your insurance coverage, including those on your employees, from an investment or financing perspective. Often opportunities to reduce costs are available and overlooked in acquiring insurance. Policies may be changed, consolidated, discontinued, or altered. Deal with insurance planners and not just claims takers. Insurance can be a liability or a valuable asset.

14

Business Valuation

There comes a point in the life of almost every small business when, for a variety of reasons, the owner is interested in placing a value on that business. This chapter will present an overview of the reasons for valuation and methods of obtaining it for small businesses.

REASONS FOR VALUATION

Certainly, if you are making a determination to sell a portion or all of a business, it is important to have an idea of the value of that business. It is also important to recognize that the sale of a partial interest of a business may not be a pro rata share of the value of the whole. For example, a minority interest of 40 percent may not be as valuable to a potential buyer on a proportionate basis as a controlling interest of 51 percent.

Even if the business is not going to be sold, there may be other "quasi-sales" reasons for putting a value on the business. For example, you may wish to establish employee stock option plans, whereby over time the employees become shareholders in the business. Such an employee stock option plan (ESOP) requires an annual valuation of the business in order to establish a value for the shares placed into the ESOP for the employees.

Another reason for a valuation is your anticipation of "going pub-lic"—positioning to sell stock in a public market. Valuation will tell you the approximate value per share to be expected from the market for the stock.

Other reasons for placing a value on the business have to do with estate planning by the owners of the business. In order to make a de-termination of the size of gifts that owners may wish to make in various years, it is important to have an annual evaluation of the gifts as they are made. You may wish to have a valuation made in order to determine the gift taxes to be paid or the best ways to save on those gift and estate taxes. The valuation may also be used to determine a way of recapitalizing the stock in order to let the current owner(s) retain control of the business, while passing the value of the business, or its appreciation in value, into the estate. You may want a value in anticipation of the purchase of life insurance to be used to provide for continuity of the business in the event of the death of a key individual. Life insurance is often used to cover an agreed upon buy-sell arrangement among owners in the business, in the event of the death of one of the principals. Through a regular valuation process you have current values to use among the owners as well as with tax people.

Valuation is necessary when you have the opportunity or the desire to spin off a part of the business into a separate legal entity or when you are acquiring or merging with another legal entity. Condemnations also require valuation to make a determination of business damages associated with the taking of property by a governmental entity. The legal reorganization of the business, either through bankruptcy or other proceedings, may require a formal valuation. Finally, two of the more unpleasant reasons for valuation have to do with ownership disputes. Sometimes these disputes among partners lead to dissolution of that partnership. Divorce, where the business is a part of the estate of the couple and that estate has to be divided between the divorced parties, also requires valuation.

VALUATION METHODS AND THEORIES

Without a doubt, the single most influential publication in the area of business valuation is the *Internal Revenue Service Ruling 59–60*. Although the revenue ruling was written specifically for estate and gift tax purposes, the concepts applied in the ruling have been generally held to be of use in any valuation for business purposes.

Section Three, .01 states:

A determination of fair market value, being a question of fact, will depend upon the circumstances in each case. No formula can be devised that will be generally applicable to the multitude of different valuation issues arising in estate and gift tax cases. Often, an appraiser will find wide variances of opinion as to the fair market value of a particular stock. In resolving such differences, he should maintain a reasonable attitude in recognition of the fact that valuation is not an exact science. A sound valuation will be based upon all the relevant facts, but the elements of common sense, informed judgment and reasonableness must enter into the process of weighing these facts and determining their aggregate significance.

One might note that the paragraph is directed toward estate and gift tax cases but its strictures can be and have been more widely applied. The processes described in the revenue ruling are applicable to sole proprietorships and partnerships as well as corporations. In fact, later rulings gave broad, general application to these concepts.

Section Three, .03 states: "Valuation of securities is, in essence, a prophecy as to the future and must be based on facts available at the required date of appraisal." "Prophecy as to the future" refers to the concept of future value, which is dependent upon income potential.

Section Four lists eight separate factors that should be considered in any valuation process. While these factors may not be all-inclusive, they are essential and should be considered whenever a valuation is being performed.

1. *The nature of the business and the history of the enterprise since its inception.* The history will show the entity's stability or lack of stability, its growth or lack of growth, and its diversity or lack of diversity. The amount of detail that should be considered will increase as the date of appraisal approaches. Recent events are of greater help in predicting the future than events in the past. The financial results of the business events of the past that are unlikely to recur in the future should be discounted, because value is most closely related to future expectancies.

2. *The economic outlook in general and the conditioned outlook of the specific industry in particular.* Every business fits into the general economy and must be looked at with consideration of where the economy appears to be going. However, some businesses do not respond in direct relationship to the economy in general. Therefore, it is very important to look at the economic impacts on the specific industry as well.

3. *The stock and the financial condition of the business.* If available, balance sheets should be obtained in comparative format for a period of two or more years. Balance sheets as of the date of the appraisal, or at the most

recent possible date, would also be helpful. From the balance sheets the appraiser should be able to determine such things as the liquidity status, the book value of fixed assets, working capital, solvency, and net worth.

4. *The earning capacity of the company*. If available, income statements should be obtained in comparative format for a period of five years. Such income statements should show gross income as well as principal deductions by major product lines. Particular emphasis may be placed upon salaries of owners or officers of the business. In addition, income available for dividends and dividends actually paid will be of particular interest, as will increases in retained earning and adjustments necessary to balance retained earning against the balance sheet: "Prior earnings records usually are the most reliable guide as to the future expectancy. Resort to arbitrary 5- or 10-year averages without regard to current trends or future prospects will not produce a realistic valuation."

5. *Dividend paying capacity*. The primary emphasis in dividend paying capacity should be the ability to pay dividends rather than on dividends actually paid. It should be recognized that in many forms of businesses dividends are avoided because of tax consequences. However, the ability to have paid dividends may be an important way to determine the value of the business.

6. *Whether the enterprise has goodwill or other tangible value*. Goodwill is, after all, a name for excess earning capacity. To determine *whether* a business has goodwill is difficult; to determine the *value* of goodwill is even more so. The value of goodwill rests upon the ability of the business to earn a return greater than the industry's average return on its net assets.

7. *Sales of stock and the size of the block of stock to be valued*. If there have been sales of stock, those sales can be used to help determine the value of the business. If parts of the business have been valued, those interests may also be used to establish the value of the whole business. However, sales of an interest in closely held businesses, sole proprietorships, or partnerships are not always arm's length transactions. Therefore, such sales must be considered carefully before being used to establish the value of the business as a whole. The concept of "blockage" has to do with minority interests. A minority interest may not always receive an estimate of value proportionate to the percentage of ownership that the block of stock represents.

8. *A market price of stocks in corporations engaged in the same or similar lines of business having their stock actively traded in open markets*. When it is possible to find comparable companies whose stock is traded on the open market, this information can be helpful in determining the value of the

business. However, as the nature and size of the business are usually unique, it is very difficult to find truly comparable companies.

METHODS OF OBTAINING VALUATION

Now that we have discussed the reasons for valuation and the elements to be considered when obtaining one, it is time to look at the practical means of obtaining one.

Discounted Cash Flows

A strictly discounted cash flow method of valuation is future oriented and is based upon a limited-life projection. The method may be used effectively if it can be applied to limited-life income streams and situations such as:

1. A project type of business that has a certain finish date.
2. Contract term-oriented businesses.
3. Situations where early cash flow is the most important issue.
4. Situations where return of investment (payback) is the key concern.

The method may also be used if an approximation of a pro forma balance sheet can be made at some future date. The value of the residual assets are discounted as a part of the process.

Earnings Capitalization Approach

The earnings capitalization approach is intended to indicate what one would pay to receive a given amount of earnings. It is very similar to the method used for valuing an insurance annuity contract.

In order to use the method, 1) a "comparison" return for competing investments must be available, and 2) a risk differential must be considered.

The return considerations will include a basic "rent on money" as well as an inflation factor and a risk for the particular investment. To determine the basic rent on money, consider such things as: daily savings accounts, annual certificates of deposit, five-year treasury notes, 20-year AAA corporate bonds, and the yield on blue-chip stocks.

First determine the amount of return (in percentage) that the money should earn, then determine the amount of money the business will return. There are, of course, many ways to estimate that return. One can look at the income from a single year, the average of three to five years of history, a projection of the next several years, or a composite of any of the above.

Once the income from the business has been estimated and a necessary return has been established, the calculation is simply to divide the income by the necessary return expressed as a percentage. The resulting number is the value of the business.

The approach is fairly simple and does not resolve a number of problems such as how to adjust the income for certain tax and other considerations or the impact of negative earnings.

Adjustments to Income Statements

Before using any income statement numbers for valuation purposes, it is important to consider adjustments that may be necessary for those numbers to reflect accurately the value of the business. Among the items that need to be considered and adjusted for are:

1. Excess compensation to the owners.
2. Excess fringe benefits to the owners.
3. Potential inventory value accumulations.
4. Bad debt write-offs.
5. Depreciation methodologies employed.
6. Extraordinary write-offs.
7. Synergistic economies.
8. Corporate income taxation.
9. Investment tax credits.

Price/Earnings Multiple Method

The price/earnings method is often used to value publicly traded companies, and less so for closely held companies because:

1. Such stock rarely has a ready market and, in fact, may be restricted.
2. Reported earnings may have been significantly adjusted for tax purposes.
3. The size of blocks of stock may differ widely.

4. True comparables from a public area are hard to find. However, the price/earnings multiple method may be used as a good test of reasonableness of the capitalization rate method discussed earlier.

Adjusted Book Value Method

The adjusted book value method is an attempt to make a determination of the appraised value of the assets of the business. Typically only those assets used in the operation of the business itself are used to make comparisons against competitors. Among the balance sheet items that will potentially require appraisal increments will be inventories, real estate, and equipment. Each asset of value is looked at independently, and an appraisal of the current value of that asset is made. Among the balance sheet adjustments that may be necessary in using this method are:

1. Inventory.
2. Bad debts.
3. Fixed assets.
4. Patents or franchises.
5. Investments and affiliates.
6. Goodwill and intangibles.
7. Future royalties.
8. Low-cost debt service.
9. Tax loss carry-forwards.

Accounting Considerations

Both the income statement and the balance sheet may have been significantly affected by accounting policies employed by the business. Among the accounting policies that need to be considered and adjusted for are:

1. Consolidated financial statements.
2. Depreciation methods.
3. Inventory accounting.
4. Marketable securities.
5. Accounts receivable.
6. Amortization of intangibles.
7. Research and development.

8. Pension funds or profit sharing.

9. Foreign exchange.

10. Income tax deferrals.

11. Deferred compensation.

12. Installment sales.

13. Overhead allocations.

Dividend-Paying Capacity Method

The dividend-paying capacity method mentioned in *Internal Revenue Service Ruling 59–60* is an attempt to determine the dividends the company could have paid over some period of time, perhaps five years. It considers such factors as:

1. The cash needs of the company for working capital.

2. The cash needs of the company for expansion and growth.

3. Contingencies and executory contracts.

4. Debt.

5. Salaries paid to owners.

Having considered these items and adjusted the dividend paying capacity accordingly, you should determine an appropriate yield. The appraiser, in considering a yield, should consider comparable companies and the yield that could be realized from alternative investments. When the dividend-paying capacity in terms of dollars is known, and an appropriate yield in percentage terms has been given, divide the dividend-paying capacity by the yield expressed as a percentage, to arrive at an estimate of value.

Comparable Method

When the comparable method is used, one must be sure sales of the stock are from "comparable" companies. This means that they are truly comparable in terms of the nature of the business, the size of the business, the earnings of the business, and the size of the block of stock being traded.

If the business being valued has had recent purchase offers of its own stock, such values may be used—with appropriate cautions. You should determine the changes that have occurred since that purchase offer and be aware of the amount of ownership involved. It is also important to look at the financial structuring of the offer to make sure that it, too, is comparable. And, be sure the offer was a valid, arm's length transaction.

You would want to consider recent sales to know for certain to whom the sale was made as well as any sweeteners or side deals that may have been involved.

Goodwill

There are many definitions of the concept of goodwill. Basically, goodwill is the ability of an entity to earn a higher than normal return on its investment in an asset. Among the ways that have been used for placing a value on goodwill are:

1. The accountant's method.
2. The profit opportunity method.
3. The cost to create method.
4. The cost savings method.
5. The cost of purchase method.

The accountant's method is simply one of plugging a value in for goodwill after values have been assigned to all other assets. The amount of the goodwill is the amount of the purchase price which cannot be otherwise assigned to specific assets.

The profit opportunity method attaches a profit to a specific and tangible asset such as a patent, and determines the present value of that profit over some period of time.

The cost to create method is similar to the construction cost method or the replacement cost method in real estate valuation. One must first identify all the costs that would be associated with creating the intangible asset. Often the intangible asset has no carrying value on the books and its cost to create will be in addition to what is shown on the books.

The cost savings method has to do with an asset that creates an opportunity for the business to save money because of the ownership of a process, patent, etc. The methodology involves the present value of savings over some period of time.

Cost of purchase method is simply an estimate of what it would take if the firm went out into the market and bought a similar asset today.

SUMMARY

There are many reasons for needing to place a value on the business—sale of part of the business; establishment of an employee stock option plan; estate and gift tax planning; settlement of a divorce; death of a principal.

Valuation methods have been very much influenced and guided by the *Internal Revenue Service Ruling 59–60*. The ruling acknowledges that valuation is in the mind of the beholder and each case must be governed by the facts at hand without the application of a specific formula. In determining a value under this ruling, consideration should be given to eight factors: the nature and history of the business; the economic outlook for the economy and the business specifically; the financial condition of the business; the earning capacity; the dividend paying capacity; the amount of goodwill or tangible value; the sales of stock; and a market price of comparable businesses.

A discounted cash flow method of valuation may be used if the business has a limited-life income stream. Another method frequently used is an earnings capitalization approach, which is similar in financial appearance to a method used to value an insurance annuity contract. Two things are necessary: a comparison return for competing investments; and a risk differential. The method is relatively simple but does not resolve how to adjust the income for certain tax and other considerations.

A method used for publicly traded companies is the price/earnings multiple method, used where the stock has a ready market value, reported earnings do not have to be significantly adjusted, and there are two comparable companies.

The business could be valued using the adjusted book value method. In using this approach, you undertake to determine appraised values for assets. In this approach, significant adjustments may be needed to account for your accounting policies and practices.

Included in Revenue Ruling 59–60 is a method of valuation using the dividend paying capacity of the business over some period of time. When using this method, some factors may be considered: working capital needs; expansion and growth cash needs; contingency needs; debt; and salaries paid to owners. By using the dividend paying capacity and an appropriate yield, you can approximate value.

Finally, comparable businesses can be used to determine value. Finding truly comparable businesses requires comparisons of such factors as size, earnings, and the nature of the business itself. Valuation is the best guess of what the business is worth. It can only be approximated. The methods given here, however, should group several estimates within an acceptable range from which the worth of the business can be determined.

__15__

Professional Advisors

$\mathbf{A}$s noted at the outset of this book, all businesses need to plan; and businesses that plan well are businesses that take maximum advantage of opportunities. But making a successful go of any enterprise is a continuing process demanding expertise in many disciplines. The creative genius who started the business may not be skilled in negotiating with labor or with material suppliers; he or she may not be an expert on the tax consequences of decisions or on legal obligations.

Typically, businesses of all sizes use people from outside the business to advise management. The ways in which these advisors are selected are as varied as the businesses themselves. These methods vary from formal requests for proposals (RFP's) for consulting services, to a phone call to one's lawyer or accountant that begins "I've got a quick question for you . . ." and ends some more than short time later with a free answer. Sometimes the expression "You get what you pay for" applies to free advice.

Small businesses often lack the in-house capability to perform the analysis and research associated with the more difficult business decisions. Individual or informal advice may not adequately address a problem that has consequences across the board. The best-qualified advice may come from a team of advisors, each knowledgeable in his field, and each with a knowledge of the business. The problem facing small businesses is assembling such a team. Often consulting and advisory businesses will not have the necessary mix of disciplines within their organization. Few accounting firms or engineering firms have lawyers as part of their normal business operation. Your objective should be to recruit and manage a well-rounded team of advisors.

The first step in assembling an advisory team is to determine your "strength on the bench"—which disciplines are represented by qualified individuals on the staff. These individuals may or may not be used in the team. You may want fresh ideas from outside the business, preferring to use in-house staff as reviewing or critiquing authority.

However, participation by in-house staff with the team can be very valuable in ensuring that the team is considering the proper components of the business and is working toward the appropriate objectives. In-house expertise often can address information problems of the team and more cheaply provide the missing information. Also, in-house staff can be very effective as an information source in helping to identify internal problems.

BUILDING A TEAM OF ADVISORS

You are striving for expertise in all areas related to the business. It makes sense for the advisors to work with and for you as a team. Even though there may be some overlapping of expertise in specific areas, such overlap may lead to healthy, differing opinions.

The following areas of expertise should be considered:

Law

In proper long- and short-term planning many major (and minor) considerations will have legal consequences.

Organizational Form. Each form—a sole proprietorship, partnership, subchapter S-corporation, limited partnership, or any other of a large number of business forms—has legal advantages and disadvantages. The consequences should be explored *before* you commence operation.

Contracts. Contracts can have significant implications for you in both the sale and acquisition of products, materials, and services. The terms can commit you to long-term arrangements affecting significant portions of your resources.

Patents. Everything from how to obtain a patent to the purchase, sale, and leasing of patent rights can be complex legal transactions of a very specialized nature. Few generalist lawyers have ever dealt with the U.S. Patent Office. Still fewer are licensed patent lawyers. Many "patent attorneys" can not otherwise practice law.

Copyrights. The practice of copyright law is another specialized field of the legal profession, subject to special rules and procedures.

Leases. Like contracts, leases are often long-term commitments of resources that may have significant consequences to you even after the business may have ceased to exist. For example, a retail store or restaurant may have to execute a three-year lease with rent increases and renewal provisions. If after two years the store has the opportunity to move to a better location the lease may not permit you to move. Or, at least, you will still have to pay for the first location. The lease may have binding consequences.

Zoning. Where you wish to locate or to expand or if you want to change the nature of the business may be prohibited or restricted by existing zoning requirements. Zoning can be changed or variances obtained by petition to and approval of a zoning board.

Labor Agreements. Labor agreements are contracts between management and labor for the provision of a service in exchange for a price. Labor agreements are very specialized contracts being governed by substantial federal labor law. Labor law practice is itself a highly specialized area of the law.

Warranties. Warranties are typically assurances about the product or services. Warranties can be expressed in the terms and conditions of sales, but more often there are implied warranties. The Pinto automobile is a case involving an implied warranty of fitness and safety. In essence, the claim is that Ford produced a car that was unsafe for transporting human beings. It therefore violated an implied warranty. Implied warranties arise as a result of a business holding itself out as a provider of a product or service.

Lawsuits. It was once said that "When the first lawyer moved to town, he nearly starved to death. When the second lawyer moved in, they both got rich." Lawsuits can be both offensive and defensive. They can be very effective at forcing action or mandating inaction.

Banking

We have discussed at length the necessity of establishing a sound working relationship with a banker. By working with a banker and understanding the bank's needs and requirements, you may be able to forewarn the bank of some anticipated changes in status. An association with the bank will also give you financial advice that may extend beyond the in-house abilities of the bank itself. For example, selling stock or bond issues may be arranged through a bank with a broker.

Insurance

Insurance might be nothing more than order taking or claims processing, but it may be more. Insurance, as briefly discussed in Chapter 13, can constitute risk management and financing for the business. Some of the areas for you to consider include:

General Liability. This is a policy intended to compensate for losses associated with the general operations of the business.

Product Liability. Here you are insuring against damages occurring to persons and property by defects in the product. The famous case in this area is the exploding pop bottle case. There, a person was severely cut when a bottle of pop, which presumably had been overly carbonated, exploded. The asbestos and Pinto cases are similar examples. The real problems are the risk and extent of liability. Most insurance policies have limits on the recoveries allowed. Often, the judgments exceed those limits. The cost of liability insurance is directly related to the amount of coverage and inversely related to the deductible. You must seriously consider this trade-off.

Casualty. Insurance can be purchased to protect against large losses generally due to disaster (fire, hurricanes, high winds, hail, etc.) As with all insurance, you must balance the risk of loss against the cost of protecting against that loss.

Life and Health Insurance. The size of the business affects the type and nature of the insurance. If the business is owned by a few principals who are the chief operating personnel of the business, then the loss of one member could have serious consequences. As you grow larger, providing employee life and health insurance becomes an employee benefit, which may become part of a package offered to induce hiring. It may also be necessary for negotiations with union representatives. Often employee life insurance can be a valuable source of low-cost financing for the business. If you insure your employees with a policy carrying a cash surrender value, and offer it as a benefit to the employee as a term policy, then you may be able to borrow against that policy.

Pensions. You may set up self insurance or purchase policies that will pay an annuity at some later date to retiring employees.

Loss of Business and Credit Insurance. You may wish to protect against unusual bad-debt losses in extending trade credit. Credit insurance is available, although not to cover against losses normally incurred in the industry. These losses, sometimes called primary losses, are distinct for each industry. Insurance is usually restricted to certain acceptable risks, as determined, for example, by a Dun & Bradstreet rating. The cost of this form of insurance varies directly with the risk of the accounts accepted and is calculated as a percentage of sales. The decision to purchase credit insurance depends upon the probability of large credit losses, your ability as a self-insurer to bear those losses, and the cost of the premiums.

Marketing

This is an area where your participation may be market directed. If you sell a highly visible consumer product (soft drinks, jeans, breakfast cereal, etc.), the services of advertising and marketing consultants usually becomes significant. As the products enter the secondary markets (chemicals, extrusions, fasteners, etc.) the need for marketing changes. New consultants and advisors can be used. The nature of the function changes significantly and so may the magnitude of the expenditures. Advertising may be restricted to trade publications and catalogues. As a result, a marketing consultant may be a substantial and necessary component within the team concept.

Accounting

With the complexity of today's businesses, the answer to the simple question "How much did it cost to make?" results in the simple answer "It depends." Actually, that is an accurate answer because it does depend on how you look at costs and revenues. The costs for regulation, taxes, and operations may well all be different. The reasons are varied and complex. For example, a machine used by a regulated entity may have to be depreciated on a straight-line basis for regulatory accounting purposes.

For tax purposes the firm will probably take the fastest depreciation permitted under the tax code. For operations, depreciation may have no relationship to time because it may simply be a function of use or of technology changes.

Because of the sheer complexity of our economy, the rapidly changing regulatory and tax environment, and the speed of technological obsolescence, you may have to call upon expert accounting assistance to meet these challenges.

Others

From time to time, you may find it extremely useful to consult with other people such as:

Customers. Often the best source of information concerning product quality, perception in the market, price, advertising, and the like may be customer surveys, questionnaires, and interviews.

Former Customers. Owners of your product who have switched to competitors' products can sometimes provide valuable information on market perception and buying habits.

Suppliers. Suppliers can give valuable insight into procurement costs and problems which may have future pricing consequences. They may also have ideas for substitute products or materials. Finally, suppliers may have knowledge concerning the needs and requirements of competitors.

Engineers. Engineers can provide help ranging from minor engineering changes to entire operating plans. For example, engineers can be consulted on something as simple as finding a cheaper fastener for joining two components together, whereas a mining engineer may be called upon to help design a 20-year mining plan. In some cases, governmental regulations may require the filing of engineering plans prior to the commencement of operations.

SELECTING INDIVIDUALS

Having determined the type and number of disciplines that need to be represented on the team, the next questions is whom to select and how to select them. Some of the criteria include:

Level of Experience. The level of experience is probably the most important criterion. There simply is no substitute for experience. Here the old adage applies: "It is good to profit from your own experience, but it is better to profit from the experience of others." Very often, consultants with experience in solving the problems of others may efficiently help to solve yours.

Secondary Areas (Overlap of Expertise). Often an individual with various specialties (e.g., law, engineering, and business) may be able to fashion solutions creatively using a multidisciplinary approach. For example, an accountant-lawyer may be able to write a contract with creative delivery and payment clauses that will have a favorable tax effect.

Availability. When considering hiring a consultant or getting an advisor, be sure that you get what you pay for. You may hire a lawyer only to find that on the day of your important hearing, he has a conflict and sends a partner who knows little of your case, or, worse, an associate who knows nothing.

Sometimes your consultant may have other business commitments with greater financial rewards and your project has to wait. One way to avoid this is to schedule and confirm in advance. Also, be explicit in your expectations. Make sure they can't say "We didn't know that was what you expected."

Cost. Cost is listed fourth but it is usually the first or second in importance. Generally, you try to get the best advice within a budget. Commonly referred to as "bang for the bucks," this figure is negotiable but you must ensure that you are getting what you want and paying what you expected to pay to get it.

A good contract lawyer can be of assistance. For example, you may withhold a percentage of final payment to assure that the product or service meets your specifications and needs. Often contracts will permit draws based upon satisfactory completion of identifiable milestones. Sometimes guarantees and warranties are conditions of payment.

Another consideration of cost is the competitive price offered for services. There is no harm in asking "What is it going to cost? What can I expect to pay? How will I be billed? Who will work on the project and what rate do they bill at?" Ask for a breakdown of the estimated cost of the project by task, by individual. Question contingencies and miscellaneous costs.

Conflicts of Interest. You should establish a conflict of interest policy. Once the policy is established it should be written, discussed, and distributed to all vendors of services seeking to work for you. Conflicts of interest can be especially difficult to assess because the experience of others is what you are seeking from an advisor. If that advisor has worked for a competitor his advice may be doubly valuable. But remember, if they talk *to* you, they may talk *about* you, and others may profit from information about you. Evaluate what they tell you about others. Is it the kind of information you want others to know about you? It might be valuable to expect from the advisor a commitment to nondisclosure of trade or confidential information. Most advisors have no problem with this.

Concordance with Your Advisors. You should be able to develop a good working relationship with your advisors and feel mutual respect. An advisor is an advisor—he does not run the business nor is he responsible for making a success of it. The best advisors are those who work themselves out of a job. You should strive for self-sufficiency resorting to experts only for extraordinary situations.

Hire advisors who expect to help the business on an "as needed" basis but are willing to keep in touch or stay current on your status. This can be encouraged through fee arrangements called retainers.

ORGANIZATION AND STRUCTURE

How the advisory team fits into the organizational structure can be answered in many ways. Some businesses have adopted the team as part of the staff function of the firm, giving it official status and requiring it to comply with the company's structural rules. Others treat advisory teams in an informal manner. Some of the advantages to an informal association of advisors include:

1. *Greater independence of thought and operation.* When an advisory body becomes institutionalized it loses some of its autonomy. That is not to say that the advisory group should not have definite lines of reporting, accountability, and responsibility. It simply means that it may not be bound by rigid structural constraints.

2. *By being an informal functioning entity, without line authority, it is clear that advisors are advisors and not decision makers.*

3. *More freedom of action.* Informal organizational structures permit the team to cross different lines of authority. This permits better problem solving. Often problems cross lines of authority and are systematic rather than isolated.

4. *Fewer controls.* Most advisory team functions should not be bound by notice of meeting, elections, and minutes requirements. These, although needed in a structured organization, are often a burden to problem solving. Unstructured, free thinking may lead to quicker solutions to problems.

5. *Planning versus review.* Advisory teams are generally more beneficial when used for planning rather than only review. Planning is less reactive to existing or past conditions, and as such must be responsive to environmental changes. If advisors are put in a review mode, then a more structured formal approach is better. For planning, the team must be responsive to unplanned opportunities as they arise.

6. *Compensation.* Although late in the list, compensation should be anticipated, considered, and discussed early in the process. Agreement should be reached on a workable approach for paying advisors. It should be remembered that not all advice is rendered at meetings and that preparation is necessary to delivering most good advice. Generally fixed retainers are used to compensate for those unstructured work requirements, but other methods may be devised.

7. *Uniformity of compensation.* Different advisors are paid differently. Pay is a function of individual contracts and services. Several advisors may work in a team but uniformity of pay is not automatic.

The goal is to get what you pay for. You are hiring advisors because of their skill and independent thinking. They should not be tied to thinking of how things have been done in the past. It may be just such thinking that has gotten the firm into whatever dilemma you now face. An objective review of the current status may be necessary, but advisors should not be restricted to thinking "That's the way we've always done it."

WORKING TOGETHER

Assembling a multidisciplinary group of advisors may cause as many problems as it solves. Consider the following sources of possible trouble:

Differing Work Styles. An awareness of how other people work is usually helpful in getting things done. For example, an individual who is concerned with detail should be able to work and respect a creative individual who focuses more on the big picture. There is, however, a big gap between "should" and "do." Therefore, have explicit expectations and discussions concerning work styles and what is expected of each member. Often a facilitator has a place on the team to ensure a unified attitude among the participants. This person, regardless of expertise or discipline, can apply the synergy to the various parts and personalities on the team.

Turf Problems. From any professional's viewpoint, there are overlapping areas of expertise. For example, lawyers and accountants may both have significant tax experience. Coming from differing perspectives can cause problems but it may also create opportunities. You may not want unity of thought from your advisors but you certainly do not want open warfare. One method of avoiding or minimizing open hostilities and turf battles is to obtain a list from the potential advisors of individuals (of other disciplines) whom they have worked with in the past. Also, confidential conversations and interviews with the consultants will bring out areas of possible difficulties in working relationships.

Attitudes toward Risk. Some individuals are more averse to risk than others. Because the object of using advisors is to get advice, and not to take risks, this should be a minimal problem. However, the concern is that the advisors should be pulling in the same direction. One of the objectives of the advisory team is to consider the risk effects of the solutions. The decision concerning the minimal acceptable risk is management's decision; whether the advisors agree on the risk effect should be of some concern to you.

Time Availability. Because advisors are not full-time employees, their time is not necessarily yours. Competing interests occupy the advisors' time; advisors are interested in selling their time and may have scheduling problems in meeting your needs. Here is where a coordinator is essential. Pulling the team together may at times be very time consuming and tax patience. Request availability schedules when recruiting and interviewing. But be aware that most schedules are subject to change.

SUMMARY

Asking for and getting the right advice is a learned skill. From the start, you need to evaluate your in-house skills, strengths, and weaknesses, and should seek advice for those weaknesses. You may wish to test the quality of your strengths by working with advisors in those areas. The selection process for advisors can be more difficult than selecting employees. The evaluation of their skills may come too late in the process to seek better advisors.

As with hiring employees, advisors bring their own prejudices and opinions as to how things should be done. They may be hard to work with or they may not have the same risk and business philosophy as your management. But as with any business decision, the risks of a bad decision can be minimized through assimilation of data, analysis of qual-ifications, checking with references and former clients, and examination of credentials. Finally, you should be willing to commit the resources necessary to see the project through—although you should also be ready to bail out in the event that the advisor is ineffective.

INDEX